Post-Courier Books

The Civil War at Charleston
62 Famous Houses
The Battery
Charles Towne — Birth of a City
Lord Ashley Cooper's Dictionary of Charlestonese
Battleground — South Carolina in the Revolution
Nature Watch — In the Carolina Lowcountry

NATURE WATCH

In the Carolina Lowcountry

By

LYNNE LANGLEY

Edited by Warren Ripley

Published by
The News & Courier
and
The Evening Post
Charleston, South Carolina

A Post-Courier Book

Contents—

FALL

WINTER

Introduction —

In a too-routine world, nature provides a sense of renewal, a fresh perspective, an invitation to explore and discover.

Nature continually changes not only the wilds but the most familiar backyard scene. Tides redecorate beaches with collectables, wildflowers or delicate seed pods transform field and forest, spiders spin transient webs, birds sculpt nests and curious mammals may dodge into view at any moment. Even a little knowledge of critters, plants and seasons helps explain some of the surprises and unravel the mysteries. While wildlife and plants remain free, they become less unpredictable.

If watching nature constantly presents something new and unexpected, the seasons lend a framework of reliability. Spring may arrive early or late, but come it will. Violets fade into wisteria and native azaleas, butterflies emerge to visit the blossoms, brilliant warblers migrate and songbirds serenade. As alligators bellow for mates, long-legged wading birds crowd into rookeries. Mushrooms appear after summer showers while wild orchids unfurl in swamps and woods.

In autumn, squirrels hoard nuts and deer snort challenges. Leaves brighten during the Halloween and Thanksgiving seasons as bats scout for insects and wild turkeys search for acorns. Shells wash onto beaches and the plant world presents holly, mistletoe and pine for the holidays. While much of the country suffers under a blanket of snow, Lowcountry foxes, raccoons and beaver court. Eagles nest in winter, owls fill the night air with their hooting and salamanders creep out to lay their eggs during chilling rains.

This book is designed as a guide to the rituals, events and activities of fauna and flora. The emphasis is on Lowcountry species, the plants and animals that live not just in the South Carolina lowlands but in much of the Lowcountry stretch from Jacksonville, Fla., to Jacksonville, N.C. Species from the Carolina midlands and mountains also are included. Weather influences precisely when a given wildflower will bloom or fruit each year or when a wintering bird species will arrive, but the seasons as outlined generally encompass these months: Spring, March through May; Summer, June through August; Fall, September through November; Winter, December through February.

The information is based on research, interviews with wildlife biologists and botanists, field trips, nearly 400 Nature Watch columns and other natural history stories published in the Post-Courier Newspapers. May the book encourage readers to observe and value the natural world.

LYNNE LANGLEY
Charleston, S.C., 1987

Acknowledgments—

The study, research and field observations of many South Carolina biologists have contributed immeasurably to this book. It would not have been possible without their information and expertise.

Thanks go to the biologists with the South Carolina Wildlife and Marine Resources Department, particularly to the Nongame and Heritage Trust Section and to nongame biologists Sally Hopkins Murphy, Thomas M. Murphy, Philip M. Wilkinson and John Cely. Biology professor Dr. Julian R. Harrison of the College of Charleston has assisted with reptiles and amphibians, Dr. Richard D. Porcher of The Citadel with plants, Dr. Dennis M. Forsythe of The Citadel with birds, Charleston Museum curator Albert E. Sanders with mammals and Charleston Museum curator Dr. William Post with birds.

Through their monthly reports over the years for Nature Watch, naturalists Lin A. Dunbar and Perry E. Nugent have provided detailed information included here, Mrs. Dunbar on the flowering and fruiting of plants, Nugent on the seasonal activities of birds. Many other biologists also have supplied material, used initially in Post-Courier Newspaper articles, that was very helpful in preparing this book.

For their assistance with photographs, thanks to Charles Towne Landing, Drayton Hall, Cypress Gardens, the Charleston Museum, Magnolia Plantation and Gardens, Dr. Richard D. Porcher, Dr. Julian R. Harrison, Jean Pfaff and the South Carolina Wildlife and Marine Resources Department.

Post-Courier photographer Wade Spees searched out subjects ranging from turtles and toads to wildflowers and birds for this book while Stephanie Harvin took a number of wildlife and beach photos. Thanks to them and to their fellow Post-Courier photographers Bill Jordan, Tom Spain and Brad Nettles. Post-Courier artist Laura Jones designed the cover and the art for the four seasons while fellow artists Bill Thompson and Gill Guerry sketched wildlife.

Finally, my gratitude to my husband, Bill Langley, for his proofreading, continuing support and abiding respect for nature.

Photo and Art Credits —

Spring

Saucer Magnolia or Tulip Tree.

Wildflowers—

Spring creeps into the Lowcountry. A blaze of crocuses, daffodils and saucer magnolias warm the spirits with spring fever while South Carolina is still in the throes of winter.

But the promise is made. Although frost may strike again, tiny buds are struggling to open and early shoots are up in February. Begin looking for tender dandelion greens, the curly or toothed leaves of wild mustard, chickweed in the yard or disturbed areas, rounded leaves of henbit and wood sorrel that resembles clover. A wide variety of plantains also pop up from a basal rosette of leaves.

In early March, spring takes hold with more conviction. Wild violet flowers begin to show, first in sunny spots and later in the woods. Those early greens have added little blossoms in lawns and fields alike. Henbit has upright clusters of small, purple flowers while the white petals of chickweed surround a yellow center. Joining the display are clover-like black medick with yellow blooms, white clover and vetch, a wandering vine with eight to 12 pairs of delicate leaflets and spikes of pea-like lavender flowers.

Animals are munching their fill of spring onions and poor-man's-pepper, whose short spikes of white flowers will turn to round, green disks and later dry to brown pepper seeds.

Bare trees that lined the sides of roads are taking on pastel shades of green, yellow and pink as buds swell. And maples, usually the earliest of all, add a brilliant red. Then comes the parade of flowering pear, plum and peach trees, redbud and buckeye. And the Lowcountry is greening nicely with new leaves and young grasses by St. Patrick's Day.

Buckeye has bright red, tubular blossoms in upright clusters. But when redbud unfurls, its tiny pea-like blooms are a lovely lavender, lining branches as if trees had been painted for spring. Often obvious, wild plums and wild pears both show off white flowers. But peaches, usually hidden away in the woods, have brighter pinkish blooms. White flowers on blueberries promise fruit later in the summer and blackberry blossoms will unfold just as blueberry flowers droop.

As March progresses, the ground will be dotted with little bluets, delicate, pale blue flowers with four lobes around a golden center. Whorls of three to 10 lavender-blue flowers surround the square stem of lyre-leaved sage. The exposed lower lip of each sage flower offers a landing platform to bees, industriously gathering spring pollen.

Soon the brilliant yellow, trumpet-shaped blossoms of Carolina jessamine, the state flower, are dotting fences, bushes and trees. The woody vine is poisonous as are leaves and delightfully fragrant flowers. In woods, thickets and meadows, wild geraniums begin showing loose clusters of two to five lavender flowers with five rounded petals.

Carolina Jessamine.

For a real treat, check savannah areas and pine lands for the bearded grass-pink, which looks like a candidate for a corsage. Of South Carolina's 45 orchid species, the grass-pink is one of the handsomest with light pinkish-purple blossoms, a fringe or beard on the lip and a deeper throat.

Spring comes later to forests, where the Southern twayblade orchid comes to life with very small, reddish-brown flowers that don't resemble orchids. Among the first to open in the woods, white bloodroot flowers have numerous white petals rising on a short stalk; the thick horizontal stem below contains a bright red liquid. The illusive purple trillium produces a solitary flower of three maroon or reddish-brown petals and three green sepals above a whorl of three diamond-shaped leaves. The unpleasant smell draws carrion flies to pollinate the blossom.

Also check shady spots for another flower with dull coloring: Carolina allspice has brownish blossoms, bud-like centers surrounded by a series of very slender petals. When crushed, the egg-shaped leaves of the woodland shrub smell spicy.

The date of Easter may vary as much as the flowering of the first wisteria and azaleas, but the wild Easter lily or atamasco lily is almost always in bloom for the season. Preferring wet meadows, this member of the amaryllis family has six pure white, lily-like petals around golden-tipped stamens. Known locally as naked ladies, the flowers pop up from the ground without any clothing of leaves. If Easter runs late, stars-of-Bethlehem also are out; sepals and petals of this lily form a six-pointed white star about 1-inch wide.

Easter, or Atamasco, Lily.

Just as the weather is warming and windows open wide to admit those wondrous breaths of spring, pine pollen strikes. The yellow pollen is the bane of hay fever victims and tidy housekeepers alike, but the tiny grains from male cones must blanket the area to assure female cones will be fertilized. Pine cone collectors and wildlife, such as squirrels, will appreciate the result come winter.

As April nears, the Lowcountry's classic spring flowers burst forth. Giant ropes of fragrant, lavender wisteria fill yards and wilds. The white haze of dogwood shows in woods, along roads and in yards. And just after cultivated azaleas begin putting on their display, equally lovely but more subtle wild azalea flowers open on bare branches. Standing 2 to 6 feet tall, often in the woods, native azaleas or pinxter flowers have light pink, vase-shaped blossoms that smell heavenly.

Glossy yellow buttercup flowers appear in moist areas. A bit later butterweed, a member of the sunflower family, produces clusters of yellow, daisy-like flowers in clumps that resemble chrysanthemums. Growing in moist ditches, the plants may stand chest-high. Bright yellow Indian strawberry flowers with five petals and five sepals pop up in waste places and disturbed areas. The trailing plant later bears tasteless fruit resembling a small strawberry.

More showy during peak flower bloom are the large, white, single flowers of Cherokee roses. Originally introduced from China, these evergreen roses escaped from gardens long ago and now thrive along fields, woods and roadsides.

In damp woods and swamps, Jack-in-the-pulpit is playing its hiding game. A green or purplish-brown spathe folds over to hide the fleshy spike of tiny flowers.

In similar habitat, pitcher plants put on a much more vivid display. The glorious hooded pitcher plant has yellow, 2-inch-wide, umbrella-like flowers with five petals and five sepals. Each blossom rises on a leafless stalk amid clusters of hollow, tubular leaves. Nectar lures insects and other small organisms along the wing of the leaf and into the hood. Struggling to escape through spots that appear to be openings, exhausted insects drop to the base of the leaf and are digested by a liquid the plant secrets.

The crimson pitcher plant, whose similar flower is brownish-red and nodding, attracts victims with colorful leaf openings and by nectar. Insects fall into water collected in the hollow, pitcher-like leaves. An enzyme produced by the plant digests the prey, a supplement to food drawn from sandy bog soil.

For sheer color, crossvine and trumpet honeysuckle rival the cultivated azaleas of the season. Crossvine has bright red, tulip-like flowers and pairs of leaves branching from the stalk. Flowers on the vining trumpet honeysuckle resemble those of the familiar white or Japanese honeysuckle, which will bloom in a few more weeks. Red outside and

White, or Japanese, Honeysuckle.

yellow inside, the trumpet-shaped flowers cluster at the ends of stems on this slender, climbing vine that hummingbirds often visit.

In April, fields may take on a blue or red glow with wildflowers. *Rumex* or sorrel produces spike-like clusters of reddish flowers, each only one-twelfth of an inch long. Blue toadflax takes credit for the vistas of blue. Small blossoms with two lips dot the slender stems of plants thriving in sandy soil. A bit later, wood sorrel will be along in purple and yellow varieties with heart-shaped, clover-like foliage.

Also check fields for oxalis, yellow varieties opening first and later blue types. The half-inch-wide flowers with five petals stand above clover-like leaves divided into three heart-shaped leaflets.

In marshes and ditches, the white flowers of spider lilies are borne on stalks with narrow, foot-long leaves that resemble straps. The spidery flowers may reach an impressive 7 inches; the six slender, radiating lobes actually are three petals and three petal-like sepals surrounding a distinctive cupped center that holds the stamens.

While irises usually thrive in marshes or other damp areas, two members of the iris family prefer fields. Both

Spider Lilies

yellow-eyed and blue-eyed grasses bloom in late spring. The blue variety with thin, grass-like leaves wears three petals and three petal-like sepals, each with a thorn-like point. But the yellow variety has long, ·iris-type leaves. The half-inch flowers have three petals around a protruding center of tufted stamens.

Beaches become a riot of color in late April with brilliant pink phlox, tight clusters of trumpet-shaped flowers growing near the ground. The large, yellow flowers of evening primrose line a long, leafy tube that takes two years to develop. The lemon-scented flowers on this plant standing 2 to 5 feet tall are open only from evening until noon; they're replaced by similar but smaller sundrops, which pop out during the day.

Coreopsis may raise its daisy-like heads along beaches, roadsides and waste places. The central disks are reddish-purple while the yellow ray flowers are toothed. In a few weeks, showy gaillardia will be sunning its red rays or petals tipped with yellow. The central disk of the flower always wears the same color as the rays, which occasionally are all yellow.

Late in the spring, spiderworts may crop up almost anywhere. Three triangular, violet-blue petals stand out behind yellow stamens atop a stem about 15 inches tall. Firm in the morning, the eye-catching flowers wilt and turn to jelly later in the day almost as if injected with spider venom. The long, narrow leaves bend in the center so the plant sometimes resembles a giant spider, crouching on the ground in wait for an insect to pollinate its flowers.

Familiar honeysuckle, an import from the Middle East, comes to the fore around May. The vine with fragrant, tubular flowers is as common and prolific as jessamine but is not poisonous. The delicate honeysuckle flowers age from white to cream to light yellow. Another sign that

summer is on the way, huge white heads of flowers dot elderberry bushes, growing 3 to 12 feet high along roadsides. Tiny, fragrant flowers form large, flat heads that will later become glistening, round, blue-black berries.

What looks like a wild iris growing up to 2 feet tall in swamps and marshes is blue flag, a violet-blue flower with attractive veining and

Elderberry Flower.

yellow on the base of sepals. The sturdy stalk of flowers, each bloom up to 4 inches wide, rises from among tall, sword-like leaves that often lie on the ground or in the water.

Another purplish flower of late spring is daisy fleabane, a small daisy-like bloom with 40 or more light purple to off-white petals around a yellow center. In dry areas, the purple flower of late spring is the thistle, whose bright flowers will turn to white, shaggy heads of fluff and seed.

In pinewoods, hummocks and thickets, flame-like flower clusters appear atop coral bean plants, their prickly stems standing 2 to 5 feet high. The plant has arrowhead-shaped leaflets, tube flowers and later bright red seeds that are considered poisonous.

Equally bright are swamp roses, double pink roses that look as though they've escaped from a garden and are ranging along banks of streams and ditches.

The final sign that summer's near are lush, waxy, fragrant, white blossoms of magnolias; dramatic white bloom spikes atop yucca or

Magnolia Blossom

Spanish bayonet plants and day lilies growing along roads and in yards. During an early, mild spring, all three could be blooming by mid-May, but in most years the triumverate will be flowering well into June.

Purple Martins

Migration—

Early in the spring something stirs inside the birds that seemed so content in their wintering grounds. Perhaps the lengthening days or a mysterious internal clock triggers the pituitary glands. Reproductive organs begin to swell and birds become restless. They feed almost constantly and build up deposits of fat to see them through the journey ahead.

Migration may have begun eons ago when the northern descendants of today's migrants fled south during the ice age. Or most migrant birds may have been tropical rather than northern species. With abundant food, bird populations may have burgeoned out of control and competition may have grown fierce. As glaciers gradually retreated, birds may have moved north and discovered not only food but longer summer days to gather it for hungry young.

Despite man's increasing studies of bird migration, questions still outnumber answers. At least some birds apparently rely on landmarks to guide them along their way. The sun plays a roll for day-time migrants such as shorebirds, the moon and stars for night migrants such as songbirds. But some birds also appear able to navigate, to determine their position even in an unfamiliar area and then to reach their destination. Birds might make use of the earth's magnetic fields or the position of the sun to map their routes on something akin to an internal grid. But all these theories remain unproven, making migration one of the true mysteries of nature.

Each spring birds set a pace that is frantic in comparison to their often leisurely trips south in the fall. Fewer birds may pass through the Lowcountry now than in fall since the favored spring route is near the mountains. But sheer beauty, a flurry of sound and color more than make up for numbers. Birds in their lush breeding plumage race for summer homes to establish their territories and find mates, to display bright feathers and to perform their most melodic courting songs.

Ducks feel the urge first. Even early in February eider and harlequin ducks are leaving the Lowcountry for summer breeding grounds in a frozen North. Although still here, others such as wigeon and ruddy ducks are showing their breeding plumage. Throughout the month, more ducks will be taking off, flying a distance, lingering where food is plentiful but heading decisively for nesting grounds.

February already is time to set out wood duck nesting boxes and purple martin apartments. Birds begin sizing up spots to raise families well before the first twig or grass blade is chosen for the nest.

In the average year, purple martin scouts begin arriving here in the last week of February. The shiny violet-black males and duller females will grow in number until late April or early May when all attention turns to nesting.

Ospreys appear about the same time as martin scouts; some of the magnificent fish hawks spend the winter here but numbers grow with spring migration. And in early March, some year-round residents begin singing songs of courtship; among them is the lovely yellow-throated warbler with its bright yellow throat.

Along the shore, March is a prime birding month. Look for the arrival of assorted gulls that wintered in Florida, least bitterns, Wilson's plovers, upland sandpipers, glossy ibises, least and roseate terns, yellow-crowned night herons, black-necked stilts, pectoral sandpipers and stilt sandpipers. Sandpipers sometimes migrate along the shore in spectacularly large flocks; interesting transients also may appear in late March. And winter residents, such as dunlins and black-bellied plovers, don showy breeding plumage before heading for northern nesting grounds.

As March progresses, more birds will serenade and more summer residents will flock to the Lowcountry.

Leading the bright warbler clan is the parula with its lemon-yellow throat and chest and its buzzy trill of a song. Brilliant prothonotary, hooded, Kentucky, Swainson's, prairie, black-throated green and blackburnian warblers will follow in March and increase in April. So will great-crested flycatchers, kites, yellow-throated and red-eyed vireos, waterthrushes and wood thrushes, pewees, orchard orioles and summer tanagers. Ruby-throated hummingbirds, yellow-billed cuckoos, indigo and painted buntings and blue grosbeaks all should arrive later in March.

Among the most glorious are male summer tanagers, solid rosey red birds that outshine male cardinals, and male prothonotaries with golden-orange heads, necks and chests. Male indigo buntings are a flash of bright turquoise blue if seen in the sunshine, far more brilliant than the dark but distinct blue of male blue grosbeaks. Male painted buntings earn their name with bright red underparts and rump, green back, purple head and red eye-ring.

Herons and white ibises begin gathering on the Drum Island rookery beneath the Cooper River bridges. Numbers on the island will grow from late March until nesting reaches a peak in early May.

In early April, shorebirds such as least and sandwich terns should fly in. Willets arrive a bit earlier, often joining godwits in a migration from South America. Incoming willets swell the small population that wintered along beaches, freshwater and salt marshes, even coastal lakes. Purple gallinules are taking up residence on ponds, former ricefields and almost any place pickerel weed grows. Also watch for Eastern kingbirds, nighthawks and chuck-will's-widow, the last giving a night call that sounds like an Eastern whip-poor-will.

Willet

The entire month of April is a birder's dream with about 100 different species coming, going or passing through the Lowcountry. In the annual spring bird counts of April, a truly industrious birder can tally 150 to 170 different species in 24 hours, two dozen warblers alone. More summer residents arrive each day, year-round and summer varieties begin nesting and everyone sings incessantly.

The hubbub will continue into early May, when migration dwindles to a halt and all efforts are turned to laying eggs and toting food to baby birds. The constant search for food keeps adults on the wing and perhaps more visible than at any other time of the year.

Otters —

In rivers, lakes and swamps each spring, river otters chatter shrilly to one another, announcing their romantic intentions. Males roll about on the shore, flattening vegetation and depositing musk on twisted tufts of grass. And couples, sometimes loyal mates for more than a year, chuckle softly to one another in affection. To these delightfully playful mammals, spring days mean not only courtship and breeding but also the birth of young.

An otter in the Carolinas bears two to four kits between late winter and April and promptly evicts the father from the den they usually share. He remains nearby, however, and soon will be romancing her again. They mate not long after the kits are born, but fetuses do not implant for several months. Active gestation is a mere 63 days.

River Otter

The female digs a permanent den in a bank then excavates entrances above and below water. She fashions her nest of leaves, grass, reeds and sticks. On occasion she may even nest in a favorite resting spot such as a beaver lodge, the burrow of a muskrat or other animal, a hollow log or the recess under an overhang. The male returns to the den in the summer, when the kits are about half grown, to help feed and care for them.

Newborn kits arrrive very well furred but quite helpless; their eyes remain shut for 21 to 35 days. The devoted mother nurses them for three to four months and guards them well when they begin exploring outside the den. If a human approaches, the female will quickly corral her kits, rush them back to the den, station herself in the entrance and growl a warning.

Because young are born over a fairly long season, they may be from one-third to two-thirds grown by early summer. Youngsters disperse when they are 8 months to 1 year old. They may leave their parents in the fall or may still be lingering with their mother when she is ready to deliver a new set of kits. Being such peaceable, sociable, fun-loving creatures, otters may simply enjoy one another's company and so stay together. The only signs of trouble in paradise come during breeding season, when adult males may scrap.

Lutra canadensis has proven himself quite intelligent and curious. Intelligence is often considered a prerequisite for play and that in itself suggests otters are smart. Whether alone, with a mate or with siblings, otters are likely to be cavorting.

The sleek, dark brown animals make slides along banks for a fast escape into the water. But the slides routinely become playground equipment for young and adults. Kits will endlessly follow one another down an 8-inch-wide slide until it is scoured into a chute. In colder climates, river otters toboggan along icy slicks. With front feet tucked, the body becomes a torpedo of blunt snout, thick neck, elongated body and thick tail tapering at the end. Rolling, diving and surfing in fast currents also seem to delight the frolicsome mammals.

The animals are beautifully adapted for their life in and under water although they run well and are quite comfortable on land. The streamlined otter has webbed toes, a rudderlike tail and valves that keep water out of his small ears and nostrils. The fast, powerful swimmer can remain submerged for several minutes at a time, swim forwards or backwards equally well and make dives or turns with grace. The otter also treads water tirelessly and will scout the shore from mid-stream with only his head visible.

Full-grown otters may reach 35 to nearly 52 inches, about one-third of which is tail. Weight ranges from 11 to 30 pounds with females being lighter and smaller than males. The body is covered with a rich coat of short, dense, oily underfur that protects the otter from cold water in winter. The long, glossy guard hairs look nearly black when wet. But when dry, the otter is dark brown with a lighter belly and silvery-gray throat.

Otters have a fairly large home range, which they may travel as a family during the late spring and summer if not longer. The mammals often move up and down a river drainage system and may spend a season or a few weeks in one pond then move on to another. Meandering trails about 8 inches wide often lead from the water to a rolling spot to a slide and another body of water. In the process, otters may wander quite far from the water. But water means safety. If a human approaches, a secretive otter is likely to leap into the nearest river or pond or silently sink beneath a trail of bubbles.

All but invisible, an otter does leave signs on land such as partially eaten fish and depositories. Several otters often use a log or tree over a bank as a common depository, marked by collections of scat and piles of fish scales, fish bones or crayfish parts.

While fish is the mainstay of the diet, otters also catch crayfish, crabs, frogs, snakes, small mammals and other goodies. Potential food may turn into a game as an otter grabs a turtle, paws the tightly closed shell and tosses it about in the water. Otters hunt and feed primarily between dawn and mid-morning and toward evening. A pair of otters may team up to drive a school of fish into an inlet, the equivalent of fast food for an otter. With a quick snap, an otter often catches a fish broadside with his 36 very sharp teeth. Otters are not particularly fussy about the type of fish they eat, but slow-moving carp, suckers and shiners prove easiest and so are taken more often than the species sports fishermen seek. Otters carry large meals to the bank to feast but roll over on their backs and munch on smaller snacks while floating.

Young otters are sometimes taken by alligators, bobcats, other large carnivores and perhaps occasionally a raptor. Parasites and diseases are a minor problem.

Man has been the otter's chief predator. The animals once thrived in almost every stretch of clean freshwater in the Carolinas and even in brackish water. Trapping, development, habitat destruction and water pollution all began taking a toll on otters. The beauty and thickness of otter fur led to overtrapping in the past. Then otters were hit by the indiscriminate use of pesticides, which drained into the water, poisoned fish and crayfish then built up in otters feeding on that prey. Not only did man develop waterfront land, which sent otters scuttling, but boating and other activities further fouled water. In some areas, particularly northern and central states, there is concern about today's populations and the future of the river otter, which has been listed as an endangered species in Virginia.

In South Carolina, however, otters are thriving and numbers stable. Regulating trapping and banning dangerous pesticides have helped otters in the Carolinas and elsewhere. South Carolina has even provided animals to some of the states now trying to restock former otter habitat. The coastal plain has the greatest number of otters in South Carolina, but every major river drainage in the state has at least some of the playful mammals. And the Charleston area has one of the highest concentrations of otters on the entire Eastern seaboard.

Shells collected on a South Carolina beach.

1 — Banded Tulip, 2 — Lettered Olive, 3 — Shark Eye, 4 — Atlantic Cockle,
5 — Knobbed Whelk, 6 — Ark, 7 — Duck Clam, 8 — Pen, 9 — Clams.

Beaches —

Early spring may be the best of times at Lowcountry beaches. The sand still holds remnants of fine winter shelling, weather is warming and the crowds of summer have yet to arrive. Water's edge belongs to the sea creatures, creeping in to breed and leave behind bizarre looking egg cases.

The first of March, when shells remain abundant, shark eye egg capsules may begin washing in. Later in March, egg cases of oyster drills, dove shells and augers may dot the shore while whelk egg cases appear throughout the winter and spring.

As the water near shore warms in late April, creatures migrate. Seashell species that are small head toward shore and search for mates. But many larger shelled creatures are heading for cooler, deeper water after wintering just under the sand in very shallow water.

Compared to birds and mammals, the snails and clams inhabiting shells may not have much personality. But they do have a remarkable ability to transform elements from the ocean, sand and their own bodies into works of art and marvels of balanced engineering.

If magnified about 7,000 times, a vertical cross section of a shell resembles a brick wall; calcite crystals are the bricks held in place by a mortar of protein. Water temperature determines how quickly crystals are formed and what size they will be.

The blood of a mollusk is rich in a liquid salt or calcium carbonate and the fleshy mantle, a sac of skin covering internal organs, concentrates the calcium. Crystallization takes place in a protected area between the mantle and layers of the old shell. Solid crystals may form on other crystals or in a lattice of protein, a soft, brown material called conchiolin. The operculum, or opening of a snail shell, is layers of this same protein hardened into a horn-like strength.

As it grows, the shell critter builds its home. At least some creatures, such as whelks, also can repair damage to their shells which often are chipped when prying open bivalve shells to reach the succulent clams inside. Food provides the pigment or color distributed by the blood system. Pigment cells add color and pattern as a shell grows.

Scattered throughout the body, these cells are concentrated in the mantle; the color-depositing cells migrate along the edge of the mantle and pigment is produced intermittently. If a pigment center stays in place on the edge of the mantle, a stripe forms along the shell. If the cell wanders, the stripe will be oblique. And if pigment is produced only periodically, then splotches, dots or streaks will color the shell. Intensity of color may change as the mollusk grows, often because of a change in diet or salinity of water.

Among the more common pigments are orange to yellow carotenoids (the same pigments that brighten autumn leaves, carrots and daffodils), black to tan melanins (pigments that tint human skin) and indigoids that once were drawn from shells to dye royal clothing a rich purple.

Tubes of almost infinite variety house gastropods, the largest class of mollusks including more than 50,000 shells such as snails and whelks. The snail inside winds in a spiral around a central axis and builds an elongated tube of shell. Each turn or increasingly large whorl is separated from the next by a suture and the pointed apex often contains the original tiny larval shell in which the animal first emerged from its egg.

Lettered Olive, the S.C. state shell.

Very shiny shells, such as olives and cowries, normally are covered by the mantle, which protects and polishes the surface while the animal is alive. Once the inhabitant dies, its shell grows dull as waves and currents grind it against sand, rocks or other shells.

Hermit crabs may move in, breaking apart the internal structure of the shell so the new home will fit the needs and the body of the crab. Such weakened shells are more easily shattered by waves and eventually broken down to become sand. In time, shells tumble in breakers and wash up on the beach, where the sun bleaches colors. Just a bit of baby oil rubbed on the shell will bring back much of the original color and luster.

Lowcountry shells include bivalves, primitive chitons covered by a series of plates, deepwater tusk shells shaped like an elephant's tusk and gastropods, perhaps the most interesting of all the classes. A univalve or single-shell animal, the gastropod usually has a tough, flattened, muscular creeping foot and a well-developed head with tentacles, eyes and a mouth that may be at the end of a long tubular extension, the proboscis. It may be equipped with a radula or organ of minute teeth to shred food. Most gastropods also have one or two siphons to bring in water and discharge waste.

Gastropods that prowl the ocean and land on Carolina beaches include slipper shells, limpets, turrets, wentletraps, augers, baby's ears, periwinkles in marshes, shark eyes, margin shells, simnias, tulips, doves, fig shells, whelks, murexes, Atlantic distorsios, oyster drills and olives such as the South Carolina state shell, the lettered olive.

Each bivalve, on the other hand, is a pair of shells attached by an elastic ligament and often by a hinge of teeth that lock together. As they tumble in the waves, bivalves usually split into two shells, occasionally dissimilar but often mirror images.

Among the more common ones in South Carolina are assorted robust arks, turkey wings, mussels, oysters, cockles, quahogs, Venuses, tellins, a wide variety of clams, sparkling jingle shells and scallops. Less frequently coquinas, bittersweets, delicate pen shells, lucines and very fragile angel wings may reach the beach.

Instead of a head, eyes, radula or jaws a bivalve has a foot at the front end. Tubular siphons or other openings in the mantle bring in water and food particles and expel waste. Many bivalves also have a byssus or bundle of fibers on the foot that will anchor the shell to a rock, another shell or other object. While some bivalves, such as the oyster, find one spot for life, others, such as the giant Atlantic cockle, use a muscular foot to burrow and to move over the sand. And some, including most adult scallops, can be downright speedy, jet propelling through the water when disturbed or threatened by a predator.

In spring mollusks that can move are often searching for mates. The immobile Eastern oyster, in contrast, changes sex one or more times during its lifetime, releasing eggs during the female stage and fertilizing them during the male stage. Atlantic slipper shells often live in stacks. A hormone, produced by the large female on the bottom, causes the shells above to remain male and release sperm. But should the lady grow old or ill and the hormone level drop, a slipper or two directly above quickly become female and begin making the hormone.

Primitive shells, such as chitons, release huge numbers of sperm and eggs into the water while more advanced gastropods, such as whelks and shark eyes, fertilize their eggs internally, usually after copulation. Excellent mothers, some shelled animals even guard their eggs against predators. Female cowries, occasionally seen on Carolina beaches, sit atop their large egg clusters to protect them. Some snails retain their eggs in a brood chamber and give birth to live young. Sundials, which live in Carolina waters but rarely are seen on the beach, keep their young in their outer shells.

Many of the more highly evolved species lay fertilized eggs in masses or capsules; a single capsule may float about or remain attached to a solid object. Other mollusks produce a string of capsules, each containing from one to nearly 1,000 eggs.

Inside the egg, the shell gland of the larva develops, eventually becoming the edge of the creature's mantle. By the time the larva emerges from its capsule, the creature may not resemble its parents or may, in the case of channeled whelks, be a duplicate of the adult shell.

Before or after young emerge, their capsules may wash up on the beach. Shark eyes often appear in early March while whelks, oyster drills, dove shells, augers and the like arrive in April.

Female whelks may spend a full week in spring and fall laying a string of up to 150 capsules 40 inches in length. The flat, rounded, tannish-yellow cases are attached to one another by a filament running

Knobbed Whelk (top) and Channeled Whelk with egg cases.

along one side. The pungent ropes resemble telephone cords or a human spinal column. Several specialized glands help the female enclose 20 to 40 eggs in each capsule.

Before releasing the string, the whelk buries one end. During the productive fall breeding season, more than in spring, capsules often break loose during storms and wash up on shore. Once dry, the durable cases are easily opened to disclose tiny versions of adult whelks. The miniscule whelks feed on albumin and nurse eggs, which the mother provides in each capsule. But hungry whelks also may turn cannibalistic before emerging. An opening in the egg case remains plugged until young whelks are ready to enter the ocean world. So if beached capsules each bear a tiny hole, young hatched successfully.

Shark eyes, rounded shells of typical snail shape, leave hundreds of golden eggs in the sand. In early March, a female may even be seen near water's edge laying her eggs in a hardened collar of mucus and sand. The eggs will remain securely lodged there until they hatch.

The single pill-shaped capsules of dove shells, which feed on algae and animal debris, often are visible on rocks along Breach Inlet. Containing about six eggs, each capsule is cemented to seaweed or rocks. Young shells are a single wide whorl and only as adults do the white to dark brown shells spiral to a pointed top.

Each spring shiny little simnias, colored bright yellow or purple to blend with the sea whips on which they live, crowd oblong clumps of capsules on branches of the whips. Each capsule contains several hundred eggs and young emerge swimming.

Another rite of the spring beach, sand dollars often migrate in early April along spots such as Kiawah and Capers islands. Some perish and drift onto the beach in smooth, white condition. But many more hide less than half an inch beneath the sand at low tide. Above the echinoderms, which are not true shells, five small holes appear in the sand. The live greenish dollars are covered with fine cilia or delicate spines on the upper side. The spines protect the animal from sand as it burrows while longer spines on the underside help this relative of the sea urchin dig and push its way through sand. Bristle-like hairs on the perimeter of the test, or shell, also pass organic material to the small mouth in the center.

By late spring hosts of sea creatures are migrating inshore after a winter in the deep. And as the ocean water hits 70 and beckons swimmers, the warmth also is drawing crabs, shrimp, fish and even sharks toward beaches.

Gulf Fritillary butterfly on Marigold.

Butterflies —

With the flush of spring flowers come the butterflies, fragile insects fluttering by in search of nectar. The season begins slowly, with dramatic swallowtails usually appearing as azaleas unfurl. By the first week in May, spring butterflies are reaching a peak. An ever-changing population will continue well into fall as new species take wing for just a few days or stay for months.

Being true insects, butterflies go through four life stages and an amazing metamorphosis. Most winter as eggs or equally inactive pupae, safe from the cold that will claim adults. In their season, females often lay their eggs on a plant variety that hungry larvae will munch when spring arrives. Larvae have but one purpose when they hatch — to feed. Each as colorful and distinctive as the winged creature it will become, caterpillars may dine primarily, or exclusively, on one type of plant.

Some caterpillars occasionally may eat dried animal matter or take live prey, but most depend on tender, leafy material. The larva has powerful jaws, functioning legs on the thorax and up to five pairs of prolegs on the abdomen, leg-like structures that will later disappear.

Once it is well fed, a butterfly larva forms a chrysalis. Modified salivary glands opening on the lower lip, silk glands fashion a covering that will protect the pupa through the winter or, in some species, for a briefer time in the summer. The chrysalis, which varies in color and often is sculptured, remains attached to a plant on which the larva was feeding or to a nearby support that offers shelter.

After a rest and perhaps with the warmth of spring, the former caterpillar emerges as a delicate winged creature. The monarch caterpillar is striped with thin bands of yellow, white and black and decorated with a pair of flexible, black filaments near the front and back ends. Inside its chrysalis, it develops brownish-orange wings with black veins and black or dark brown margins spotted with white. An exotic-looking blue-black, almost shiny, caterpillar with a row of large red spots, many white dots and branching spines takes on the dreary name of mourning cloak. It leaves its chrysalis with purplish-brown fore or front wings edged in dirty yellow and with brownish-gray hind wings flecked with pale gray resembling weathered wood.

After struggling from a chrysalis, the fully-grown butterfly waits for the insect equivalent of blood to fill the intricate pattern of veins in its wings, actually membranes covered in pigmented or prismatic scales that will rub off like dust to the touch. Major portions of the body and legs are covered with scales.

Butterflies are most active from late morning to mid-afternoon and much prefer hot, sunny days. When not dipping the long, coiled tube or proboscis into flower nectar, a butterfly may be stopping by a puddle for a drink.

Numbering more than 125,000 known species of butterflies and night-flying moths worldwide and 12,000 in North America, the order *Lepidoptera* includes many varieties yet to be classified. The insects range in wingspan from ⅛ inch to 10⅝ inches and may live for just a few days or for more than a year. Monarchs, first seen here in late April, can fly from Canada to Mexico and back to the southern United States. Millions migrate in autumn to escape oncoming cold. On the route north the next spring, females lay eggs that will produce adults in just four weeks.

Yellow sulphurs, often one of the first butterflies seen in spring and the last seen in fall, may even survive a mild winter and be looking for mates when warm weather arrives.

Courtship may not be the lively, vocal game of birds, but solid yellow sulphurs have their own rituals. Floating over meadows, a male sulphur will spot a potential mate and begin flying close beside her near the ground. One sulphur circles the other and both immediately begin spiraling up around each other. Borne on a wingspan of about 1½ inches, the butterflies rise together, sometimes as high as 60 feet.

Suddenly one butterfly drops, as if weighted, to the ground while the other drifts down slowly. The female of the pair usually has mated already but leads the spiraling perhaps to discourage a courting male. The male gives up and falls to the ground when she flies too high for him to follow while she descends gracefully and returns to her egg-laying duties. These aerial dances continue throughout the spring and summer. Eager males spend the season flying about rapidly and will approach almost any other butterfly regardless of species or sex. Only at close range is the male sulphur able to recognize a potential mate or, more likely, to see his mistake.

Some of the most glorious Lowcountry butterflies are often the first to emerge in spring. Large swallowtails seem to escape their winter

Swallowtail butterfly visits Zinnia flower.

chrysalises just as azaleas pop into bloom. Archetypal butterflies, members of the swallowtail or *Papilionidae* family bear the same name as the French word for butterfly, *papillon.*

Eastern tiger, Eastern black and palamedes swallowtails have distinctive points or tails at the bottom of each hind wing. Tigers, wearing the yellow wings and black, tiger-like stripes of their namesake, have wingspans that may reach nearly 6 inches. In the South, dark phase female tigers are common, their brownish-black wings bearing yellow and blue spots near the outer margins.

Black swallowtails, with wingspans of 2¾ to 3½ inches, have black fore wings marked with a double row of yellow spots. Spots in the inner row are larger and more triangular in males, smaller in females. Hind wings of this low-flying butterfly bear a row of yellow, crescent-like marks and, in males, a row of larger yellow spots, smaller in females. The area between the spots is washed with blue. The butterfly dines on nectar from clover and cultivated flowers while caterpillars enjoy the foliage of parsley, carrots and celery.

The palamedes is primarily black but marked with blue. Thistle plants and purple vetch seem to attract the palamedes as do garden flowers, which are prized by a wide variety of butterflies.

Swallowtails may be seen into the fall, but spring mourning cloak butterflies mate early in the spring, lay their eggs on food plants such as willows and often die before summer. Prospective mates sometimes spiral as sulphurs do but more often chase one another for short distances. A member of the largest family of butterflies, mourning cloaks are nicknamed "four footed" because their third front pair of legs is small and held against the body. Like some other butterflies, the mourning cloak usually produces two generations in the South. Adults of the second generation are thought to overwinter, hidden in crevices of bark or rock. The butterfly comes to life early in spring and sails the open woods with rapid wing flaps and graceful glides.

Pearl crescents prefer flitting about open areas, feeding on butterfly weed and orange milkweed flowers and stopping at roadside puddles. The insect's wings are mostly brownish-orange marked with dark brown and colored somewhat differently below than above. The underside of wings is brighter orange and has fewer marks on the fore wing of individuals hatched in the summer generation and darker marks in the spring generation, appearing by early April. Hind wings are more silvery and dull brown in the first generation but more yellow in the second.

Separate generations of various butterflies may look identical. But, as with pearl crescents, the top of a butterfly's wings will be at least somewhat different from the underside. The latter often is more luminous or bright than the topside, a pleasant fact since butterflies usually pause with their wings upright and together.

Angle wings are orange with brown spots above but brownish-gray with silver markings below. The question mark angle wing has silver streaks that resemble a question mark while the comma has silvery punctuation.

Various butterfly species also fly distinctively although it may take an expert to distinguish between some patterns. Angle wings have angular scoops, protrusions and a small tail at the back of each hind wing. The insects fly very irregularly almost as if hampered by the strange cut of their wings.

The satyr has no such excuse, but its flight is nearly as erratic. Appearing a bit later in spring, as do angle wings, little wood satyrs are light brown, brightened only by two prominent eyespots on each wing. Below, wings are paler and marked with several, smaller eyespots along the outer margin. On a wingspan of just 2 inches, the satyrs swoop close to the ground then zip up through openings in plants. Very similar in appearance but slightly larger, the wood nymph is abundant in spring and summer. The fore wings often are dressed up with a yellow patch containing two blue eyespots.

Hairstreaks, which begin to show in April, are named for the narrow bands on the underside of their wings. They streak through the air with swift darts on their search for beans and hops. The small common or gray hairstreak, which can produce three or more generations here, is grayish-brown with a large orange spot on each hind wing.

Spring azures, also known as common blues, can't be mistaken. The only predominantly blue butterflies in the Lowcountry, tiny males have pale sky blue coloring above and are metallic brownish-gray with small dark spots below. The female's fore wings fade from dark blackish-gray in front through the blue range into nearly white, but her hind wings are pale bluish. The first generation each year is brightest with progeny in the summer looking paler.

Painted ladies, which first appear in spring, have fore wings of orange above with numerous black markings and a few white spots. Below the wings are grayish, marbled with white and black and dressed up with bright pink at the base. Hind wings are orange above but dotted with four round eyespots below.

When it comes to eyespots, the pearly eye shines. Its light yellowish-brown fore wings have a row of four dark brown spots outlined in yellow; hind wings have six spots. Beneath, wings have dark brown spots in eye-like patterns. Speedy fliers, males lie in wait on tree trunks and dash out at other butterflies. The males, with a wingspan of no more than 2 inches, will battle furiously over territory.

Red admiral males also are territorial and often chase away other males. When the dark wings are open, a wide orange band forms parentheses; white dots mark the outer top edge of the fore wings.

Silver-spotted skippers and viceroys also appear as spring advances. The skippers are small, chocolate-brown butterflies with an irregular golden band below and smaller yellow areas above on the fore wings and a silvery-white, irregular spot below on hind wings.

Viceroys are almost dead ringers for monarchs. Wings are brownish-orange above with blue-black to dark brown margins and veins and a few white dots. The viceroy probably evolved to mimic the color of the monarch, which is poisonous to predatory birds.

As spring fades into summer, many of these butterflies will vanish and reappear as new generations rush through their life cycles. And still more varieties will grace the summer landscape. Even after cold weather strikes in fall or early winter, the pure yellow of sulphur butterflies will glide by, searching for the last vestiges of wildflowers or camellias in the garden.

Carolina, or Green, Anole displays dewlap.

Lizards —

The spring sun draws lizards out of winter hiding to bask and forage, then soon after to court and mate. By late spring lizards will begin laying eggs and small versions of adults will be emerging in late June or July.

The familiar Carolina, or green, anole, the alternately green or brown lizard mistakenly called a chameleon, claims his territory by flaring his red throat fan or dewlap and bobbing his head. Each species of anole around the world moves his head in a different pattern, recognized by competitors and potential mates alike. The act usually drives an intruding male away from the resident's territory, about one square meter of land he actively defends. Should the visitor linger or creep even closer, the two will fight, thrashing about and sometimes crashing to the ground as they grapple. The defending male is usually the winner.

On the other hand, the apparent intruder may prove to be one of the two or three females living in the male's territory. The female begins forming an egg when she sees the male's display and what might have become a battle quickly turns into courtship. Because sperm remains viable for eight months or more, the female only needs to mate once each spring. But she is capable of laying an egg every two weeks for the entire breeding season so must be courted and witness a male's showy fan twice a month.

Rain appears to stimulate egg laying. A female on a branch may casually drop her egg, leave it on the bark or climb down to lay her egg in leaf litter. The egg hatches in about 7 weeks and the newborn lizard makes his way alone. As he grows, he repeatedly sheds his skin in thin white patches. He may even consume the skin, perhaps to recycle vitamin D or other compounds.

Dining on insects, the anole sips water from dew and raindrops. An anole kept in captivity may not recognize water presented in a bowl and may die of dehydration unless surroundings are sprayed with water.

The anole's nervous system can trigger his color changes in just minutes while hormones accomplish the same end more slowly. In winter, when anoles sometimes come out to bask and occasionally to feed, the lizards are brown to gray. In warm months, anoles can turn brown but usually are green, a very intense green when courting or defending territory.

If the area is overcrowded with lizards, a social hierarchy or pecking order will develop. Only dominant males attract mates. Subordinate males fail to breed, thereby reducing the population.

Being opportunistic feeders and thriving in a wide variety of habitats, lizards are the most sucessful of all reptile groups. Some 3,000 species ring the world, particularly the tropical climes. South Carolina has 11 known native species; the Texas horned lizard was introduced and has taken hold. And a 13th species of lizard was recently discovered but has yet to be named and described to science.

Lizards are most closely related to snakes. In fact three species of glass lizards in South Carolina and the new nameless lizard lack legs and look more like snakes than lizards. Most, however, have four legs and all are covered in dry scales. But unlike snakes, lizards have movable-eyelids, ear canals and middle ears. Lizards cannot unhinge their jaws, as snakes can, to swallow enormous prey. Lizards hunt actively, more like snakes than like salamanders or frogs that wait for dinner to pass by. Sight is the most vital of the senses, but smell also is important, especially to members of the secretive skink family.

Many lizards, including anoles and most glass lizards, have fracture zones in their tails, permitting the reptiles to race away safely while a predator is preoccupied with a twitching tail. The main artery in the tail constricts spasmodically, reducing the loss of blood, while a flap of loose skin folds over the injury. The lizard can regenerate his tail in a matter of weeks.

Like snakes, lizards bask in the sun to raise their body temperatures then retreat to the shade to cool off in the summer. Year-round, lizards typically spend the first hours of daylight soaking up sun and warmth, easily raising their temperatures to 98.6 degrees and so belying the term coldblooded. Anoles and their relatives, members of the iguana family, even have the remnants of a third eye atop their heads, a sense organ telling the animal when he is hot enough and should move from the sun. Only once he is warm will the lizard search for food.

Texas Horned Lizard.

Particularly dependent on high temperatures are Texas horned lizards, which normally live in and around Texas. Texans apparently brought the fearsome looking lizards to the Lowcountry as pets. Texas servicemen also introduced the horned lizards to Fort Moultrie and Sullivan's Island during World War II. Also known as horned toads, the animals sometimes are sold in pet shops but seldom can be properly fed in captivity. In the wild, however, the horned toads have prospered. Members of the same iguanid family as the Carolina anole, the horned lizards are now seen regularly around Sullivan's Island, Isle of Palms, James Island and Garden City.

Thought to stop eating when temperatures fall below 70 degrees, horned lizards are active primarily on summer days then hide in burrows during cooler weather. The species prefers dry, loose soil so takes readily to open, grassy, sunny areas among and just behind beach dunes. Plunking himself down on a busy anthill, the lizard scoffs up large live ants with his long tongue.

Measuring 3 to 7 inches long, the squat, short-tailed lizard is pale yellowish to grayish brown or tan with black blotches and a thin light streak down the middle of his back. He is crowned with spines and wears two rows of pointed scales that resemble spines on his sides. Perhaps most unusual, the horned lizard can eject a thin stream of blood from his eye, a sign he is angry or irritated. At will the lizard can increase the blood pressure in his head to jet the blood up to 7 feet.

While some horned lizards give birth to live young, the Texas variety lays 13 to 37 eggs between May and July. The female digs a burrow and deposits her eggs 2 to 7 inches below the surface. When young hatch about six weeks later, they measure slightly more than 1 inch.

Horned lizards and male broad-headed skinks are the most fierce looking of South Carolina's lizards, but none of the 13 is poisonous. However the broad-headed skink, which may be aggressive and tends to bite if captured, can draw blood. Adult male broad-headed skinks may reach 13 inches. The rusty brown lizard has a very wide red-orange head that becomes intensely red during the breeding season.

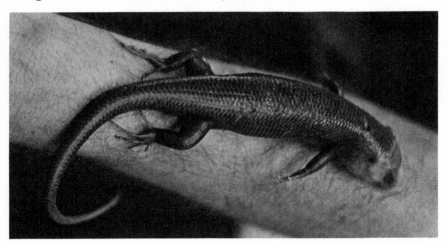

Broad-Headed Skink.

Young look like an entirely different species. The body is black, lined lengthwise with yellowish-white stripes and tipped with a brilliant blue tail. A youngster can leave his tail wriggling in front of a predator and run to safety. The tail apparently causes extreme nausea, enough to stop the predator from ever wanting a juvenile skink again. Females are relatively dark but retain stripes on their sides and a narrow head. The ferocious broadhead routinely goes hunting high in trees and has even been seen shaking wasp nests to free a meal of pupae. His scales are so bony that he seems unperturbed by the stings of defending adult wasps.

Although young skinks may make themselves very evident around a porch or warm, brick steps, adults often play it scarce. In extreme drought and heat, skinks all but disappear under leaf litter and become inactive to reduce their need for water and food.

Two very close relatives look almost identical to the broadhead, particularly young and females. All three are sleek lizards with smooth scales, giving them a shiny look. Both the five-lined and the Southeastern five-lined skink grow only 5 to 8 inches long. Adult males are black or brown with five light stripes that may fade to uniform brown with age. The males have narrower red-orange heads than the broadhead and tails remain blue to gray.

Of the three, the Southeastern five-lined is probably the most common variety on coastal islands and the least arboreal. Cats occasionally feed on the skink and afterwards may temporarily become paralyzed or lose their balance. The plain five-lined, the most common of the skinks in much of the Lowcountry, climbs little except to bask on stumps or the bottom of tree trunks. Spiders, insects, worms, even lizards and small mice are favorite foods.

Sometimes mistaken for salamanders, ground skinks are active year-round but spend most of their time on the ground, often hidden in leaf litter. The smallest lizards in the Carolinas, only 3 to 5 inches, the long-tailed skinks are brown with black stripes along their sides. Females lay from one to seven eggs almost every month from spring through summer but abandon their nests after laying.

Other skinks stay with their eggs, usually laid in a depression or cavity in the ground, an old sawdust pile, a tree cavity or a rock cavity. The female routinely curls around her eggs to defend them and will brace intruders. But she does not incubate the eggs, which are warmed by the decaying sawdust or leaves around them.

The coal skink probably resides in the mountains of South Carolina, but there is only one official state record for this threatened species. Particularly secretive, the skink generally remains buried in leaves on rocky, wooded hillsides and usually near water. Growing up to 7 inches, adults are brown with four light stripes extending from neck onto tail. A dark band on each side separates the light stripes. Males may have reddish heads. Young are almost coal black and have a blue tail.

Aptly named, the six-lined racerunner has six light stripes separated by dark greenish-brown to black bands. A seventh narrow, light stripe may run down the middle of his back. Females have white throats, males green or blue. The belly in adults is white or blue-white, the tail brown with stripes but light blue in young. Most active in the morning, when he basks and hunts for insects, the lizard burrows into the soil at night. Most common in sandy areas such as Kiawah and Edisto islands, the long-legged lizard moves in jerky bursts of speed.

Legless glass lizards very readily release tails that may shatter into several pieces. Although the tail is more than half the body length in some species, the animal can grow a new tail in a matter of weeks.

The most common of the glass lizards in the coastal plain, the Eastern glass may grow to 42 snake-like inches. Foraging in the early morning, glass lizards are most visible before 9 a.m. or in the late afternoon. Omniverous, the animal dines on assorted insects but also wrestles young mammals; he most often hunts near marshes and other wet areas near highways. Wearing white markings near the edges of his back scales, the lizard has an unusual fold or groove on the side of his body, which distinguishes the lizard from a snake. The female stays with her clutch of eight to 17 eggs for their two months of incubation.

Throughout the state, the slender glass lizard haunts the margins of woods and open areas. The longest of the state's glass lizards and the most common one in the Piedmont, the slender may reach 47 inches, much of which is tail. The slender looks much like the Eastern but has dark stripes or speckling below the groove, which the Eastern lacks. Mating in May, the slender lays six to 17 eggs in June or July and broods them. Preferring dry grasslands and dry, open woodlands, the lizard will fight to escape if he is grabbed and will quickly drop a tail more than two and a half times as long as the body and head.

A rare animal, the island glass is usually seen only in McClellanville, on Morris Island and in a few Beaufort and Jasper county sites. Often seen under debris on sandy beaches, the island resembles the Eastern glass but tends to be more spotted with white and is only 15 to 24 inches. Heavily marked with white bars on his neck, as the Eastern also can be, the island does not appear to shed his tail readily.

For a time the fence lizard also seemed somewhat rare, but the animal now appears to be thriving in pine forests and open pine woods. The arboreal lizard not only likes fences but also clings to the bark of pine trees. Measuring up to 7 inches, the lizard has a dark band along the rear of his thigh. His color varies from gray to brown to rusty with stripes and sometimes a hint of crossbars or spots. Males usually have blue throat patches and blue patches bordered with black on the belly. The lizard's favorite meal is beetles although he also will eat assorted insects, spiders and snails.

Bird Songs —

Just after dawn on spring mornings, the Lowcountry erupts with bird song. As predictably as dogwoods bloom, birds choose that time and season to chorus with supreme zeal, urgency and variety.

Attracting a mate and claiming a territory are paramount to these songsters, all males eager to advertise their virtues. It was long thought that males sing only to draw mates and indeed some polygamous birds do round up more mates when their songs are particularly elaborate. But ornithologists now know that birds are territorial and use song in spring — sometimes also in fall and winter — to drive competitors away. Indeed those same polygamous birds that captivate so many mates with more intricate songs also prove to have larger territories than their less musical rivals.

Light intensity is thought to trigger the vocal outbursts. Singing peaks for about half an hour as the black of night lightens to gray and birds awake. Songs slow as morning progresses and birds all but fall silent in the noon-day heat. But the orchestra tunes up again just before birds turn in for the night.

The songs are prompted by hormones that cause the sex glands of males to swell, sometimes up to 400 times normal winter size. As the spring courtship and breeding season passes, hormones drop and so does song. Some species cease their vocal displays not long after mating while many continue at least through nesting season. Still other dramatic songsters, like the mockingbird, go into an equally vigorous fall display, put on perhaps because a low level of hormones has begun to flow, because days are again the same length as during breeding season or because migrants are invading the territory. Birds may continue singing a bit even in winter, particularly on warm, spring-like days. And winter nesters such as owls are heard most often during the cold months.

While man's voice comes from his larynx, a bird's song flows from the syrinx at the bottom end of the trachea. Birds have two sources of sound while man has one. And birds do not use tongue and mouth to affect sound as man does; instead muscles control the syrinx. The system is at its complex best among songbirds, a small portion of the world's nearly 9,000 species. Magnificent vocalists like the brown thrasher are able to sing two melodies at once, each half of the syrinx producing different notes at exactly the same time.

Of all the Lowcountry songbirds, the brown thrasher and its close relatives give the most marvelous performances. The thrasher, mockingbird and gray catbird — all of which nest in South Carolina — belong to the *Mimidae* group and are considered mimics.

The brown thrasher, *Toxostoma rufum*, lives throughout the state year-round and willingly nests close to houses. The bird defends its nest almost as insistently as a mockingbird and may fly at people who have the audacity to walk in and out of a house by a thrasher nest. Measuring about 10 to 12 inches in length, the bird has cinnamon rufous upper parts, wings and long tail. Undersides are white to buffy with dark brown streaks on the breast and sides.

The bird is sometimes confused with smaller thrushes such as the wood thrush which gives its own beautiful song to announce spring is here. The series of melodious, flute-like phrases ends in a trill. After a moment's quiet, the wood thrush repeats the tune in slightly different form.

As early as February, the thrasher begins to sing from a lofty spot, far above the ground where the bird is usually seen tossing fallen leaves in its search for insects. The song is a wondrous variety of musical sounds, each resembling another bird's notes. The thrasher repeats the call, pauses briefly then moves on to its next melody and repeats that. The performance may continue for some time without duplicating a stanza. The late South Carolina ornithologist Arthur T. Wayne has written of the thrasher, "To my ear the song...is sweeter, richer and wilder than the mockingbird and as a musician he is simply incomparable."

The Eastern mockingbird, in contrast, usually proclaims each phrase three or more times and can't bother to pause between phrases. Full of curiosity as well as melody, the mocker continues tirelessly at most any time of the day and, not infrequently, the night. In what seems sheer exuberance, a male will stake out a high, exposed spot in his territory and mid-song will fly several feet straight up then slowly spiral down on outstretched wings. The white patches on wings and tail are well displayed in these shows, in flight and as the gray bird struts the ground and periodically flashes its wings.

The mocker shows amazing variety. The songs of 36 species have been counted in one mockingbird's repertoire. The bird's Latin name, appropriately enough, is *Mimus polyglottos*. Mockers are thought to learn or develop their vocabulary by listening to other bird songs and, sometimes regretably, to other sounds around them. If a car in the neighborhood backfires regularly, expect the local mocker to pick up the racket. Mockers in downtown Charleston routinely give grackle calls while brothers in suburbia will be experts at cardinal songs. Mockingbirds even seem to orchestrate their compositions. One very melodic bird song will lead to another lovely tune, but beware that first raucous note because it probably signals a string of accusations, hollering and other screeching.

The mocker isn't known for its delightful personality, either. Extremely territorial, a male will patrol the boundaries of his property and attack intruders. Mockers have died in the vain attempt to fight off their own reflections in glass or mirror. Both male and female will defend their nest area and have been known to terrify resident cats with pecking and people with dive-bombing.

The gray catbird's vocalizations are less dramatic. Although it's a common permanent resident throughout the state and named *Dumetella carolinensis*, the bird isn't often seen close to the coast in summer. The dark gray bird with black cap and rusty undertail coverts produces a long but irregular stream of musical and mechanical notes or phrases. It sometimes seems to mimic other birds outright and often gives a cat-like mewing from a tangle of growth. An imitation of a cat's whine often brings the bird into view. Like its relatives, the catbird is very comfortable near homes and in gardens, where it dines on a variety of insects.

Most other area songsters have only one or a handful of songs, notes so distinctive that birders often rely on song more than appearance to identify a bird in the field.

A few like the familiar cardinal have a rather rich vocabulary from which to choose. Field guides may claim the cardinal says only "what-cheer, cheer, cheer" or "purty-purty-purty-purty" or the word "sweet" repeated four times. However, cardinals have never read bird books. In spring the bright red males can come up with a wide variety of songs and some birds seem more talented, if not inventive, than others. Hidden away in a flowery azalea bower beside his would-be bride, a redbird may court with a long, complex score of trillings, warblings and soft notes totally unlike the usual cardinal chatter.

The many Lowcountry nesters that are not true songbirds have their own vocal measures. The secretive yellow-billed cuckoo, rarely seen but easily heard even from a distance, gives a rapid drum roll of hollow notes that slow at the end. Nicknamed the rain crow, this cuckoo often announces approaching storms. And mates call out from a tree perch before delivering a meal of caterpillars to spouse or youngsters on a flimsy saucer of a nest.

Still other birds, such as many woodpeckers, prefer drumming to singing. And pelicans, known to make sounds only as youngsters, rely on head bobbing and bill clapping to court.

Whatever the beauty of the song, ornithologists have long wondered and often tried to prove whether birds learn the appropriate notes from parents or instinctively know the proper sounds their species should make. The answer, apparently, is both. As a test, baby birds have been taken from their parents and raised by adults of another species. Such a foundling grows up to give the song of its adopted father. Other nestlings that aren't exposed to bird songs are able to make only some of the sounds of their species.

In addition to the songs of spring, birds have less luxurious and somewhat less individualistic calls, simple notes that both males and females give at any time of year. For the thrasher, the call is a sharp "smack," for the mocker a harsh "chack," for the catbird a mewing, for the cardinal a metallic "chip" or "cheep."

Mates and members of the same flock call to one another; a male cardinal at a feeding station may "cheep" to his nearby mate and answer her responses all the time he is dining. Birds living in flocks give what are known as contact calls. Mates call to one another and their young with recognition notes and baby birds quickly are able to distinguish their parents' calls from those of other adults. Young birds, whether on the nest or newly fledged, use calls to gain their parents' attention and food.

Of necessity, birds also call when danger threatens. Small birds, which seem to face threats on all sides, have two types of alarm cries. The thin, high-pitched call signals a predator or peril from above such as a hawk. The more abrupt, harsh call means the problem is approaching from below, perhaps a snake or cat. Each type of alarm is similar among many species so birds can recognize the danger calls of one another. When bluejays set up a ruckus because a cat is on the prowl, sparrows and warblers and woodpeckers are warned as well.

Like man, birds also can send messages visually with assorted posturings and displays. But while many wild creatures rely on sight and smell for much of their communication, birds all but have a language. Mates can recognize one another through songs, young distinguish their parents by their calls, birds verbally warn one another of danger and males can tell rivals to stay away and females to come hither. In short, birds have all the basics of life covered in their small but beautiful vocabularies.

Charleston Museum specimen.

Striped Skunk.

Skunks—

After a winter of relative inactivity, skunks take a new lease on life in early spring. Males begin searching for mates almost before shaking the chill of winter and by late spring mothers are parading a straight line of little replicas behind them. This springtime bustle, of course, means skunks and people may run into one another, a meeting probably more feared by man than beast.

Truth to be known, skunks are pleasant critters, low-key, shy, even friendly and playful. They are never happier than when left alone to mind their own nocturnal business. The animals appear self-confident — and little wonder — but not the least bit aggressive. Aggression is often a sign of rabies rather than normalcy. Unless threatened, skunks will not pull out the heavy artillery for which they are famous. Sudden moves frighten them, and mothers defend young fiercely so the best tactic is to freeze if a skunk suddenly appears with or without babies in tow.

The musk of striped and spotted skunks is actually a butyl mercaptan, a sulfurous compound that makes the eyes burn and can temporarily cause blindness. Charleston pastor and naturalist, the Rev.

John Bachman, co-author with John James Audubon of the massive work *The Viviparous Quadrupeds of North America*, described the luminous musk as "an attenuated stream of phosphoric light." The musk gives the striped skunk his Latin name, *Mephitis mephitis* or "noxious gas" doubled.

Victorian naturalist Ernest Thompson Seton described it this way, "Imagine a mixture of strong ammonia, essence of garlic, burning sulphur, a volume of sewer gas, a vitriol spray, a dash of perfume musk, all mixed together and intensified a thousand times. This will give a faint, far, washed-out idea of skunk musk."

The oily musk also has been used as a long-lasting fixative in perfumes, which linger for the same reason skunk odor clings to a victim. Ammonia or tomato juice removes the skunk smell from clothing, carbolic soap and water from skin.

Two scent glands at the base of the tail are surrounded by special muscles, which the skunk can contract to douse a foe. The glands of the striped skunk hold about a tablespoon of yellowish musk, enough to fuel five or six sprays. This member of the weasel family would rather let danger pass than spray it; in fact a skunk usually gives warning signals before getting serious. The elevation of his tail is a clue to his mood. The tail is usually slightly raised as a skunk wanders about. When very trustful and calm, a skunk will lower his tail. To issue an alert, the cat-sized mammal first stamps his front feet and may click his teeth. Then he lifts his tail but holds the tip down. When the tip rises, beware.

The striped skunk curves his body into a "U" shape so both tail and eyes are pointed at the intended victim. And the skunk characteristically aims for the eyes. He can propel his musk 18 feet and usually is quite accurate. If the first blast doesn't discourage the enemy, the skunk can unleash four or five more doses. As a rule, these natives of America do not use their musk when fighting one another and prudently arch their tails before spraying so as to avoid getting the scent on themselves. The skunk can release his spray even if being held off the ground by the tail.

The Eastern spotted skunk, which lives in the Piedmont, uses a slightly different technique and has an even stronger smelling musk. If a predator does not flee when the skunk raises his tail, *Spilogale putorius* turns his back, stands on his forefeet and arches his tail foreward. Then he spreads his hind feet, looks back, takes aim and sprays his target, with accuracy of at least 12 feet.

In addition to man and cars (the skunk's single greatest killer), predators such as bobcats and fierce great horned owls may take the mammals. With a weak sense of smell, the owls do not seem particularly bothered by the skunk's most potent weapon unless the musk strikes their eyes. Relying on the musk, a skunk has little need for other defenses. He ambles rather than runs, averaging about one mile an hour and rarely hitting six. He neither hears nor sees well and, perhaps conveniently, has a rather poor sense of smell and taste.

The striped skunk does not climb, but the spotted can hustle up a tree. Being smaller and faster than a striped skunk, the spotted version has four to six solid white stripes on his head and neck that disintegrate into an irregular pattern of spots. The body is covered with very fine fur, much more silky than the pelt of the striped skunk. The long, bushy, black tail usually ends in a white tip. Spotted skunks, measuring 13 to 22 inches and weighing 2 to 4 pounds, are quite social as skunks go. Several may den together during the winter, often in burrows dug by other animals or in hollow logs or brush piles.

The striped skunk, which lives throughout South Carolina and most of the United States, has a single white stripe on his head that usually breaks into two parallel stripes down his back. Coloring can vary considerably, one skunk having fairly narrow stripes and a black tail while another is mostly white on his back and tail. Size ranges from about 21 to nearly 28 inches, a third of which is tail, and weight from 2.5 to 11.5 pounds. Carolina skunks, which may live only a couple of years in the wild, tend to be larger than those farther north; males are somewhat larger than females.

Striped skunks seem to be on the increase in the Lowcountry as well as the mountains, where they are more abundant. Skunks usually avoid wetlands so are seldom seen right along the Atlantic Coast. The animals are very much at home in a variety of habitats — fields, field edges, forests, cultivated land and suburbs — preferably within a couple of miles of water. Whatever the spot, a skunk will either select or dig a burrow, perhaps a hole abandoned by a groundhog or fox or perhaps under a fallen tree, stump or woodpile.

Particularly fond of insects, striped skunks also dine on mice and other small mammals, snakes, frogs and eggs of ground nesting birds. Vegetation such as fruits and berries make up a far smaller percentage of the diet. A hefty set of long claws helps skunks unearth nests and rip through rotting wood in search of insects. Usually silent, skunks may grunt softly when eating but also can snarl, growl, churr and twitter depending on mood. The very carniverous spotted skunk eats primarily small mammals but also takes grubs and other insects, corn, mulberries and grapes. Skunks eat a tremendous number of insects such as grasshoppers and so can be counted as a friend to man, gardens and farms. But skunks are a known host of rabies. A rabid skunk may act aggressive or may attack a dog pursuing him, as dogs so often do.

In February or March, male striped skunks begin looking for mates, which means skunks are out, about and more visible than in early winter. Spotted skunks are on the trail in late March. When he finds a willing partner, the suitor usually moves into her den for a few days or sometimes for most of the 59 to 77-day gestation period. The female then advises him to leave so she can reline the den with dried grasses and leaves.

From two to 10 half-ounce kits arrive blind and covered with sparse black and white hair. In about three weeks, eyes and ears should open and at a month young are trying out their legs. If upset, a month-old skunk will even stamp his feet and act as if he is going to spray with his still tiny musk glands.

Young are weaned by 8 weeks and ready to follow their attentive mother in single file strings. The very protective female will snarl and stamp her feet at any potential threat. If the enemy lingers, she will raise her hind legs, click her teeth and ultimately arch her tail over her back and brace her hind feet to spray the intruder. Much of the time, youngsters quietly follow their mother and imitate her poking, prodding, sniffing, pawing and general exploring for food.

The family will stay together into autumn, when skunks begin overeating to gain weight for the winter ahead. By late fall, young resemble small versions of adults and are as confident, yet gentle, as their parents.

In winter, skunks become less active. A skunk may dig a hole, take over an abandoned animal hole, crawl under an outbuilding, move into a woodpile or crevice or slip into a hollow stump or log. He often will return to the same den he used the winter before. Although skunks do not hibernate, they are inactive in northern winters. In South Carolina, skunks may sleep more in winter than in warm weather, but they do appear after dark. Striped skunks would rather forage during new moons than during brighter full moons; spotted skunks, being even more nocturnal, are far less active on moonlit nights.

Resurrection Ferns at Drayton Hall.

Ferns—

Early in spring as the first wildflowers herald an end to winter, bracken ferns begin popping through sandy fields, pinelands and hardwood forests. By late March or early April, the woolly fiddleheads of cinnamon fern and royal fern are rising. And as spring marches on, tightly curled fiddleheads gradually unfurl into lacy, compound leaves.

Often associated with moist, shady areas, the Lowcountry's 32 species of fern and closely related allies live in a wide variety of habitats including swamps, rocky hillsides, marshes, unshaded fields and ponds. These primitive plants may be small today, but relatives towered as tree ferns some 250 million years ago in the Carboniferous Period when ferns were the dominant plants on earth.

Although ferns are vascular plants that produce their own food, they remain lower on the evolutionary chain than the flowering plants that predominate today. Ferns reproduce not by seed but by spores. The sporangia or spore-producing structures distinguish ferns from all other vascular plants and help to identify one species from another. Many bear sporangia on unusual structures, others on leaf-like fronds. These fertile fronds look exactly like sterile leaves except that brown dots or sori, clusters of sporangia, dot the underside.

Each sporangium may contain 50 to 2,000 spores and a single plant may produce as many as 50 million spores in a season. Reproduction begins in late spring for the rare adder's tongue, which has a single broad leaf that looks distinctly unlike a fern. Most ferns, however, produce their spores in summer and fall. Sometimes carried considerable distance on a breeze, a spore grows into a tiny, heart-shaped leaf bearing no resemblance to a fern. The leaf contains male and female organs to form an embryo, which in time becomes a recognizable fern.

In addition to casting spores into the wind, ferns spread to nearby spots on underground stems or rhizomes, from which thin, wiry roots reach down and fronds or leaves grow up. These spreading underground rhizomes may form blankets of ferns while the short, erect rhizomes of other varieties are often mistaken for rootstocks.

The cinnamon fern is the first to produce fertile fronds in early spring, when the plant is at its spectacular best. Bright green at first, the fronds turn a lustrous cinnamon as they ripen and disappear by late spring. To identify the fern in summer, look for masses of brownish wool on the stalk-like petiole and on axils of leaflets of sterile fronds with deeply lobed pinnae or segments. When crushed, the tufts of hair smell something like cinnamon. Growing in damp or waterlogged shady sites, the fern may grow into jungles 4 feet tall.

The robust royal fern, which shares the genus *Osmunda* with the cinnamon variety, often grows to about 4 feet. Found in freshwater marshes, swamps, abandoned ricefields or along ditches, the fern has

leaf segments divided yet again into segments, a two-pinnate frond with serrations on the margins of segments. Like other Lowcountry ferns, the royal has been used in a variety of ways over the years. At one time area ferns were taken as medicines, applied as compresses and astringents, even made into dyes. The rootstocks are still used today, packaged as osmunda fiber for growing orchids.

Fiddleheads.

The most common fern of coastal pinelands, bracken thrives even after fires have blackened an area; the underground rhizome is protected from fire and from the winter cold that kills the leaves or fronds of bracken and so many other Lowcountry ferns. But in spring, as after a fire, fiddleheads magically appear and soon blanket the ground with green.

Comfortable in dry, sandy fields, pine, mixed hardwood or hardwood forests, the bracken is a sign of poor, barren soil since the fern rarely lives in the rich, moist areas most ferns prefer. Having a great many varieties, bracken is the most familiar fern in the world and occurs on all the continents except Antarctica. The variety that lives here may have two-pinnate or three-pinnate fronds. Sporangia are produced in a line along the edges of the blades, but reproduction is primarily from the rhizomes, which may grow 50 feet in a year and may reach 10 feet underground.

Other deciduous ferns that resprout each spring include the spider brake or Huguenot fern, a native of China and Japan, that sends up fronds in late March or early April on short, very scaly rootstocks. Delicate rattlesnake ferns in moist, shady woods have stalked fertile spikes that mature in spring and begin to wither by midsummer.

The netted chain fern looks much like the sensitive fern but the former has alternate lobes on fronds while the latter has opposite. When held up to the light, sterile fronds clearly show a network of veins. The chain fern likes shady, wet areas such as swamps, low woods and stream bottoms. The sensitive fern, found in damp or wet places in full sun or shade, has long-lasting fertile fronds lined with bead-like structures that hold sori.

Virginia chain fern, which grows in waterlogged soil where few if any other ferns could survive, thrives in sunny spots such as roadside ditches. Spreading rapidly, it resembles cinnamon fern, but fronds rise individually from the rhizome while cinnamon fern fronds cluster in a dense circle. In rich, deciduous woods, along streams and at the edges of bogs and swamps, colonies of broad beech ferns often grow with beech or magnolia trees. Fronds are broad and triangular with the lowest pinnae or segments pointing down.

A final deciduous fern, the southern lady fern is quite common near the coast but challenging to identify. In moist deciduous forests, the fern has many lobes and teeth, giving pinnules, segments into which pinnae are divided, a very jagged look.

Of the Lowcountry's evergreen ferns, undoubtedly the most familiar is resurrection fern, which rambles along the branches of live oaks. It's also seen from time to time growing in soil or moist, shaded cracks in brick. Actually an epiphyte, this fern doesn't draw food from its host but instead depends on rain. In dry periods, the fern folds its 6-inch-long leaves, which are divided into just one set of segments. Looking gray and withered, the fronds reopen to their green fullness, a sort of resurrection, when rain arrives. Large, round, brown spore cases dot the underside of the leaflets.

Also an evergreen, ebony spleenwort is identified by its black rachis, the stem-like center of the frond bearing leaflets of one segment. The fern is common in moist to dry woodlands, in shady or sunny areas, even in gardens, where it prefers relatively poor, well-drained soil. The small, tufted fern has short infertile fronds that lie almost on the ground around a central, erect fertile frond. Both types of fronds are green year-round, but fertile fronds often become ragged in the winter.

Christmas fern has been used as a Yule decoration, but the name may also come from the fact leaflets are shaped like Christmas stockings. Preferring shady conditions and rich, moist, loamy soil, the plant may form colonies but more often grows singly, as twins or triplets. Fronds with a single division of segments form circular, arching clumps. In winter, fertile fronds wither while sterile, green fronds may recline on the ground after frost strikes. New fiddleheads arise in early spring from the base of old leaves; a rainy July may bring on a second crop of fiddleheads in August.

The small, delicate grape fern is named for its sporangia, said to resemble bunches of grapes. Sporangia develop in fall and appear to be another plant, independent of the surrounding sterile fronds. Growing in moist woods, the fertile fronds soon wither and new sterile fronds appear late in the year. Varying considerably, the much-cut sterile fronds may take on a bronzed tone in winter.

Last and most unusual is the aquatic plant known as mosquito fern, introduced in hopes of controlling mosquito reproduction. The fronds of this floating plant are bright green in shade, which the fern prefers, but turn reddish in the sun. Mosquito fern has quarter-inch-long fronds that overlap. Pairs of lobes are of slightly different sizes, the larger one being submerged to act as a float and the smaller one standing above the water. The top leaf hosts a colony of blue-green algae in a cavity; able to fix nitrogen, the algae aids the fern that hosts it.

The little fern will stick to the legs of wading birds, which carry it from one site to another. Growing quickly under ideal conditions, it may cover the entire surface of a pond or lake and can clog pumps, block boats and interfere with fishing. On the other hand, the ability to fix nitrogen has proved mosquito fern a valuable green manure crop for southeastern Asian ricefields.

Baby Box Turtle.

Turtles —

The first sunny, warm days of spring are reveille in the turtle world. Emerging from a burrow or river bank, crawling out from under piles of leaves or other debris, turtles bask in the sunshine like northern vacationers determined to soak up every possible ray.

Freshwater turtles, terrapins and tortoises may move slowly at first, but the spring warmth soon raises body temperatures and quickens metabolism. Shelled bodies can be downright speedy, appetites swell and thoughts turn to courtship. By late spring, some varieties already are laying eggs of future generations.

Such varieties as the yellow-bellied slider, snapping turtle, chicken turtle, mud turtle and two soft-shelled turtles all live in ponds, lakes or slow-moving rivers. Diamondback terrapins prefer brackish water, spotted turtles take to swamps and damp meadows. An endangered species, the gopher tortoise entirely avoids water and box turtles with their high, domed shells remain resolutely on land. But all are particularly visible in spring as they try to shed the winter chill.

Like all other turtles, these species have expanded ribs incorporated into a protective shell and, unlike all other animals, turtles have limb girdles inside the rib cage. A horn-like beak serves in place of teeth. The dry, scaly skin is typical of other reptiles such as snakes and alligators, which also are coming out of winter hiding and soaking up the spring sun.

Chicken turtles, so named because they are said to taste like fowl, begin the season early. A female may excavate a hole and lay her first clutch of 15 eggs in mid-March with more eggs to follow during the summer. Home is most often ditches and ponds in pine forests, always quiet water rather than rivers. With extremely long, striped necks and narrow shells up to 10 inches in length, chicken turtles have a dark carapace or upper shell crossed by a net-like pattern of light lines. Generally shy, the chicken will bite if disturbed. It's most often seen basking, wandering on land or crossing highways.

Box turtles, which sometimes dig a comfortable wintering hole in a residential garden, are among the most common and visible turtles in the Lowcountry. Willing to spend an entire lifetime — 60 to more than 100 years — in a yard that supplies adequate food, water and shelter, a box turtle may become accustomed to human neighbors and even to gentle handling. But if threatened, a box turtle will draw in head, feet and tail then slam its shell closed with a hiss of escaping air. The box is the only turtle that has a broad hinge dividing its plastron or bottom shell and allowing the turtle to close the shell tightly.

Living entirely on land, the 1-pound animal has a black or brown 4 to 8-inch domed shell heavily marked with yellow, orange or olive. Solitary except during breeding, males have concave bottom shells to aid in mounting females, which have flat or convex plastrons. Males may have red eyes while females' are brown.

Waddling about on tiptoes and searching for assorted vegetation, insects, frogs and snakes, box turtles have a very fine sense of smell, sight and touch. The female puts that skill to use in digging her nest, a night-time task for the day-time turtle. When the flask-shaped nest feels right to her hind feet, she lays four to six leathery, pink eggs then quickly covers the hole and tamps the area to disguise the nest. Like other turtles, the box leaves her eggs to incubate in the sun. Baby turtles instinctively dig up and out of the nest chamber and, quite alone, face a world of predators. The youngster's only protection is its shell, said to support 200 times its own weight in the case of a box turtle.

Unlike the box, the snapping turtle is nocturnal and aquatic. Although common here, snapping turtles are rarely seen except during spring. In April, the turtle crawls from a winter hiding spot beneath a mud bank or under debris. Females come out by day and males wander from pond to pond in search of mates. About June, the female will dig a shallow nest to hold about 25 eggs. If they aren't unearthed and gobbled down by raccoons, the eggs will hatch in about three months and young will begin a sometimes lengthy trek to water.

Weighing up to 57 pounds with a shell measuring from 8 to 19 inches, the snapper is the largest freshwater turtle in the Lowcountry. More aggressive than most and sometimes downright vicious, the snapping turtle also has an unusually large head with powerful jaws. The tan to dark brown carapace, often obscured by algae, bears three long ridges, more prominent in the young and worn nearly flat with age. The bottom shell — for anyone foolhardy enough to pick up a snapping turtle and look — is yellow to tan. Watch for the long-tailed turtle in warm shallows, where it may lie buried in mud with only eyes and nostrils exposed. Excellent swimmers, snappers dine on a variety of fish, birds, small mammals, aquatic plants and even carrion.

Yellow-bellied sliders also are highly aquatic, but they emerge to bask, often in groups or stacks, on a favorite log. The handsome turtles have bright yellow bottom shells, dark top shells that may be marked with yellow and yellow markings on heads. Males usually have longer tails than females and always have long claws, used to entice claw-less females during courtship.

Yellow-Bellied Slider Turtle.

Common throughout the Lowcountry, the sliders are most easily seen on Kiawah, Capers and other islands, where they often grow much larger than on the mainland. Youngsters dine on protein, such as water insects, shellfish and tadpoles, but adults turn to a vegetable diet. Widely sold by dime stores over the years, sliders have been raised by the millions on turtle farms. Few such pets ever survive to reach a mature size of 5 to 11½ inches.

Sliders mate fairly early in the spring then often lay about 10 eggs on a river bank or sometimes in the dirt of a roadbed. Hatchlings usually climb out of the nest cavity in a couple of months but may overwinter in the nest. The nest often is considerable distance from the slider's favorite habitat, shallow streams, swamps, ponds, sluggish rivers and lakes with soft bottoms and plenty of vegetation.

In rivers and lakes such as Marion and Moultrie, spiny softshell turtles abound. Closely related Florida softshells are less common in Lowcountry waters. The leathery, soft, oval shell of the spiny resembles a flat pancake marked with circular spots. The Florida variety has a striped head and dark brown to dark brownish-gray shell. The shell bears many small bumps and sometimes a suggestion of large, round spots. Neck and head are extremely long and hold a snorkel-like snout above the water while the turtle is submerged in sand or shallow water. Armed with sharp claws and strong jaws, these turtles also have aggressive dispositions and are best left to their own devices.

Mud turtles are abundant in the calm water of lakes and ponds and on occasion in brackish water. Nesting early in the summer near the water, the vegetarian turtle lays three to five eggs that may not hatch until the next spring. Tiny turtles appearing in early spring undoubtedly are nocturnal mud turtles newly emerged from eggs that overwintered. Most, however, hatch in late summer or early fall and may be grabbed by such enemies as raccoons, birds, alligators and even larger turtles including snappers.

Maturing at 5 to 7 years, adults measure only 3 to less than 5 inches. The smooth carapace is olive to dark brown, the plastron yellow to brown. During the warmest months, the mud turtle is sometimes visible beneath the water as it prowls the bottom. Should its soft-bottomed, watery home dry up, the mud turtle may strike out cross country and will readily cross roads in its search for a permanent body of water. Or, it may burrow into the mud and estivate, a dormant summertime version of hibernation.

Similar in size to the mud turtle, the spotted has a black top shell usually sprinkled with round yellow spots. The head, neck and limbs are spotted; the plastron is a creamy yellow with large black blotches along the border. Males are recognized by their brown eyes, tan chins and long, thick tails while females have orange eyes and yellow chins. Thriving in marshy meadows, wet woodlands, boggy areas, ponds and shallow streams with muddy bottoms, the handsome turtle is out early in the spring to bask. It winters under the water in soft mud, debris or burrows. In the heat of summer, it all but disappears under the cover of dense vegetation.

Living in brackish water, diamondback terrapins began declining around the turn of the century when man killed and ate large numbers of the terrapins. More recently, the animal has suffered as its coastal marsh habitat was developed. Today the terrapins are most often seen in saltmarsh estuaries, tidal flats and lagoons behind barrier beaches; mud flats are the favorite basking sites. Dining on clams and marine snails and worms, these coastal turtles nest in April and May. Females lay an average of nine pinkish-white, leathery eggs in nests as deep as 8 inches at sandy edges of marshes and dunes. Maturing at about 7 years, females measure from 6 to more than 9 inches while males are much smaller.

The light brown or gray to black carapace is ridged; scutes, the bony plates of the shell, bear deep growth rings that give a sculpted look. The oblong plastron is yellowish or greenish with dark flecks or blotches. The gray neck and head are peppered with black.

No list of Lowcountry turtles would be complete without the gopher tortoise, the state's only tortoise and an endangered species in this state. The only tortoise in this country that digs extensive burrows, the gopher has a domed, dull brown to tan shell with few if any markings. Adults may grow to 15 inches in length and more than 10 pounds in weight. Hind legs are round and stumpy, almost elephantine, but front legs are scaled and flattened for digging.

Gopher Tortoise.

And dig the tortoise does. A record burrow for the species is 47½ feet long; large adults easily excavate burrows 30 feet long and 10 feet deep. The burrow ends in a chamber where humidity and temperature remain constant, about 75 to 80 degrees. The tortoise spends the coldest winter days and the hottest part of summer days in the chamber, where it also can escape if a forest fire strikes. A number of other species also rely on the gopher's burrows. Several rare and threatened species have been found living in gopher holes and such animals as snakes, lizards, frogs, toads, crickets, rabbits, skunks, opossums, mice and quail are known to move into vacated burrows.

With the warming temperatures of April, the gopher begins leaving its burrow regularly to forage for the plant food it eats exclusively. Although young need relatively nutritious plants, adults can survive on such tough fare as wiregrass and prickly pear cactus. Shunning water, the tortoises obtain all the liquid they need from food and dew.

As soon as he emerges in spring, the male gopher begins scouting for a mate. From April into early June, a male will seek out the opening of a female's burrow and will sit there bobbing his head up and down quite patiently for hours at a time. A willing female eventually will emerge from her borrow to accept the suitor. She most often will lay her eggs during June in a hole she may dig in the mound at the entrance of one of her burrows. As soon as youngsters hatch, in a bit more than two months, they instinctively begin to dig. Before long, a small gopher is working on a burrow where it will spend the winter.

Gophers, which inhabit a small area in South Carolina to Florita and west to the very eastern extreme of Louisiana, have been dwindling for several reasons. In Florida, where populations are strongest, the tortoises have been hunted extensively and numbers have fallen rapidly. In this state, gophers have very little habitat, dry sand ridges and sandhills found in only three main sites, about 2,000 acres of Jasper and Hampton counties including the Tillman sand ridge. Life is best for gophers in areas that burn periodically, forests with scattered openings in a canopy of longleaf pine and turkey oak where wiregrass and other herbaceous plants spring up. Most gophers dig their burrows in such openings, where the tortoises can bask and where the sun will incubate eggs.

Living as long as 50 years, the tortoises grow slowly. It takes females about 15 years to reach 8 inches, their breeding size. Gophers nest at most once a year and lay only two to seven eggs. Many of the eggs or young fall prey to raccoons, foxes and snakes. South Carolina is thought to have between 500 and 1,000 gopher tortoises, deemed this state's most endangered species.

Opossum.

Opossums —

One of the Carolinas' most common mammals is a 50-million-year-old throwback to the days of the dinosaur. North America's most primitive mammal and only marsupial, the opossum is also famed for his prehensile tail, which carries nesting material and grabs hold in precarious situations. And of course this relative of the kangaroo and koala bear is known for playing possum.

When confronted by man or danger in general, an opossum at first may hiss, drool and make a great show of baring his 50 very sharp teeth, more teeth than any other North American mammal. But the nocturnal opossum is largely bluffing. He will fight if he meets another male but does his best to avoid crossing paths. At heart opossums are extremely tolerant and passive. A tufted titmouse, for instance, may pluck enough fur from an opossum's back to line her entire nest without his objecting to her repeated landings and yankings.

Once an opossum has made a hissing show of teeth, he is likely to retreat or live up to his name. The opossum keels over, closes his eyes, sticks out his tongue and looks dead to the world. If lifted, he is unlikely to move and he shows no sign of feeling pain. The act is enough to turn predators around. Most prefer to eat food they have killed themselves so decide the lifeless opossum must not be a decent meal.

While down, *Didelphis virginiana* may literally be out. Studies show the heartbeat slows and other responses seem involuntary, much like those of a human who has fainted. Playing possum was long thought voluntary, a defense the mammal would use when he chose. But it now appears the animal goes into shock and perhaps temporary paralysis. Often accused of being dumb because of his small brain and relatively slow movements or reactions, an opossum may faint in fright, according to one theory. Or the opossum may produce a substance that knocks him out, according to a second, unproven theory. Whatever the cause, the swoon may last a few minutes or up to six hours, by which time most predators such as foxes, bobcats and coyotes have lost interest.

Opossums are far more likely to fall victim to hunters, dogs and cars than to wild creatures. Because opossums eat virtually anything, they amble onto highways to feed on road kills and are struck by cars.

Most active in spring and summer, opossums quiet down a bit in cold weather, when extreme temperatures may freeze bare ears and rat-like tail. But long before spring arrives, females come into heat and males begin tracking potential mates. Essentially nomads, opossums lead solitary lives. They may wander widely and den for the day wherever the mood strikes them. Or they may use several dens quite regularly and move primarily around and between those dens. By late January, however, a male's nightly foraging for food is easily interrupted by the scent of an available female. Guided by his very keen sense of smell, he chooses and woos a mate rather unceremoniously. There are a few reports of a smitten male's standing on his hind legs, lurching forward and thrashing his tail back and forth. But that is the height of courtship.

The male nuzzles the female's hindquarters for a time then mounts her and leans to the side; the united couple lies on the ground together for up to 20 minutes. Perfectly suited, the male has forked genitals and the female two uteri. Each animal then goes his own way, perhaps never to see one another again. If the female does not become pregnant in the 36 hours she is in heat, her estrus cycle will repeat in another 28 days. From January until July, a Carolina opossum will be in heat at least twice and will usually bear two litters of young. The season and activity peak in late January to early February and again about May.

Having the shortest gestation period of any North American mammal, the opossum gives birth in 12 to 13 days. As the time nears, the female seeks out a more permanent den than the napping spots she uses the rest of the year. An excellent climber, she may choose a hollow tree or stay on the ground in a hollow log, deserted burrow, thicket, wood or brush pile, culvert, or crawlspace below a house. She builds a nest of grass, leaves and other plant material that she picks with her teeth then takes with her front paws. She dextrously passes the material under her body to her hind feet, which have opposable toes and hold the vegetation well. Curving the end of her tail into a circle, she shoves the material into the loop and heads for her chosen chamber.

Before the first of 16 or more young arrive, the female begins licking the fur inside her pouch and a convenient pathway through her fur. In just a few minutes, she may have given birth to 20 blind, hairless young. More like embryos than true young, a litter would fit into a teaspoon and weigh only a tenth of an ounce. The babies have three tiny nubs where hind legs and tail will grow. But front legs are well developed and equipped with claws to make the 3-inch crawl to her pouch. The damp path the mother provides apparently guides her babies, which shy away from the more scratchy dry fur on either side.

Some never manage the momentous trip. Those that do immediately head for their mother's 13 nipples, arranged in a horseshoe pattern inside her pouch. Those unable to claim a nipple will perish. But a baker's dozen will each grab hold of a nipple that will enlarge to fill the tiny mouth as it grows. No longer needed, the claws fall off.

Warm, well-fed and protected in the pouch, the young increase their weight by 1,000 percent in just a week. About 10 days later, the tail and hind legs are developing and beginning to move a bit. Whiskers appear at about 36 days, some fur at 43 days. The key time is about 2 months. The baby is the size of a mouse, will release the nipple on occasion, gets his first tooth, opens his eyes and gains some control over his body temperature. Before long, the 1-ounce youngsters will feel tempted to look beyond the pouch and then to venture out. At no time do young opossums appear to play together, making them an exception in the mammal world. Play helps develop skills needed in adulthood and suggests some degree of intelligence and sociability.

By about 80 days, opossums spend little time in the pouch. When mother goes out feeding for the night, the young wait quietly in the den. Young may cling to their mother's back or sides and ride with her but not, apparently, on her feeding forays. A study showed young make jaunts only when their mother is moving them to a new den.

Youngsters begin searching for food on their own at about 3 months but den up with their mother each day. The family remains together until young are 3 or 4 months old. On occasion a female has been seen with a litter in her pouch and an older litter sharing her den. Eventually, young take off to establish their own dens and foraging areas.

Favored with high reproductive rates and cosmopolitan appetites, opossums gradually have dispersed to an ever larger area. Once residents of the South, they now thrive throughout the East, north to Ontario and Minnesota, west to Colorado and as far south as Costa Rica. The species has even been introduced into California, Oregon and Washington, where the marsupial seems to be doing well.

When it comes to food, opossums will eat almost anything and will happily sample birdseed, dogfood, garden produce and garbage in yards. Regular fare includes carrion on roads, insects and earthworms, fruit and berries, birds, bird eggs, frogs, snakes and some mammals. Persimmons are a passion but opossums also enjoy apples and corn. The animals do develop some sense of taste and have good memories. One study showed opossums could remember a food that made them sick and would avoid it even months thereafter.

Opossums are not terribly fussy about living quarters and will adopt open woods, brushy waste areas, farms, city parks and subdivisions. Low, tangled woodland with a stream or other water nearby is more attractive to the average opossum than dry woods. If trees remain, water is available and food sufficient, an opossum will settle into a well-developed neighborhood. Because they are quiet and nocturnal, opossums may inspect a yard regularly without being noticed or may show up on a porch one night and look in the front door. The mammals are harmless enough and will silently wander away at a leisurely gait.

An opossum can make tracks, his pale pink feet and short legs scurrying faster than the heavy body seems able to move. Most of the time, an opossum plods along, moving both right legs at the same time and both left legs together. For safety, he is likely to head up a tree rather than strike out over the ground. He can swim well although slowly.

Despite his very small start in life, an opossum will reach 24 to 40 inches; individuals in the Carolinas average about 16 inches of body and 12 inches of hairless tail. House cat sized with short legs, the animal is covered in grizzled white fur, an inner coat of black-tipped fur and a longer coat of white hair. One opossum may seem nearly white, the next one almost brownish or black. With a face that can look coy, fierce or just vacant, the opossum has a pink nose, light whiskers, black eyes and dark ears that are leathery.

His eyesight is less than perfect but serves him well enough in the dark. His senses of smell and touch are far keener and he hears well except for low notes.

Paw prints look like astericks because the first toe of the hind foot is opposable and lacks a nail. The opossum carries his tail low with tip down so his trail shows a solid line between footprints. The prehensile tail serves almost as a fifth leg when the opossum climbs. He curls his reassuring lifeline around a branch when the going is unsteady or a delectable piece of fruit is beyond easy reach. He also can hang upside down from a branch by his tail at least briefly.

Able to breed as yearlings, many opossums may only survive about a year in the wild. But they are known to reach 7 years if they can play possum or otherwise avoid their many predators.

Mourning Dove and offspring nested in potted plant on piazza.

Nesting—

While many animals build nests of a sort for their young, no creatures go to quite so much trouble and effort as birds. For their weight, most birds gather and arrange an amazing amount of material to hold eggs and young.

Birds may have begun building elaborate nests as the feathered creatures evolved from cold-blooded to warm-blooded animals, no longer abandoning their eggs as snakes and turtles. Rather than relying on heat from the sun, birds had to incubate or warm their eggs themselves. Nests might have become necessary to hold eggs and adult, provide protection and insulation from below and hide eggs and young from predators. The first bird nests probably were nothing more than a slight depression in the ground, similar perhaps to the sand scrapes many terns and gulls still use as nests.

Danger abounds for such ground nests so birds instinctively may have begun choosing more protected spots in grass clumps, shrubs and ultimately trees. A nest in the grass might not have demanded much effort, just a few loose blades to contain the eggs. But higher spots suddenly required major construction. Birds may first have built rather clumsy, flimsy nests not very different from those of some herons, egrets and ibises today. Eventually, however, at least some birds became architects and weavers, able to combine different materials into a dense, smooth, perfect cup or a giant pile that lasts for years and serves as a beacon to returning eagles and ospreys.

Today birds build a variety of cup nests in trees or cavities, cups in buildings or on the ground, larger free-form nests in trees or on ledges, suspended or hanging nests, domed nests with side entrances, mud nests on buildings and rocks or little nest at all. Cavity dwellers, relying on holes in trees or bird boxes, may pile up considerable nesting material as bluebirds do or virtually none in the case of many owls and vultures. Geese, gulls, turkeys and some other gamebirds often put little effort into nest building and seek sites on the ground.

For birds in fairly open spots, the construction method is sideways-throwing or sideways-building. Once a site is chosen, the female, or both birds, begin picking up potential nest material during their travels and dropping it near the spot. Sitting on the future nest, the architect draws in the gathered items and tucks them around the nest. Shorebirds and terns often build their nests in this way. Birds such as ducks and geese are a bit more elaborate — the female pulls down from her breast to line the nest.

Gull-Billed Tern nest.

Birds nesting above the ground search elsewhere for material, sometimes at considerable inconvenience. The swallow-tailed kite, an endangered species, breaks sizable branches from trees and hauls them great distances in its feet. The kite refuses to pick up a dropped branch whereas other birds routinely search the ground for likely twigs and grasses.

One of nearly 200 species of birds nesting in South Carolina, the familiar cardinal gathers much of its material on the ground and builds only a few feet up in a shrub. Quite comfortable nesting near a house, the female first chooses heavier sticks, which she tries to wedge or balance against branches. The first few attempts may fail and the expectant mother flies or hops to the ground to retrieve the twig. Even when the first three or four stems seem safely in place, ends crossing one another and resting on branches, the female may make the wrong move and see her efforts tumble. Meanwhile, the male is usually nearby singing his best spring songs to notify every other cardinal that the area and the female are his.

For several days, the female works diligently although she spends her nights away from the nest. Once the base is established, she finds more delicate twigs and then supple material she can bend, wrap and tuck to form the kind of cup nest so many species build. As the cup takes form, she hops in and twists her body about, perhaps to check the fit and also to push lumpy spots into a smooth interior.

Many birds that build cup-shaped nests actually sit in the structure most of the time as they build so they can pull in loose ends and form a beautifully round, even nest. Once the foundation and walls are set, the bird begins interior decorating with such soft materials as grasses, mosses, leaves, feathers, spider webs, even bits of cloth or other man-made material. To attract birds to the yard, try putting out pieces of yarn or fabric: It may be appropriated within a few hours.

As the bird adds lining, she sits in the cup with her bill and tail up, moves about and presses the nest with her chin and the coverts under her tail. Then she pushes down with her bill and tail to firm the rim of the nest. Shoving back with her feet, she makes the extra room needed for her eggs.

In the Carolina Lowcountry, the nest building season is kicked off in late fall as bald eagles return to their nest sites. The endangered birds lay their eggs from late November into early January in huge nests sometimes measuring 15 feet high and 9 feet across.

Owls aren't far behind: Great horned owls often are on eggs in late January, barred owls in January or February (as late as March in the Piedmont), but little screech owls not until early April. Although she can and sometimes does build a nest, the fierce great horned owl usually usurps the deserted nest of a hawk, crow or osprey and occasionally shares an eagle nest when the eagle and her young are still in residence. These raptors may nest in winter to take advantage of relatively open deciduous woods; as young hatch and squawk for food, parents find easier hunting for rodents, mammals and other prey.

Nesting in the Carolinas begins in earnest in March. Year-round residents generally get a jump on the season, before many summer visitors have arrived or claimed territories and mates. Cardinals, blue jays and others are searching for material in late March. Piling grasses in nest boxes about the middle of March, bluebirds are incubating eggs late that month or in early April. Pine and yellow-throated warblers as well as yellowthroats, all common permanent residents, should be nesting late in March.

In choosing their summer range, migrants undoubtedly have sought the best habitat for raising their young. The earlier a summer resident arrives, the sooner it is likely to lay eggs. The last to appear are busy with first nests about the time second broods are being raised by many permanent residents including cardinals, bluebirds and blue jays. Such birds as brown thrashers, house sparrows and robins are even capable of a third set of young. And mockingbirds routinely raise three broods, the first in April, the second in June and the last in late July or early August. The parula warbler, the first migrating warbler to settle in, raises two broods with the first nesting flurry late in March. Also a summer resident, the wood thrush rushes its first set of young out of the nest in early June and may have a second nest built within a week.

Late March finds a large number of summer birds looking for sites, and wading birds begin showing up at rookeries such as Drum Island in Charleston. Ibises flock in early in April, but eggs are not laid until early May. By then, such year-round waders as great blue herons already have sizable young.

The only native duck to breed in the Lowcountry, the wood duck, has young out of the box, or tree cavity, and exploring the water in early April. Meanwhile hummingbirds are building their tiny nests in early and mid-April. Young bluebirds that hatched in late April are leaving nest boxes in mid-May while the young of year-round warblers, cardinals, jays and thrashers fledge later in May. Many songbirds are out of the nest soon after hatching, baby mockingbirds in just 1½ to 2 weeks. In fact May brings a flurry of activity as adults hunt food for voracious young.

Among the more interesting nests, the ruby-throated hummingbird's home is also one of the most difficult to see. Building in a tree anywhere from 6 to 10 feet above the ground, the hummer attaches its nest to a twig or small branch that slants downward from the tree and usually is sheltered overhead by leaves. The female, seldom receiving help from a male that probably is polygamous, builds a nest of plant down, fibers and bud scales. The nest is lined inside with soft plant down and camouflaged outside with lichens. The hummer spends about five days in early to mid-April building the nest and may continue building or repairing throughout the nesting season. The cup is probably attached to a limb with spider silk, which is also used to bind the nest. One hummer observed in Francis Beidler Forest near Harleyville repeatedly brought long strands of spider web to her nest. Sitting on the edge and sometimes hovering above it, the female resembled a sewing machine, the needle or bill flying up and down to stitch the nest together.

At the other extreme is the osprey, a fish-eating hawk that returns to the same nest year after year. Adding at least a little material each year and repairing damage, ospreys often use large, ungainly sticks for the nest base then line the top with grasses, vines, sod and inner bark. Over time the nest may grow from a few inches or a few feet to 10 feet high. Listed as a threatened species until 1985, the hawks with wingspans up to 6 feet are recovering and now outnumber natural snags and dead trees where the birds normally would build. So they are turning to such man-made structures as loudspeakers, communication towers, floodlights, movable offloading cranes, radio towers, chemical plant towers and nautical aids.

Some little warblers come up with ingenious disguises and labor-saving tactics. In mid-March, handsome yellow-throated warblers are examining Spanish moss strands as low as 8 feet or more than 100 feet above the ground. The expectant female gathers cobwebs or caterpillar silk, works her way into a likely clump of moss and begins weaving fibers together. She incorporates bits of bark, rotten wood and fine grass into a nest that is completely concealed. A nest is disclosed only by the squeaking of babies or the coming and going of attentive parents, which disappear into the thick, drooping strand of moss. In the Piedmont and other Carolina sites where Spanish moss does not grow, these warblers build open nests of bark strips, grasses and plant down, a cup saddled on a horizontal tree branch.

The related parula warbler often chooses Spanish moss in which to build a pendant nest. Vireos, however, build more obvious pendant nests, hanging well below a branch and often swaying in the breeze. The white-eyed vireo seeks a forked twig in a low shrub from which to suspend a cone-shaped nest. Woven of small pieces of soft wood, bark shreds and other material, the nest is lined with dry grass and fine plant stems. The female binds the structure with cobwebs.

White-Eyed Vireo on nest.

The state bird of South Carolina, the Carolina wren builds a domed nest with a side entrance, similar in style to nests of meadowlarks (which build in arches of grass) and house sparrows (which messily toss together balls of weeds and trash). The wren builds a more precise dome of leaves, twigs, rootlets, mosses, weed stalks, strips of inner bark and debris, all lined with soft material ranging from moss to wool. The wren readily appropriates some unusual sites for her nest, which normally would be in a natural cavity such as upturned roots or woodpecker holes. Wrens routinely build in hanging baskets of plants (something mourning doves also try on occasion), shoes left outdoors to dry, tin cans, pipes that vent appliances, any nook or cranny around a house or inside an outbuilding. More than one wren has moved into a garage, pumphouse or cellar then each day at dawn demanded the owner open the door and let her out. And heaven help the human if he closes the door before the wren pair deliver the last feeding of the day.

Orioles weave deep pouches or baskets that hang from forked or

Two Oriole nests — Baltimore (left) and Orchard.

drooping branches. Fine material such as grasses, plant down, even hair and string make a comfortable home for the young.

The mockingbird constructs a loose, outer layer of thorny twigs and softens it with an inner layer of leaves, plant stems, moss and rootlets. The male begins several nests to woo a female; she makes the final choice of a site and the pair builds their nursery together.

Mockers construct cup nests as do many birds including sparrows, some thrushes, grackles, blackbirds, even smaller herons and egrets. Cup nests are even built in holes, cavities or crevices by some wrens and sparrows, purple martins, tufted titmice, prothonotary warblers, starlings, bluebirds, vultures, kestrels, woodpeckers and many owls.

Using a natural tree cavity, woodpecker hole or birdhouse, titmice carefully line the cavity bottom with bark strips, dead leaves, moss, grass then a padding of hair, fur, bits of string and cloth. Purple martins, often using gourds or apartment houses put out for them, collect grasses, twigs, paper, bark, leaves and string for a nest. Both the male and female do the building then line the egg cup with fine grasses and fresh green leaves. Female bluebirds, rarely helped by their males, collect a large amount of fine grasses and weed stalks to form a loose cup in a nest box or natural cavity.

The cavities used by many birds initially were the work of woodpeckers. A pair of pileateds share the task of drilling a new nest hole each year, in the area and sometimes the same tree as the previous nest. These large birds spend considerable time excavating a cavity as deep as 2 feet, but the adults bring no material in to line the nest. Nor do red-headed woodpeckers add material to nest holes that both sexes drill. While other woodpeckers use primarily dead trees for their nests, the endangered red-cockaded woodpecker hollows a cavity in a live pine tree infected with and weakened by red heart disease. Mating for life, these birds also chip away bark below the nest hole; resin flowing from the holes turns the tree trunk whitish and probably discourages hungry snakes from invading the nest.

And finally there are mud and saliva nests built by assorted swifts and swallows. Chimney swifts use their glutinous saliva, which hardens nesting material, to bind a thin half saucer platform of twigs to chimneys, barns, attics, old wells, garages and other structures.

Male and female belted kingfishers take turns digging a burrow from 3 to 15 feet into a bank. The adults spend up to three weeks tunnelling in and then hollowing out a dome-shaped chamber up to a foot wide and 7 inches high. The burrow may be reused for several years with later eggs resting on a nest of fish scales, remnants of food youngsters devoured the year before.

The rough-winged swallow also prefers to burrow into an exposed bank. From 2½ to 6 feet into the soil, the bird builds a bulky foundation of twigs, bark, roots and weeds lined with fine grasses. Lacking a bank, this swallow is satisfied to use a cave, cranny under a bridge, culvert, wharf, drainpipe, gutter, even the side of a building. John James Audubon discovered the rough wing and took the first, or type, specimen near Charleston. A few years later, Charleston minister Dr. John Bachman sent Audubon swallow eggs collected from an unfinished brick house in that city. Ingenious swallows had appropriated holes that scaffolding left in the walls.

Rabbits—

Spring is the best of times for rabbits. After a relatively sparse winter, they suddenly find a smorgasbord of tender, lush greenery that may coax the mammals into view early in the morning, at twilight and through the night.

Spring means Easter, the time of year thoughts most often turn to this long-eared, puffy-tailed hopper. And early spring brings not only courtship but a litter of young, the first of six litters a female, or doe, may produce during the year.

Charleston Museum Specimen.

Cottontail Rabbit.

Both the common cottontail and the similar marsh rabbit of the Lowcountry have earned their reputation for prodigious reproduction. A single breeding pair and their young could bear 350,000 rabbits in five years if none of the bunnies died.

Of course that doesn't happen. In captivity rabbits have survived more than five years, but in the wild more than 80 percent don't celebrate a first birthday. An estimated one-third to one-half don't live even 20 days to leave their nest. Heavy rains drown youngsters, farm plows and lawnmowers kill others, predators may dig up and consume an entire nest. Enemies such as large hawks, snakes and foxes take some adults while others succumb to diseases such as rabbit fever.

The average cottontail won't begin breeding until her first spring, but precocious individuals mature at two and a half to three months. From that day on, the female will be ready to mate approximately once a month and to give birth to an average of four or five young, occasionally as many as nine.

Males, or bucks, which usually range over the territories of several females, are usually gathering as a doe gives birth. She comes into heat immediately and will be fertile for only about an hour. Should she fail to become pregnant, however, the cycle will repeat every seven days until she does.

Immediately after giving birth, she covers her young with a blanket she makes of fur and plant material. Then she leaves the nest and may face a brace of suitors. One is usually dominant and the others may wait at a distance. Or a buck may hop forward to issue a challenge. The two males may circle each other, looking for a chance to bite and scrap. Or both may rear up on their hind legs, try to strike with their forepaws and kick with strong hind legs, which do far more damage than front paws. With legs capable of leaping 5 to 15 feet, one cottontail may even jump over the other and slam him from above with a proverbial rabbit punch.

Once the fight is over, the victor has anything but an easy courtship. The pair may appear to be playing as one leaps straight up and the other races under the jumper. But in fact the female is trying to bite the male's flanks and he is trying to avoid the painful attacks. Even once the female has been wooed and won, the buck may be literally charged out of position by another male. Breeding takes only a few seconds and then the female, biting and nipping once again, drives the male away, perhaps only to accept another suitor or two.

Only as darkness falls will the female return to her nest, suckle her naked young and cover them once again with the warm blanket. About 4 inches long, the pink newborn are helpless with sealed eyes and half-inch-long ears pressed flat against their heads. Weighing barely an ounce, the young grow very quickly on a diet of milk four times as rich as cow's milk. The mother will return once or twice during the night and again at dawn to nurse her nestlings.

Meanwhile, the nocturnal animal forages nearby and keeps very keen eyes and ears attentive for predators. She rotates her large ears to pick up sounds from front, back and side. With oversized, protruding eyes, she can see in almost all directions without moving her head. The sense of smell is less important to rabbits in detecting danger. Although only 2 to 3 pounds and at most 18 inches long, she will fight off predators such as dogs and foxes with her hind legs. If that fails or the enemy is too strong, she tries to draw attention away from the nest by running a zigzag course.

Safety also comes in knowing her home range, which may be as small as a backyard. A male or a female without a nest to protect may freeze at any sign of danger. The coat serves as camouflage and the tail as a decoy. If flushed, a rabbit zigzags and the flashing white tail may distract a predator. The speedy rabbit ducks into hiding or stops and hunkers with tail hidden while the confused hunter keeps searching for the puff of white. Older rabbits may be cagey, ducking under a barbed wire fence just as a hawk or owl makes its dive. Many raptors found caught on wire fences each year are thought to be victims of cunning rabbits.

Protected by their mother, nestlings grow quickly. A week after birth, they are covered in soft fur and have a white blaze on the forehead that adults lose. Eyes open and ears pop upright. At 2 weeks, the bunnies begin to venture from the nest, explore, play and investigate a wondrous world of new foods. Although the youngsters continue to sleep the day away in their nest, by 16 to 20 days the rabbits are independent of their mother. Already weighing about 2 pounds, the young soon disperse and each begins working on a form or shallow depression. Like their mother, the young will spend days hiding and resting in the form, often trampled or scratched in tall grass or weeds, under a brush pile or other cover.

Meanwhile, their mother is expecting her next litter. Gestation takes a mere 28 to 32 days for cottontails, 39 to 40 for the marsh rabbit, which has a longer breeding season to compensate. She seeks a likely nest spot in an open area such as a meadow, lawn or backyard garden. Using her front paws, she scoops out a bowl 5 inches deep and 5 to 7 inches in diameter. The doe collects grass and leaves to insulate the nest and pulls fur from her chest to make a soft lining. Then she forms a blanket of the same materials to keep her future family hidden and warm.

Leaving her nest, she spends the next few days feeding in her territory. Labor begins suddenly and may catch her too far away to reach her nest site. (An entire litter may be born in just 45 minutes.) If so, she diligently cleans her newborn with her tongue, nurses and carries each to the nest in her teeth. She then covers the family and scampers off to her prospective mates.

Cottontails are quite comfortable in a variety of habitats including backyards, pastures, meadows, marshes and swamps, farmlands and abandoned fields, cemeteries, thickets, clumps of weeds, shrubbery and open woodlands. The advent of clean, modern farming techniques has destroyed some favorite habitat, however, and the number of cottontails is lower today than a century ago. The Eastern cottontail thrives throughout the East except for New England while the marsh rabbit is limited to Florida and to coastal areas north to Southeastern Virginia.

Within those areas a cottontail will settle in almost any place he can find enough food. Not a fussy eater, he dines on a combination of leaves, grasses, sedges, flowers, stems, buds, berries or bark. If desperate in winter, a rabbit may girdle a young tree, pick up crumbs from a bird feeder or take woody stems from such plants as goldenrod and dogwood. Rabbits have even been known to eat rubber-coated ignition wires from automobile spark plugs, rendering the auto temporarily useless.

Gardeners complain about rabbit damage and experiments have shown the long-eared rascals are tough to discourage. Bunnies don't seem to be bothered by the likes of mothballs, ground hot pepper, bone meal, creosote paper, or jars filled with water and commercial products.

On the other hand, studies have shown crabgrass is a rabbit's absolute favorite, which should make the mammal a welcome addition to many lawns. Rabbits also are fond of dandelions, daisy fleabane, ragweed, lespedeza and other greens not planted in gardens.

Well adapted for hopping, rabbit paws don't assist in eating. Instead the deeply cleft upper lip, which inspired the term harelipped, pulls food free. Teeth only meet on one side of the mouth at a time. Rabbits chew with a transverse motion that makes their noses appear to wiggle. Rabbits have two pair of incisors, one behind the other, on each side of the upper jaw. That distinguishes rabbits and hares, members of the *Lagomorpha* order, from rodents of the order *Rodentia*, with which rabbits were classified until recently.

After quickly devouring a meal, a rabbit hops to its shelter and excretes moist, greenish pellets of partially digested food. Much like a cow chewing its cud, the rabbit then eats the meal a second time to extract every possible nutrient.

In the Carolinas, Georgia and Alabama, cottontails are most common, but marsh rabbits abound along the coast. Swamp rabbits live in the extreme western tip of South Carolina.

Eastern cottontails are grayish-brown to reddish-brown above with a white belly and undersides. The nape is rust-colored. The tops of the feet are whitish and, of course, the short tail is cottony white below. Ears measure as long as 2¾ inches.

The darker marsh rabbit has reddish-brown upperparts, a dark cinnamon or rufous nape. Rump, top of tail and back of hind legs are chestnut brown to dark rusty-reddish. Most of the belly is buff to light brown, but the middle of the abdomen is white. Although about the same length as cottontails, marsh rabbits have noticeably shorter ears, just 2 inches long.

Marsh bunnies like the sea islands, wet bottomlands, brackish swamps and brakes so are less often seen in yards than are cottontails. Excellent swimmers, marsh rabbits often hit the water to avoid predators or to feed. They have been reported swimming strongly 700 yards from shore. Favorite foods include grasses, cane, bulbs, leaves and twigs. The rabbits make well-beaten trails through dense marsh plants and can tear along their paths faster than cottontails move. But when feeding, marsh rabbits often stand on their hind legs and slowly step one foot at a time.

For her rather large, covered nest, a female marsh rabbit collects soft blades of grass and fur. The doe often builds near water but about 30 feet away from the high water mark. Being so oriented to water,

Charleston Museum specimen.

Marsh Rabbit.

the nocturnal rabbits alter their activity according to tide, move to higher ground on flood tides and back to lower ground on ebb tides.

Both marsh and cottontail rabbits thump the ground with their hind feet as a danger signal. Otherwise, marsh rabbits are silent, but cottontail mothers make soft, grunting sounds to their young. Adult cottontails sometimes utter a high-pitched, shrill scream when fighting one another or when captured by a predator such as a great horned owl, fox, bobcat, mink, weasel, skunk, large hawk, snake, dog or man.

Facing a host of dangers, a lifespan of less than a year in the wild and a lifestyle that sometimes sounds a bit tough and hard-hitting, rabbits nonetheless are bascially gentle creatures. Lush fur, delightfully long ears and large eyes all give the bunny a look of cuddly innocence. And its incredible ability to give life with such abundance may make the rabbit a very fitting wildlife symbol for the spring Easter season.

Summer

Summer scene at Edisto Beach.

Beaches —

As the long, hot summer settles in, beaches swarm with people seeking a suntan, a breeze, a cooling dip in the ocean or a spontaneous party. But those obvious drawing cards can pale in comparison to the show put on by sea and shore critters.

Small pools may be filled with tiny fish and hermit crabs, land crabs dodge in and out of their sandy burrows, bizarre animals that look like plants often dot the beach and mysterious marine life lurks in the shallow water. The more a beach-goer hunts, the more there is to discover.

On the back edge of the shore, Indian blanket and black-eyed Susans grace the sand. The nearby dunes are protected by tall clumps of panic grass, beach elder and sea oats that will soon draw birds to golden heads of grain. The roots of sea oats help hold sandy dunes in place and it's against the law to remove the protective plants or harvest the oats. The dunes form a last refuge, a line of defense against storm tides and the inhospitable stretch of sand between land and sea. Life is challenging for animals here.

In the dry back beach that is rarely covered by water, ghost crabs

Ghost Crab.

hold sway. Tunnelling several feet under the ground, the square-bodied crabs emerge from their round holes at night and sometimes on cloudy days. The speedy crabs race out to prey on almost anything from sea turtle eggs to mole crabs to carrion that washes up. Their grayish to straw-colored shells, about 2 inches wide, blend so perfectly with the sand that the crabs appear and disappear like ghosts. Watch them gather as the sun sets or sit quietly on the beach beneath a full moon to view the crabs at their busiest.

In the same stretches of dry sand, pale beach hoppers or beach fleas may be bouncing through the sand. And some 30 to 40 species of shells may decorate the sand from the dunes right into the water.

The intertidal beach, exposed at low tide and covered with water at high tide, is often laced with holes. Ghost shrimp, up to 4 inches long, hide in burrows with entrances as wide as half an inch or as narrow as the diameter of a pencil. Bubbles sometimes rise from the holes, which often run 3 to 6 feet deep and make the shrimp almost impossible to excavate. The animals secrete a sticky substance that cements their sandy burrows. At the bottom is a shell-lined chamber leading on to other burrows. Nearly blind, the ghost shrimp has tiny eyes and a face only a sightless mother could love. More closely related to hermit crabs than to shrimp, ghost shrimp feed on tiny bits of organic matter.

Small holes in the intertidal zone are signs of marine worms such as tube worms. A periscope-like tube almost the consistency of parchment may extend above the hole. A tube sometimes will become dislodged and wash up on the beach or out to sea. In great numbers, tubes have been known to clog shrimp nets and displeased shrimpers compare the wet tubes to newspaper.

Where waves are breaking on the beach, mole crabs or sand fleas do their burrowing. The pale grayish crabs, with oval shells 1½ to 2 inches long, ride in on waves and quickly use their specialized diggers to build a home in the sand. Bait for surf fishermen, mole crabs also provide entertainment for children. The crabs are easy to unearth just beneath the surface and, with little coaxing, will compete in sand flea races across the damp sand. (The winner is the first one to cross the finish line or reach wet sand and dig in.)

Also riding the tide are mollusks, live shell creatures such as the half-inch-long dwarf surf clam. Colorful coquinas, more common on Florida's Gulf Coast beaches than here, wash in on a wave, turn upright as the wave retreats and rapidly burrow just below the surface. The triangular but rounded shells, about ¾ inch long, may be striped, plaid or solid colors ranging from pink to reddish-orange, yellow, green, blue and purple. Typical of many shells, brighter coquinas come from more southern waters while the coquinas found here often have dull grayish-white shells.

Breaking waves bring in a beachcomber's wealth of plants and animals, which may be tumbling in the surf or littering the damp sand. As the tide recedes, live creatures may become stranded. But often being tough, the marine animals may still be alive and will gratefully swim or crawl away if taken back to the water.

Plants such as red algae, seaweed and leafy green sea lettuce are easy to recognize as plants. So is yellowish-brown Sargassum weed, which drifts here from hundreds of miles away on ball-like flotation devices filled with gas. When it washes in, Sargassum weed may contain shrimp, small crabs, fish and live shells.

Other plant-like materials washing up on beaches are really communal animals such as sea whips, sea pork and assorted hydroids and bryozoans.

Colonial animals, including sponges, often grow in ill-defined and unexpected shapes; other brownish or grayish animal communities resemble moss or branched plants. These colonial animals in turn are home for a whole world of tiny animals. Float a sponge in a bucket of water and innumerable little critters may emerge and scurry around. Anything from delicate brittle stars to sea slugs to colorful anemones to insect-like isopods and amphipods may be hiding in a sponge.

The most common bryozoan on the beach is rubbery, branching, brownish, fleshy clumps of fat grass. It usually covers the stems of rockweed and other plants or may live on rocks near the low tide line or in shallow water. Bryozoans are sedentary animals living in a colony that may be several feet wide. Each individual, or *zooid*, lives within a body covering that is continuous with or fused to neighbors. The covering may be gelatinous, membranous, rubbery, limy or chitinous much like a shrimp.

Hydroids have radially symmetrical bodies, a tube or sac with a single mouth opening surrounded by tentacles. The tubularian hydroid is a 5-inch-tall single, pink polyp growing on branching stems above a creeping horizontal stem. The feathered hydroid, on the other hand, is bushy as if topped by a feather duster. Stems are covered with a tough, hard, yellow to black sheath; the white to pink head has irregular whorls of knobbed tentacles.

Sea whips, which may be bright orange, red, purple or even white, are a branching soft coral. When alive, the colonial animals live attached to rocks or other hard objects in shallow water. The coral has a hard core of narrow stems and branches pitted with small, evenly distributed pores.

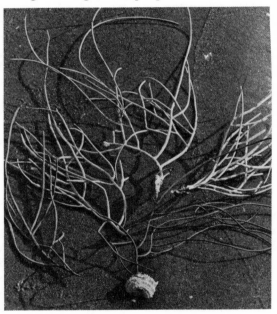

Far less attractive is sea pork, a globular colonial animal that looks like slightly rendered salt pork. Usually sandy in color or blotched with pinkish orange, sea pork breaks loose in storms, when raked by trawlers or hooked by fishermen.

As the name suggests, sea cucumbers also look more like plants than animals. But in fact sea

Sea Whip growing on shell.

cucumbers are members of the same *Echinodermata* phylum as starfish, sea urchins and sand dollars, all of which wash up on beaches here. At home in the water, a sea cucumber extends its feathery tentacles and looks almost like a flower. But lying on the beach, the cuke draws in its tentacles, actually modified tube feet, and takes on a drab, tannish, lumpy vegetable appearance.

All echinoderms are radially symmetrical and most have bodies arranged in five parts or multiples of five. Their internal limy skeletons are covered with skin and may have movable or fixed spines. What sets echinoderms apart from all other animals is their internal hydraulic system, a water vascular system that moves rows of numerous tube feet or podia. To move and feed, the animal can extend a slender foot by pumping in fluid and then can withdraw the foot by retracting foot muscles.

Inside the body, a complex system of canals is filled with sea water or, in the case of the sea cucumber, with body fluid. The animal draws in or expels sea water as needed through a sieve plate. Like higher animals, echinoderms have complex digestive, nervous and reproductive systems. But the animals lack excretory organs and instead diffuse wastes through their skin or water vascular system.

Familiar starfish are flattened animals with five rays or arms while sand dollars are round, flat, hard, but fragile, creatures. During most of the year, only the white tests, or external skeletons, of sand dollars are seen on area beaches. But during breeding, large numbers of live sand dollars may gather just under the sand in shallow water. Live keyhole urchins, the variety of sand dollar seen here, are tan, light brown or grayish and wear fine spines. On the upper surface of the sand dollar is a pattern of five sets of tube feet, one set directed forward and two each to the right and left. The round casts are marked with five narrow openings and a central five-pointed star.

Area sea urchins include the Atlantic purple with its purplish-brown spines and the variegated urchin with abundant short spines varying from green to white to pinkish to brownish-red. The variegated often is camouflaged with bits of shells, plant material and other debris. Once a dome-shaped sea urchin dies, spines fall off and the animal inside decays, leaving an empty, delicate test often marked with intricate patterns.

In early summer, horseshoe crabs sometimes blanket area beaches during mating and egg laying ceremonies. The empty shells the ani-

Horseshoe Crab and typical track.

mals shed as they grow may wash up at any time of the year, but only in summer will horseshoe crabs crawl up on land.

Mature horseshoe crabs congregate near the shore during breeding season. Males hold onto the abdomens of females with heavy walking legs. At high tide, the female digs a hole just above the low-tide mark and deposits 200 to 300 pale greenish eggs as the male fertilizes them. Several weeks later, miniature horseshoe crabs with button tails dig their way up through the sand and head for deeper water.

Measuring as long as 2 feet, greenish-tan horseshoe crabs have a convex carapace shaped like a horseshoe and a harmless, spike-like tail. Used for locomotion rather than fighting, the tail can be a life-saver for the arthropod. In shallow water, it swims about upside down, with legs up in the water. Should a wave leave the animal immobile on dry sand, a horseshoe crab can push the center of its body up with its pointed tail. Bending between the triangular abdomen and the front shoe, the body tilts and flips over onto the sand rightside up. Five pair of walking legs leave scratchy tracks on the beach as they invisibly propel the tank-like creature back to the safety of water.

These invertebrates dine on clams, worms and the like, which are ground with the burr-like bases of the legs, which surround the mouth. The animal is harmless so it's quite safe to handle...with due care not to hurt the creature. Turn it over briefly and discover an intricate array of legs with pincher tips, six pairs of overlapping flaps, mouth, pair of compound and pair of simple eyes. Then return the horsehoe crab, feet down, to the water.

Hermit crabs often linger in tidal pools or near the water. Several different varieties of hermits live along South Carolina beaches, from the giant hermit crab that can reach nearly 5 inches to the 1¼-inch striped hermit crab and the similar sized star-eyed hermit. Among the most common is the long-clawed hermit crab, measuring just half an inch.

While many other hermit crabs choose snail shells as home, the long claw may move into a little oyster drill shell, a periwinkle or mud snail. Growing 1¼ inches long, the flat-clawed hermit crab, which likes open shores and brackish estuaries, prefers moon snails and whelks above all others. Some varieties can't survive in a tidal pool because oxygen is so limited, but others scurry around as if the pool is their kingdom. Apparently always on the lookout for a bigger, better shell, hermits sometimes can be seen facing off or charging at one another. When trying out a new home, the crab extricates its delicate vital organs from deep in its shell and backs into an empty shell. The crab may even chip away the internal structure of the shell to fit its body.

Sharing tidal pools with hermits are tiny fish such as yellow or brown mud minnows. Schools of smaller silver and black striped killifish, usually 2 to 3 inches long, will literally vanish by quickly burying themselves in the sand of a tidal pool. Shorebirds often walk the edges of pools and probe the damp sand in search of crustaceans or mollusks. Following bird tracks is even a good way to find shells. A bird may leave behind a string of little shells in perfect, fresh condition but beautifully cleaned.

At low tide, trails of mollusks may be visible in the damp sand. A slight depression, sometimes forming a line but often twisting and turning, usually means a live sea shell is just below the surface. But most mollusks prefer staying in shallow to deep water, where they crawl over or bury into the sand.

Check pilings, rocks and any submerged surface for animals such as sea anemones. These pink, orange and white column-shaped relatives of hydroids and jellyfish have a pedal disk to attach to the bottom and an oral disk circled with tentacles on top. Resembling flowers in the ocean water, anemones may retract and tuck their tentacles inside. On a dry beach, the anemone is a plain, soft hemisphere with only a slight indentation on one end.

In the turbulent water near shore live a number of crabs. The 2½-inch-long calico crab is extremely active, perhaps in part because it has such a large gill area and can take in unusually large amounts of oxygen. The crab lives up to its name. Its dull yellowish, grayish or brownish shell is covered with many large, round or irregular light red spots with dark borders.

About 3 inches wide, the lady crab has a fan-shaped shell of yellowish-gray. Polka-dotted with small reddish-purple spots, the shell shines with a metallic irridescence. Known for its aggressive disposition, the lady has large, sharp pinchers so should be handled with care if handled at all.

Blue crabs, growing to 9 inches wide and 4 inches long, are grayish

Blue Crab.

or bluish-green with red spines; males have blue fingers, females red.

Living in shallows and brackish estuaries, the crab ranges from the low-tide line to water 120 feet deep. The surf crab resembles the blue but is brownish with white spots.

Blues aren't the only variety of edible crab here. Secretive stone crabs, active primarily at night, are hiding in area jetties, oyster reefs and burrows. The gray-brown backs and legs of the crabs are sprinkled with darker spots; undersides are beige, brightened with orange under their claws. Stone crabs spend much of their time in burrows excavated with claws and back legs.

Often complex with many chambers, the burrow protects a female after she sheds her shell. Since the female is ready to mate just after molting, a male often stands guard just outside her burrow. If she accepts him, he cradles her beneath him and in one mating provides enough sperm for an entire spawning season ahead, usually four or five sponges containing 160,000 to 350,000 eggs apiece.

Stone Crab. Crusher claw, left. Pincher, right.

The stone crab uses its larger crusher claw to break up such food as oysters and clams. The smaller pincher claw, the crab's defense, can exert considerable pressure. If caught by an enemy, the crab can amputate the pincher claw and swim away to safety. If the claw is removed at that correct plane, the wound heals quickly and without bleeding. State law provides for harvesting a single 2¾-inch or longer claw, which should be removed along that plane. After the next molt, the crab will have a new claw about three-quarters the size of the old one.

Another favorite of seafood fans, brown shrimp abound in shallow waters, small rivers and tidal creeks beginning in early summer. (White shrimp won't arrive until mid-September.) A female brown shrimp normally produces from half a million to a million eggs, which the male fertilizes externally. The female may spawn several times during a season and may live to spawn a second year.

Young shrimp grow in the upper reaches of sounds and bays, rivers and creeks, where they feed on decomposing saltmarsh grasses, small marine worms, tiny crabs, small fish or squid and even other shrimp. The rich estuaries of South Carolina serve as dining room and nursery for an incredible number and variety of young marine creatures, most abundant and active in summer.

Not only is summer the peak season for recreational crabbing and shrimping, but fishing is at its prime for species such as trout, bass, spot, croaker, whiting, sheepshead, flounder and even sharks.

Summer is shark season in South Carolina as 31 species ply the ocean, some near shore and some in the deep. Less potentially troublesome to man, inshore species such as sand tigers, sandbars, blacktips, spinners, lemons, sharpnoses and spiny dogfish haunt shallow waters including rivers and harbors. Such pelagic or deepwater species as blues and makos are speedy, streamlined hunters usually considered more threatening. The most dangerous shark in the Carolinas is the tiger, which can weigh more than 800 pounds and often visits inshore waters.

Guided by a very keen sense of smell rather than sight, sharks feed primarily at night and are attracted for miles by the scent of blood. Lacking bones, these almost delicate animals have skeletons of cartilage and lack strong connective membranes between their body walls and organs. But sharks are armed with up to seven rows of teeth, each containing up to 50 teeth, and a body covering of microscopic, toothlike scales. Shark species vary widely in size, lifestyle and even reproduction. Many give birth to live young, nourished either by a yolk sack or an umbilical cord. But other shark mothers deposit then abandon embryos in leathery egg cases.

Sharks swim the inshore Carolina waters from April or May into at least September, just the time people most enjoy ocean dips. The vast majority of these squaliformes will have migrated south or headed for warmer, deeper water by late November or December.

Orange, occasionally yellow, Day Lilies grow along roadsides.

Wildflowers —

Summer erupts with brilliant colors in the wildflower world. Spring blooms may be a pastel delight after winter's chill, but summer blossoms come on strong and bold.

Butterfly weed, trumpet creeper, orange milkwort and day lily are out in glorious orange shades while coral bean, despite its name, has bright red blooms. Yellow shades blossom on prickly pear cactus, woolly mullen, hawkweed, sneezeweed, coreopsis and others. And pinks include goat's rue, mimosa, marsh pink, swamp rose, meadow beauty and morning glory. Morning glories also wear purple tones as do exotic passionflowers, verbena and pickerelweed flowers that cover the water. Gaillardia is ablaze in red and yellow, lantana in pink, orange, yellow and lavender.

Many summer flowers are large and showy or mass in profusion. Clusters of trumpet creeper flowers flash from fences or shrubs and trees, along roadsides and from yards where gardeners sometimes introduce the aggressive vine for its beautiful blooms. The bright orange, trumpet-shaped flowers, each about 2½ inches long, have five lobes. A member of the poison ivy family, the creeper is best handled with care since some people have allergic reactions to its sap. Hummingbirds, however, have no such trouble and eagerly seek nectar deep in the blossoms.

Less common but equally brilliant is the coral bean, its bright red, tubular flowers forming a flame-like cluster. The erect plant has purplish, prickly stems that will grow 2 to 5 feet high later in the season as poisonous red seeds form. This tropical plant usually grows along sandy roadsides.

Familiar day lilies also dot roadsides, particularly in more moist areas between roads and hardwood forests. A native of Eurasia, the day lily has been widely cultivated here and has done so well that both orange and, less commonly, yellow varieties have escaped to the wild. Flowers usually measure about 3½ inches wide with three petals and three petal-like sepals. Apparently a hybrid, the wild day lily reproduces from the roots and does not have fertile seed. Picking the handsome but short-lived flowers should not endanger populations. By and large, however, it's best to observe and sniff rather than gather wildflowers since future generations depend on those blossoms for seeds.

Another brilliant display, butterfly weed is a member of the milkweed family. Tiny, bright orange flowers grow in large clusters atop leafy, hairy stems. Flowers have five petals that curve back from a central crown. Adding to the sheer beauty of the bloom are the butterflies that regularly visit them along roadsides and in rich woods. Standing 2½ feet tall or less, the plant also is known by the common name pleurisy root because Indians once chewed the tough root in hopes of curing pulmonary problems.

Orange milkwort plants are often hidden away in the damp sandy or peat soils of bogs, but the ball-like heads of bright flowers stand out. Each compact cluster of tiny flowers stands atop a simple or branched stem. Lingering long past their prime, orange flowers dry to a distinctive yellow shade. A little later in the summer the related yellow milkwort will send up branched, flat-topped clusters of small, yellow flowers. Clusters, which are 5 to 6 inches wide, form an umbrella over the plant with its inch-long, basal leaves.

On visits to the beach, look for lantana that has escaped from yards and for gaillardia's reddish ray flowers, yellow tips and darker central disk flowers. Plants grow 8 to 16 inches tall in sandy fields and along roadsides. The same dry, sandy conditions are ideal for prickly pear cactus plants. The broad, flattened, spiny leaves are topped with delicate bright yellow flowers that will produce purple pears in fall.

Woolly mullein also sends out yellow flowers in sandy areas and along roadsides. The tall, thick, heavy spikes of tiny flowers stand out above a rosette of thick, velvety basal leaves. During the Roman empire, soldiers dipped the dried stalks of mullein in grease and burned them as torches. For warmth, Indians and colonists lined their shoes with the soft leaves of the biennial, which blooms only in its second year.

If it looks like dandelions have been reborn in the yard or along roadsides, the plants are hawkweeds, originally introduced from Europe. A member of the sunflower family, the rapidly-spreading plant produces inch-wide yellow flower heads on stalks considerably taller than those of dandelions. Yet another member of the sunflower family, garden coreopsis brightens moist ditches, roadsides and other low-lying spots. Its five to seven fragile, yellow ray flowers are toothed at one end and blotched with reddish-brown at the base. Central disks are reddish-purple on this flower that was once widely cultivated but now is running wild. Sea-oxeyes, growing along salt marshes, produce yellow, sunflower-like blossoms. The low, gray, hairy shrubs have pairs of leathery leaves shaped like arrowheads.

Among the pink flowers of early summer, brilliant single or sometimes double swamp roses are as handsome as cultivated varieties but are content in ditches, freshwater swamps and creeks. Goat's rue flowers resemble sweet pea blossoms with pink wings and yellow standards. Blooms cluster on top of a hairy stem with small, delicate leaflets; plants grow 1 to 2 feet tall, flower clusters to 3 inches.

The lovely little meadow beauty shows off with several pink flowers in broad clusters atop a sturdy, four-sided, slightly winged stem. Measuring 1 to 1½ inches, the flowers have four petals and eight prominent stamens. Flowers literally fall apart when picked. If left on the plant until autumn, however, they turn into handsome, urn-shaped seedpods.

Mimosa trees in the wild and in yards wear poms of pale pink feathery flowers among the lacy leaves.

The wheel-shaped flower of marsh pink has five pale pink petals and a yellowish, star-shaped center edged with red. The salt-marsh pink thrives in saline or brackish marshes and meadows along the coast while the slender marsh pink takes to dunes, sandy soil and peaty soil along the coastal plain.

Morning glories appear in pink, purple, blue and white; the funnel-shaped flowers open singly or in clusters along twining vines that may invade cultivated fields, roadsides and almost any disturbed area. Introduced from tropical America as an ornamental, the plant with distinct broad, heart-shaped leaves has wandered from gardens and become naturalized.

Another tropical plant, the passionflower, is among the most beautiful of all Lowcountry wildflowers. Measuring 1½ to 2½ inches, the wheel-shaped flowers have five outer sepals and five petals ranging

Flowers and fruit of the Passionflower.

from bluish to whitish. Against that background rest two or three circles of purple and pinkish fringe. The five drooping stamens are suspended around a three-styled pistil. Although the beauty and tropical nature of the passionflower family might be reason enough for the name, parts of the flower are also said to represent aspects of Christ's passion. The 10 petal-like parts stand for the disciples except Peter and Judas, the five stamens for Jesus' wounds, the knob-like stigmas the nails, the fringe the crown of thorns. After the flower falls, a large, yellow berry forms on the climbing or trailing vines that grow in sandy thickets and open areas. A related yellow passionflower with much smaller blossoms is less common in South Carolina.

Along sandy roadsides, look for a wild verbena that is closely related to the verbena grown in many flower gardens. This wild variety reaches 3 to 4 feet with divided branches holding bursts of tiny purple flowers. They grow in eye-catching clusters that look like several good-sized blossoms.

Proving a pest when it clogs ditches, pickerelweed becomes a show in early summer. Violet-blue flower spikes rise above the water while a rhizome creeps below the surface. Pickerel fish may live beneath the plant while deer may feed on it from above.

Check ths same freshwater marsh, pond, lake or ditch habitat for lizard's tail, which like pickerelweed can grow so densely that it slows the flow of water. White, fragrant, catkin-like blossoms rise above the plants then gracefully droop like the tail of a lizard or cat. In midsummer the white flowers of alligator weed also will erupt in the ditches where the aquatic weed flourishes.

Pine bogs come alive in June with such flowers as blackroot and colicroot. The former has long, feathery, upright clusters of very small white flowers and unusual leaves, green on top but white and woolly beneath. The urn-shaped flowers of colicroot form a white spike at the end of each sturdy, round stem; on the ground is a basal cluster of pale green, pointed leaves.

Wild plants of all sizes are sprouting flowers in early summer. The smaller or less bright and distinguished, of course, require more than the eye can see from a speeding car. At a glance, roadsides may take on a blue to purple haze. But a closer look discloses the stiff, pencil-like spikes of tiny, tubular flowers on vervain.

In moist areas, button-bush is decked in small, white fuzzy balls of flowers. In swamps, marshes and moist pinelands, white-topped sedge forms a spikelet of lily-like flowers. White bracts surround a small, central white flower on a triangular stem. During July, aquatic milk-weed in swamps will produce heads of white flowers in individual circles of densely packed blossoms.

Skullcap, a member of the mint family, shows its two-lipped, bluish-lavender flowers in the axils of upper leaves. The inch-long blooms form a lengthy cluster along a square stem. And beardtongue, a member of the snapdragon family, has inch-long tubular, violet-purple to pinkish flowers that are striped inside with narrow, darker violet lines.

The stinging or spurge nettle, also known as tread-softly, is topped with a cluster of white, trumpet-shaped flowers. Best enjoy the blossoms from a distance since a mere brush against the spines of this 6 to 36-inch-tall plant will produce a miserable rash.

Light yellow blooms appear on wild lettuce plants, reaching 2 to 10 feet tall. In clearings, thickets and edges of woods, the plant has quarter-inch-wide flower heads in a spreading cluster. Like the dande-lions of spring, the blossoms produce white down that carries seeds all over the countryside.

The little Mexican clover, which bears white flowers, may reach 4 to 6 inches in height but usually forms low mats. White flowers of summer that promise fruit include blueberries and winged sumac, the latter wearing spikes of flowers that will turn to clusters of red berries.

As the summer wears on, many of the early flowers will continue to bloom. And such standard fare as Spanish bayonets, also known as yuccas, and palmetto trees both produce large clusters of white blooms that will turn to fruit. Drooping blossoms on bayonets form a large, showy spike above rings of leaves with tips nearly as sharp as bayo-nets.

Palmettos, the South Carolina state tree, have large panicles of light-green buds. The tiny, fragrant white blooms draw bees and later the round, shiny black ber-ries will attract hungry birds. In days gone by, entire trees would be killed to obtain large leaf buds, which were grated into a salad re-sembling cole slaw. Trunks also have been used for wharf pilings and docks and poles, leafstalk fibers for brushes and whisk brooms, blades from the fan-shaped leaves for baskets and hats.

Another plant produc-ing a panicle of white flowers in mid-summer

Yucca flower and bayonets.

is Hercules' walking stick. The unusual flower spike rises from the very top of the tree. Bark, leaves and twigs all are covered with spines, making it a Herculean task to use a branch as a walking stick.

In swamps and other damp places, July brings brilliant cardinal flowers, tubular, red blossoms about 1½ inches long forming a long, narrow cluster on an erect stalk. Hummingbirds usually pollinate the flowers, which insects find too long and narrow to handle. Although not rare, the plant has been dug and flowers picked so often that it has become scarce in many places. A related plant, lavender lobelia, also blooms through July in swamps, rich lowland woods and meadows. The flower clusters are very similar to the cardinal flower but are bright blue, somewhat smaller and more subtle.

Plants in swamps may be spared the drought and some of the heat of summer. But elsewhere flora often suffers and some plants find special ways of adapting. The morning glory, for instance, opens for only part of the day, closes and reopens again the next day. The handsome hibiscus, also known as rose mallow and flower-of-an-hour, closes after a very short time. Creamy with a red throat, the flower has five

Wild Hibiscus resembles cultivated plant.

petals flaring around a column of numerous stamens and anthers. The flowers, which look much like a cultivated tropical hibiscus, dot tall annual plants in sandy, dry soils along roadsides. In dry pine areas, the sensitive brier adapts by closing its leaves and by having spines, both of which conserve water loss. The plant resembles a bizarre cross between a cactus and a mimosa dressed in fernlike leaves.

Mimosa-like leaves also decorate the partridge pea with yellow flowers as long as 1½ inches. Not at all pea-like, the blooms have five slightly unequal petals and conspicuous brown anthers growing from axles of the leaves. Another obvious yellow pea flower, showy rattlebox, produces elongated clusters of blossoms near the top of an erect plant 2 to 3 feet tall. The flowers are poisonous and have been known to kill cows that nibble the plants. The blossoms later produce dry seeds that rattle in their pods, giving the plant its name. Seedbox or *Ludwigia* also has yellow blooms during the summer on plants about the size of rattlebox. Seedbox, however, grows in swamps and wet soils rather than fields and roadsides; the solitary flowers with four yellow petals and four green sepals will later bear box-like square fruit filled with seeds.

Throughout the summer and sometimes in spring, Spanish moss is forming low-key flowers in its web of threadlike leaves. Hailing from North and South America, not from Spain, Spanish moss is not a primitive moss but an epiphyte in the same family as the pineapple. Beneath the gray scales hides a green plant that

Rattlebox flowers are poisonous.

produces its own food rather than taking life from its host tree. Air and water provide all the food Spanish moss needs although it can take up nutrients from decaying tree bark. About half an inch or longer, the pale green flowers have three short, narrow petals that fade to yellow with age. The blossoms are delightfully, if subtly, fragrant at night. Later the wind will blow tiny seeds from the dry flowers to the craggy bark of a tree or shrub. Catching hold with minute rootlets, the seed will quickly sprout short roots to anchor the budding plant in its new home.

As if giving a hint of autumn long before the first cool weather arrives, sunflowers and aster-like blooms begin appearing later in the summer. Sunflowers feature showy golden ray flowers surrounding a central core of disk flowers. Black-eyed Susans send out 2 to 3-inch-wide flowers in their second year of life. Sneezeweed has yellow rays that droop backward from a greenish-yellow center. (Don't fear the name. The plant and flowers do not bother the nose, but leaves were once dried and made into snuff that induced sneezing.)

Another sunflower, ironweed, has pinkish-purple aster-like blossoms with 30 to 50 central disk flowers surrounded by bracts. Other sunflowers include *Eupatorium rotundifolium* and climbing boneset or climbing hempweed, both showing dense, flat-topped clusters of dull white blossoms. They actually resemble fluffy dandelions gone to seed more than true sunflowers. The boneset vine of stream banks, moist thickets and swamps has sweetly scented flowers ranging from white to pinkish to pale lavender.

Plants such as French mulberry and poisonous pokeweeds bloom and quickly begin producing their fruit. Elderberries and cocoa or cocos palms are heavy with clusters of berries, the latter a sweet, luscious golden shower. Wild creatures from birds to insects to raccoons and opossums feast with abandon. And even before the heat of summer ends, fall wildflowers are preparing a display that will almost rival spring.

Royal Terns on Bird Key in Bull's Bay.

Rookeries—

Summer rookeries bombard the senses. On every side, tiny bills are chinking away from inside eggs, fluffy young are racing the beach or gawking down from nests while parents are divebombing any and all intruders. Ears are assaulted with the shrieks and bleats of young and with assorted quarks, grunts, growls, guawks, squawks, screams and croakings of adults. The ripe smell of rotting finfish and shellfish, spilled overboard by baby birds, accosts the nose. Mosquitoes and biting flies assail any bit of flesh they can find while birds overhead unleash volleys of body wastes in hopes of driving out visitors.

Those unpleasantries aside, a rookery is one of the most fascinating places on earth and one of the most fragile. Low, sandy spits of land may erode. A single storm may destroy hundreds or thousands of bird nests. Drought may dry a wetland rookery site or kill the birds' supply of finfish and shellfish. Predators may discover, then decimate, a rookery. If that happens one year, birds may try again the next. But if predators strike two years in a row, adults may abandon the rookery site indefinitely.

Drum Island, beneath the Cooper River Bridges, has hosted as many as 50,000 birds in spring and summer. In 1983, George Reiger's book *Wanderer on my Native Shore* called the island the largest wading-bird rookery in eastern North America. But drought and predators have plagued the rookery since then.

Bird Key, a spit of land on Stono River between Folly Beach and Kiawah Island, grew into the largest brown pelican rookery on the East Coast. Gulls, black skimmers and other birds shared the site with the pelicans. However, the key is vulnerable to high tides.

Marsh Island in Cape Romain National Wildlife Refuge off the coast of McClellanville has logged nearly 40,000 nesting adults on just four acres of land. Marsh Island birds include royal and sandwich terns, laughing gulls, pelicans, black skimmers, royal terns, oystercatchers and even a scattering of egrets and herons. Marsh also suffers from high tides that devastate at least some nests each year.

Pumpkinseed Island in Winyah Bay has nearly rivalled Drum Island in sheer numbers. Most of the same species nest on both islands — white ibises, great egrets, black-crowned night herons, yellow-crowned night herons, tricolor herons, cattle egrets, little blue herons and snowy egrets. But the low island has felt the effects of drought and storms.

A variety of sites along the coast, in former ricefields and inland on lakes, also serve as rookeries for smaller groups of colonial nesters. Wading birds occupy about 70 known sites, most of which boast only 20 to 100 nests. Even the rare wood stork has recently established rookeries in this state. And least terns, a threatened species, are claiming some gravel roofs of shopping centers as rookeries.

About 10 percent of the bird species on earth nest in colonies despite the fact a bird's natural inclination is to defend his territory and drive away any competition. Most likely to breed in colonies are varieties that range over large areas, such as lakes or ocean, to find food. Lack of suitable nesting sites may force some birds together.

Colonial nesting also may prove useful to birds. They may share information, perhaps on the best places to feed. The safety of numbers and group efforts at defense may help adults protect eggs and young from predators. Several varieties, including some terns and gulls, apparently are stimulated by sheer numbers into breeding at the same time thus laying eggs that hatch at the same time. A predator searching for eggs has a shorter season and more nests to scout at one time, assuring more eggs will survive in the colony than if egg laying were scattered over several weeks.

On the other hand, even colonial nesters are instinctively aggressive and territorial. A male may have to spend an inordinate amount of time guarding his mate from the advances of rivals. Birds may fight over nest sites. In places like Drum Island, where sticks are the gold of the bird world, nest builders scrap over twigs or steal material from one another's nests. A colonial bird generally chooses a site just beyond the reach of a neighbor's pecking bill. But on Marsh Island, where birds nest on the ground, youngsters often go exploring and may be pummelled as they pass nesting adults.

Despite such jabs and lessons, life is amazingly peaceful on Marsh Island. Each species has its own area, the site most ideal for its type of nest. Royal and sandwich terns scoop out shallow depressions in the sand and nearly ring the beach above the high tide mark. Their fluffy, chick-like young hatch more quickly and are on the wing much sooner than those of larger species. Just inside the ring of terns, laughing gulls choose an area covered with low clumps of grass that help camouflage olive eggs flecked with brown.

Farther from the water, tricolor herons and snowy egrets seek out dense, tall clumps of grass. Until an adult lands, looks furtively around then strides into the grass, nest and young are completely invisible. Far fewer of these wading birds head for Marsh Island than do gulls, terns and pelicans. Waders all but vanish in the hubbub of the other birds, and the long-legged young remain docile in comparison to speedy young terns and fiesty baby pelicans. In other sites, snowy egrets build a platform of sticks in a bush or reeds; tricolor herons construct a stick nest in a tree, among reeds or on the ground. But not a twig can be found on Marsh Island.

On the highest ground, pelicans collect grass for their tall nests. In some spots live grass all but disappears around nests, but in other areas low clumps remain. Over the weeks, parents and then errant young virtually trample the nest into a pancake. The most experienced pelicans usually nest first and take the highest, most desirable spots. When a high tide eats away at the island, those pelican nests stand the best chance of surviving. If a storm comes at the wrong time, eggs may wash out to sea and the young drown.

Black skimmers apparently have discovered Bird Key and Egg Bank. The magnificent black and white flier lays three to five creamy eggs marked

Black Skimmer nest.

with black to lilac spots, dots, blotches and splashes. The nest is a mere scrape of sand, indistinguishable from the rest of the beach and other skimmer nests nearby. These ocean birds, which rarely stray inland, seek very low, exposed sites, free of predators but braced by high tides. When a storm tide covers such rookeries, other birds are likely to give up. But indomitable skimmers renest, sometimes laying three sets of eggs in a row before a clutch hatches and fledges. If an intruder walks into the colony, adults rise in a cloud and charge the enemy with almost deafening cries and yelps. An adult also may flop around the sand in hopes of calling attention away from his nest. The red bill, with its longer lower mandible, barely cuts the surface of the ocean as the bird gracefully zips back and forth searching for small fish.

Unlike the sandy sites ocean birds choose for colonial nesting, the Drum Island rookery develops in trees. From the ground, the island bears no resemblance to the tranquil green trees and gliding birds visible from the Cooper River Bridges.

Dappled in sunlight, the ground is littered with twigs, snail shells from dinners long gone, pieces of eggshell, handsome aigrettes and other breeding plumage. Little else is visible but birds and bird nests, from eye level to the top of saplings and taller trees. The different species build similar nests, rough if not haphazard affairs crammed into almost any spot two branches meet. Wherever slender hackberry trunks bend across one another, an egret or heron is likely to start construction. A stronger hackberry may house six sprawling nests just a couple of feet apart.

At a few days of age, young are recognizable as white ibises, great egrets, black-crowned night herons, yellow-crowned night herons, tricolor herons, cattle egrets, little blue herons, snowy egrets and some-times glossy ibises.

Of the group, the most bizarre is the tricolor heron. Long strands of reddish fluff form a reverse Mohawk along a bald strip on the head and round yellow eyes have a deranged glint. A young wading bird is all neck and legs, gawky green legs in the case of the tricolor. Through a sparse covering of long, downy strands, the body is warm to the touch and the heart races with a strong beat.

Although dependent on their parents, 2 and 3-week-old youngsters are quite capable of defending themselves. Ornithologists who band and study the nestlings on Drum are subjected to jabbing bills, flailing wings, defensive regurgitating and voiding, even talons that grip nest or branch with surprising strength.

Parents seem preoccupied with gathering food for the family: killifish and shrimp for tricolors, finfish for little blues, insects for cattle egrets, saltwater creatures and sometimes baby egrets or ibises for night herons, freshwater crayfish for white ibises.

In 1985, a severe drought caused crayfish to bury deep into the ground long before their usual aestivation or summer hibernation. Aware of that fact, less than one-tenth the usual number of ibises nested on Drum and less than 4 percent of those nests fledged young. Pumpkinseed had less than half the nests of the previous year. Several inland wading bird rookeries were entirely abandoned when surrounding ponds dried up and fish perished.

Then in 1986, a once small number of predatory fish crows swelled enormously and took to roosting on Drum. The crows ravaged virtually all the nests of ibises, herons and egrets. Many adults fled and only 443 pair continued trying to nest on the island. Crows and small mammals such as raccoons, rats and cats consumed about half the eggs laid and some of the nestlings.

As one species or rookery is failing, another may be gaining. The endangered wood stork, for instance, was first discovered nesting in South Carolina in 1981. Just eight pair shared an isolated swamp that year, but numbers have grown steadily. By 1986, 120 pair were nesting in three sites and wood storks successfully raised 270 chicks. Now listed by both the federal and state governments as an endangered species, the wood stork is thought to number less than 4,800 pair and to be in jeopardy due to water management, drained wetlands, lowered water tables and increased development.

Breeding almost exclusively in South Florida until recently, this country's only stork repeatedly failed to raise young. Stork populations plummeted by 55 percent between 1960 and 1981 alone. Grope feeders, wood storks depend on large volumes of fish in small bodies of water. The long-legged white waders with bare, black heads, black wing edges and tails literally wait for fish to swim into or against their bills. South Florida's drainage canals and water management plans manipulate water in exactly the wrong way for wood storks. A flood of released water turns shallow pools into seas, fish escape, young storks starve, and adults are forced to desert their nests and seek food elsewhere.

Storks normally breed in Florida during the winter then fly north to feed in South Carolina during the summer. But more recently, storks have been arriving early, searching for food they could not find in Florida. The birds also may have been scouting rookery sites. Storks have chosen places near former ricefields, where water flow is controlled. Water levels and concentration of fish correspond perfectly with the time the storks nest in South Carolina or, as some biologists suggest, the birds may have altered their breeding cycle to take advantage of the food supply. Whereas 75 percent of the nation's wood storks bred in South Florida through the 1970s, in 1986 some 78 percent of the birds nested from central Florida to South Carolina. And the birds are successfully raising young, providing the first hope the endangered species might increase in number.

Lowcountry storks build flimsy stick nests high in cypress trees standing in fresh water. Sometimes sharing their rookery are great blue herons, birds of similar size that begin nesting at the same time. Cattle egrets and anhingas arrive later in the spring to build nests much lower in the same cypress trees.

Nicknamed water turkeys or snake birds because of their long necks, anhingas are so aquatic that even the very young, if frightened, dive into the water. A youngster will surface several yards away in a tangle of vines and branches. Using his neck and webbed feet, a young anhinga can work his way up, over, down, back up, around and finally into his nest, where parents deliver an assortment of freshwater finfish. Lacking oil on their feathers, black anhingas can dive easily. But after a fishing expedition, adults must perch with black and white wings outstretched until the sun dries waterlogged feathers. Even as babies, anhingas practice what is known as branching, teetering back and forth on a branch near their nest.

Instead of mixing with other species, least terns nest in their own seaside rookeries, where the birds make a slight hollow in the sand and line the nest with bits of shell. The small white and gray tern with black crown, nape and stripe from bill to eye has endured ups and downs in the past century and today is a threatened species in South Carolina. In 1910, Mount Pleasant ornithologist Arthur Trezevant Wayne wrote, "As a result of the custom of adorning women's hats with birds, these beautiful little terns have become practically, if not absolutely, extinct on this coast." With the protection of the law, by 1950 the birds were deemed one of the most abundant summer residents along the South Carolina coast. Least terns formed rookeries by the tens and hundreds on sea islands, beach resorts, waterways, spoil banks and even some sandy mainland sites.

As beaches drew more people and development, however, nesting declined. Beach-goers too often walked through colonies without noticing tern eggs, so perfectly camouflaged in pebbles and sand. As numbers have fallen precipitously, rookeries along the East Coast have been posted, marked or otherwise identified to guard adults as well as eggs and young.

In the Lowcountry, the birds themselves have adopted a new tactic and congregate where people can't wander through the colonies. Perhaps attracted by the abundance of small stones, least terns increasingly are nesting on gravel-roofed buildings such as grocery stores, discount franchises, department stores and government installations.

Some store employees take a very proud, protective attitude toward their birds, which often catch the attention of shoppers. The greatest problem to surface thus far is the lack of railing around many roofs. Gravel usually provides enough traction to hold eggs. But when fluffy, speckled young go venturing around the rookery, they sometimes fall off the edge of the roof or become trapped in a gutter. Because terns normally nest on a flat beach, nature apparently hasn't equipped hatchling terns with the instinct to look before they accidentally leap.

Cottonmouth or Water Moccasin.

Snakes —

Despised or enjoyed, endured or maligned, snakes are almost universally misunderstood if not feared. Despite all their bad public relations, dating back to the days of Adam and Eve, snakes are delicate, usually gentle, ecologically beneficial creatures.

These reptiles are really simplified lizards that may have adapted eons ago to life underground or under the bark of trees. Living and hunting in burrows, snakes would have found legs useless so they disappeared. Only a few snakes, such as the boa constrictor, have two stubs where rear legs might once have been.

Rather than eyelids, snakes have a clear scale that protects their eyes underground. And while the lizard has openings for its ears, a snake has no external ear at all and, instead, hears by picking up vibrations with its entire body. And it smells with a forked tongue, concealed in a sheath on the floor of the mouth. Almost continually flicking its tongue to the ground, the snake picks up tiny bits of soil. In the roof of the mouth, two olfactory organs interpret the particles and help the snake locate food or otherwise assess surroundings.

The poisonous group of snakes known as pit vipers — the Low-country's rattlesnakes, copperheads and water moccasins or cotton-mouths — has an opening or pit between eye and nostril. That infra-red sense organ helps a snake sense the heat of warm-blooded prey by day or night. An extension of the windpipe stretches to the opening of the mouth so a snake can breathe for the several minutes it may take to swallow a meal whole.

The scale-covered reptiles move in a very complex way by using scales made of a material similar to human fingernails. While man and most vertebrates have fixed ribs, each of a snake's movable ribs is attached to a large belly scale, connected to its neighbors by muscle. A snake hooks two or more scales over tree bark, blades of grass or even grains of sand: Almost nothing short of glass proves tough going for a snake. The animal tightens the muscles to its front scales and pulls the hind part of its body forward. Then it pushes forward with the back of its body, grips and pulls forward again.

After adapting to an underground life so perfectly, snakes moved back above ground, into trees and even into water. If not hunting, seeking a mate in spring or basking in the sun to raise their body temperatures, however, most snakes choose to hide under cover such as leaf litter, a woodpile, board or log.

In this climate, serpents usually spend the winter in rotting trees and logs, loose bark on trees, woodpiles, rocks or a hole in the ground. Snakes may return to the same spot winter after winter. Some congregate in small groups or even twine into balls. To keep their body temperatures up during winter, snakes rely on a few inches of insulation from cold air and the warmth produced by decaying wood. On a warm winter day, however, snakes may slowly slither into a protected spot to soak up the sun. The reptiles may even stretch out on hot, blacktop roads, which helps to account for the number of snakes found dead on quiet rural roads. Their low body temperature in winter makes movement extremely slow so the reptiles are relatively easy taking for red-tailed hawks and raccoons.

In summer, snakes need protection from extreme heat to prevent their temperatures from rising too high. Instead of basking in the sun as in spring and fall, snakes may hide away under leaves or debris in a shady spot.

Hunger brings a snake out of its hideaway. To handle live prey — from insects to frogs, eggs, birds and other snakes — the predator can dislocate its jaw with a hinge in the back of the mouth and another in the front of the jaw. In fact rat snakes can down a dinner equivalent in size to a man's swallowing a basketball. Excess skin on the throat also expands to accommodate a meal.

Other varieties catch and consume prey live. Rows of teeth are slanted toward the stomach so any animal, struggling to escape the jaws of a snake, only becomes more thoroughly trapped. Snakes periodically shed every other tooth so the reptiles always have sharp, new teeth in prime working condition. Having grabbed, poisoned or squeezed a victim into submission, the snake moves forward one side of the unhinged jaw after the other, sliding slowly over the prey.

A snake may need four or five minutes to take in an entire mouse. The reptile will seek cover and rest for two or three days while the lump of a meal digests and the snake regains its svelte lines. Then the reptile is usually ready to hunt again, by day or night depending on the species.

Well-fed snakes grow throughout their lives but more slowly after maturing. To do so, a snake must shed its skin, left behind as a whole, opaque casing. A snake sheds its skin for the first time shortly after live birth or hatching from a leathery egg. The reptile needs a new skin in part because the old one wears out just as birds must molt and produce fresh feathers. Before shedding twice a year, most snakes soak in water for a couple of days. Eyes begin to turn cloudy and, temporarily blind, the snake heads for hiding. A chemical action begins separating old skin from new.

The reptile first loosens the skin around its mouth then rubs the area to free the skin. Anything sharp, from a holly leaf to a stick or stone, may serve as a hook as the snake works to split its skin the length of its body. Up to several hours later, a bright, shiny snake crawls out of its dull, old skin much the way a human pulls his foot out of a sock.

Because color and markings vary as snakes age, it may be difficult to recognize the poisonous pit vipers from the far more numerous varieties of harmless snakes. All three venomous vipers have a very clear neck with a distinctly wider jaw and triangular shaped head. The heads, necks and bodies of non-poisonous snakes are the same size, giving them a sleek line. Non-poisonous snakes have horizontal pupils like those of a man or dog. But like cats, pit vipers have vertical pupils, giving rattlesnakes, copperheads and water moccasins a menacing look.

The Lowcountry's fourth venomous snake, the Eastern coral, is a burrower seldom seen above ground. Related to cobras, the coral snake doesn't strike with erectile fangs as a pit viper would but instead must bite and slowly chew into its victim with tiny teeth.

The coral and the non-venomous scarlet snake, which also lives here, both are ringed with bands of red, black and yellow. The scarlet snake has wide red and narrower yellow bands separated by still slimmer black borders. The coral has wide red and black bands, each surrounded by a narrower yellow band.

The height of evolution in the snake world, pit vipers retain shell-less eggs and give birth to live young. Copperheads, water moccasins, canebrake rattlesnakes, diamondback and pygmy rattlers kill by injecting a venomous saliva into their prey. These Lowcountry carnivores wait for the victim to struggle off and die then seek out the lifeless meal with the tongue and the heat-sensing pit. Coral snakes use the same tactic but lack the pit to help them find their meal.

Only when a pit viper opens its mouth do the needle-sharp, hinged, curved fangs appear. Constantly growing replacements, the snake releases venom through a tiny hole behind each fang. The poison flows down a slit in the fang and into the prey. Rattlers and, to some extent, other snakes can control the amount of venom injected: People have been bitten by venomous snakes without receiving any poison or suffering any ill effects. But a snake makes no promises so it's best to head for a doctor quickly if bitten by a snake.

Apparently venom not only kills prey but speeds digestion and helps a sluggish snake reduce the bulky dinner in its stomach. One experiment showed diamondback rattlesnakes need a week to digest dead mice but only two or three days for live mice the snakes killed themselves with venom.

The most common venomous snake in the state, the copperhead, ranges from pink to coppery-tan with distinctive chestnut or reddish-brown hourglass crossbands enclosing light areas. Despite the fact it

Copperhead at Charles Towne Landing.

bites more people in South Carolina than any other variety, the copperhead normally strikes only if touched or stepped on. Although painful, the bites carry the least dangerous venom. Growing as long as 4 feet, the snake prefers life along the edges of swamps and areas that periodically flood. In summer it retreats to piles of debris, sawdust heaps or rotting logs. Small rodents, lizards, frogs, even large caterpillars are on the snake's diet.

The water moccasin or cottonmouth is known for the warnings it gives, an open, gaping white mouth. (Other snakes also have a white mouth lining but simply don't display the fact.) Reaching an impressive 6 feet, this snake of lowland swamps, lakes, rivers, ricefields and ditches is olive, brown or black above. The skin may have serrated, dark crossbands or no pattern at all and may have a wide, dark brown cheek stripe with light borders. Unlike other water snakes, it swims with its head well above the water. Beware because the bite of this water snake can be fatal. More active at night than during the day, the snake preys on fish, frogs, sirens, birds and other snakes.

The Eastern diamondback rattlesnake, the largest venomous snake in this country, has been known to reach 8 feet. The population is declining because numbers have been killed and its favorite habitat is being developed. Today the snake is listed as a species of special concern in South Carolina. Wearing dark diamonds with light centers down its back, the snake is famous for its rattles, actually dried portions of skin that remain attached when the snake sheds. It usually will coil and rattle its tail as a warning before striking.

More common is the canebrake rattler, which can kill and consume an adult rabbit without much difficulty. Canebrake rattlesnakes are now recognized as a southern population of the timber rattlesnake, which is different in color and markings. The canebrake is gray with a yellowish, brownish or pinkish tint and has a tan or reddish-brown back stripe dividing its chevron-like crossbands. The tail is black and a dark stripe runs behind the eye. Swampy areas, canebrake thickets and floodplains are home to the snake, which can grow up to 74 inches in length.

The pygmy rattler, on the other hand, reaches a mere 15 to 30 inches including slender tail and tiny rattle. Gray to reddish with brown to black blotches along the midline of the back, the snake has one to three rows of spots on its sides. The pygmy may also have a narrow, reddish back stripe. The top of the head has nine enlarged scales, and a bar from eye to rear of jaw usually is underlined with white. Dining on lizards, small snakes, mice and sometimes insects, the small rattler makes only a buzzing sound that doesn't travel far.

While venomous snakes generally are more aggressive than harmless ones, each variety has its own character. A rattler, for instance, usually prefers to move before a person comes near. A water moccasin is basically lazy. It doesn't flee an approaching human and ends up striking because an outdoorsman steps on it. Yet a non-poisonous water snake, often mistaken for a water moccasin, is likely to bite first and ask questions later.

The brown water snake, which grows as long as 5 feet, has been known to terrorize fishermen, but not intentionally. Fond of climbing trees to sun in the branches, the water snake has a habit of dropping unexpectedly into boats as no self-respecting water moccasin ever would. More than one panicky fisherman has shot a water snake in the bottom of his boat...then swum for shore as the boat sank. Like other water snakes, the brown is fairly aggressive. If grabbed, it not only will bite but will hold on and keep biting.

The brown water snake has rectangular, dark blotches bordered with black on its rusty or brownish-green upper parts. The red-bellied water snake has appropriately bright undersides beneath its olive-drab back. It prefers river swamps and forest edges along streams, ponds and lakes. And the banded water snake, which lives only on the coastal plain and usually in ponds, has squarish spots on the belly and red, brown or black crossbands that usually darken with age.

If a beauty contest were held, the rainbow snake undoubtedly would be the winner. Striped lengthwise with reddish pink, yellow and black, the snake haunts rivers and old ricefields where it dines on eels. The rainbow, like the mud snake, grabs prey with its mouth, encircles the victim and strikes with a spike on the end of its tail. The frightened meal reacts by rushing forward, right down the throat of the snake.

The black racer uses a different tactic when it grabs prey such as frogs, fellow snakes and small rodents. The snake fights, trying to swallow the captive before it can wriggle free. The slate black snake with white on its chin is speedy, agile and a good climber but spends most of its time on the ground.

Rat snakes, on the other hand, are true constrictors that squeeze prey. Rather than squash a victim they suffocate it by pressing ever more tightly each time the prospective meal exhales. Outstanding climbers, rat snakes sometimes show up in attics but more often in trees. Handsome red rat snakes or corn snakes, which are excellent mousers, have checkered bellies; red markings, bordered in black, splotch their backs. Yellow rat snakes, which are yellow-brown to olive with four black stripes, can easily climb 40 feet up a tree, kill a

Red Rat Snake.

squirrel and eat the mammal on a lofty branch. The snake also enjoys eggs and even visits chicken coups in search of a shelled meal. Perhaps lacking a bit in the smarts department, a yellow rat sometimes bypasses real eggs and swallows a china version, meant to induce a chicken to lay.

The favorite food of a king snake is other snakes, which should make it tolerable even to the most ardent opponent of snakes. Because they often are slow-moving, poisonous snakes frequently fall victim to king snakes, which apparently are resistant to snake venom. Despite what might seem like ferocity as a predator, the king snake is downright docile and isn't inclined to bite man. Its temperament and its shiny, striped body make it popular among people who keep pet snakes.

Another favorite pet snake that roams wild here is the hognose, a gentle snake that puts on quite a show when approached by man or predator. It first flattens its neck and hisses like a cobra. But if that bluff doesn't work or if the enemy persists, the snake will roll over on its back, extend its tongue, thrash about and play dead. If turned onto its belly, the snake flips back and repeats its performance. If kept in captivity, however, the snake soon becomes accustomed to human beings and won't put on the act. The snake's solid black back may be marked with gold and the upturned, pig-like snout is distinctive. The hognose is at home on dry land and may even show up in parking lots. There lights draw insects, insects attract toads and hognoses arrive to swallow the amphibians whole and alive.

South Carolina's snakes are as varied as the habitat they choose, the food they eat, their coloring and even their size. The little brown snake, which spends most of its time hiding underground, doesn't grow longer than 18 inches. Yet the coachwhip snake, the largest variety in the state, reaches 94 inches. Man needn't fear, however. The coachwhip is not venomous, and the opportunist dines on such things as snakes, lizards, birds and small mammals.

Sea Turtles —

On summer nights, female loggerhead sea turtles linger in shallow water just off Lowcountry beaches. If all conditions look right, a loggerhead begins her slow trek up the beach.

Her heavy shell and body, up to 300 pounds that feel light when buoyed by salt water, weigh heavily on her lungs and make every movement on land a monumental effort. She searches the sand for a spot that is neither too wet nor too shelly, where plant roots are not intruding. Using her hind flippers alternately, she digs down and brings a pile of sand up and forward. Pausing, she holds the sand in her flipper as skillfully as if it were a hand. The other rear flipper reaches back and down; as it comes forward and stops with a load of sand, the first flipper tosses its sand to the side.

Loggerhead Sea Turtle depositing eggs.

She tilts her body as deeply as she can into the growing hole. Shaped like an inverted light bulb, the finished cavity with firmly packed sides will be about 18 inches deep and 10 inches wide.

If the first site she chooses doesn't feel perfect or if she senses an intruder or activity nearby, she turns back to the water or looks for a better spot. Even when frustrated repeatedly, a loggerhead will keep trying to come ashore and nest, sometimes on the very beach or at least in the general area where she hatched 20 years or more before.

When the cavity is ready, she begins to release her leathery, pliable eggs, white spheres the size of ping pong balls. Laying two, three or four at a time, the loggerhead produces an average of 120 eggs, as few as 55 or as many as 230.

Her hind flippers fill the hole with sand her front flippers shove backwards. And her heavy body, swaying as she works, packs the nest until only a turtle scientist can recognize the signs. After her hour and a half or two hours of work, she returns to the ocean. But she leaves behind telltale tracks, a crawl that looks much like tractor tread marks measuring 3 or 4 feet in width. At least half the tracks on a beach may be false crawls, signs a turtle investigated but did not nest.

The loggerhead, listed as a threatened species by the federal government and the state of South Carolina, may lay eggs five more times before the summer is over or she may not touch land again for two years. During most of her life, she swims far out to sea. From the moment a male takes his newborn swim, he will never set a flipper on land again.

After mating in early spring, females begin gathering offshore in April. They nest from mid-May until mid-August and eggs hatch in 50 to 75 days. Tiny young, with shells about the size of a quarter, begin bubbling up from nests in mid-July. Nesting continues into early August and the last hatchlings may not appear until October.

That range of hatching times plays a major role in keeping populations of males and females in balance. The first study of its kind, conducted partially in South Carolina, found the warmth of beach sand not only incubates loggerhead eggs but determines the sex of hatchlings. Cooler sand brings male hatchlings, hotter sand females. Nests laid in late May produced no females in the 1984 study, nests in early July 80 percent females and nests in early August 10 percent females. (Loggerheads are not alone: A growing body of evidence suggests temperature, rather than chromosomes, may determine the sex of reptiles. Cool weather, for instance, produces more female alligators, hot weather more males.)

Although a beach may be awash with tiny turtles, they do not all break free of their shells at one time. Using an egg tooth, a temporary projection on the end of its nose, a turtle opens its shell a couple of days before it surfaces. The hatchling will remain underground for several days to absorb the last bit of its egg sack and to allow its shell, curved within the egg, to straighten. Then the entire group begins slowly pawing upward, sand filtering down between the young and raising the floor of the nest. As night cools the final layer of sand overhead, the hatchlings begin to emerge. Most will appear in a group, within two or three minutes.

Hatchlings instinctively head for the brightest spot they see. Over most of the 120 million years sea turtles and their ancestors have been swimming the oceans, the only glow was the reflection of moon and

Newly hatched Sea Turtles make it to the ocean.

stars on the water. Now, however, street lights and flood lights from beachfront homes may attract hatchlings to certain death on roads or in tangles of beach grass. And despite federal and state laws, poachers sometimes still take turtle eggs.

But the young face other dangers as well. Ghost crabs seize the hatchlings on land, sea birds from the surface of the ocean and fish from below. Even optimistic marine biologists estimate only one in 100 will live long enough to breed. Other scientists think one egg in 10,000 may reach sexual maturity at age 20.

Only a low percentage of eggs ever hatch. Beach erosion and high storm tides can wash eggs out to sea or kill embryos. Plant roots take a toll as do hungry ghost crabs and raccoons, the last sometimes skulking nearby even as a loggerhead is laying.

A study on Botany Bay near Edisto found that of 100 females producing more than 10,000 eggs, only 45 hatchlings emerged, all from the same nest. Programs to help threatened loggerheads and several varieties of endangered marine turtles are now trying to improve those odds.

In the Charleston area, for instance, the Edisto Island Sea Turtle Project began helping loggerheads in 1981. Supported by the Charleston Natural History Society and the Center for Environmental Education in Washington, D.C., the program records turtle crawls and nests on Edisto Beach, Edisto Beach State Park, Edingsville Beach and Botany Bay. Screens are placed over nests to protect them from raccoons. If a nest is at risk from erosion, eggs are unearthed and moved to a higher, drier site. As a result the beaches have been yielding some 4,500 hatchlings, a success rate often as high as 70 to 80 percent for all the eggs laid.

At Cape Romain National Wildlife Refuge, workers carry out similar loggerhead nesting surveys and protection measures on Cape Island. Virtually all the sea turtles nesting in the refuge lay on Cape Island, located eight miles offshore from McClellanville. Before the program began, about 95 percent of the nests on Cape produced no young. But the success rate at the turtle hatchery, where endangered nests are relocated, has been averaging 75 percent.

The Kiawah Island Loggerhead Hatchery Program, which began in 1975, found only 1 percent of the eggs laid in the wild hatched. The program raised the hatching rate to about 75 percent in a protected hatchery. Sponsored by the Kiawah Island Community Association, the program is supported by property owners including the Kiawah Island Co.

In addition, endangered species biologists with the South Carolina Wildlife and Marine Resources Department continue to study the loggerhead and to protect nests. By removing raccoons and moving nests threatened by erosion, biologists increased the success rate of turtles from 12 to 62 percent on South Island, part of the state's Tom Yawkey Wildlife Center near Georgetown.

Despite such gains, numbers of loggerheads may barely be holding their own. The turtles have suffered as beachfronts are developed and sandy shores are blocked by seawalls and groins. During their life at sea, young loggerheads face natural predators and man-made devices. Adults and juveniles just nearing maturity are accidentally trapped and drowned in commercial shrimp trawls and other fishing gear. Nesting perhaps every two or three years and taking about 20 years to mature reduce reproduction.

Females appear in Lowcountry waters during nesting season and hatchlings depart from area beaches. But marine scientists have long puzzled over where the young go in the meantime. Recent research has found young loggerheads, with upper shells no longer than 20 inches, in the eastern North Atlantic. Only larger juveniles reappear off South Carolina beaches, primarily from spring until fall.

The head and upper shell of the loggerhead are a dark reddish-brown, flippers and lower shell are light yellow. The oval or heart-shaped top shell may reach 40 inches but head and neck may extend the full length to nearly 5 feet on turtles that live an average of 80 years. The name *Caretta caretta* refers to the head of the turtle, larger in proportion to its body than that of other marine turtles. The animal feeds primarily on whelks, crabs, fish and such benthic organisms as sponges and algae.

While the loggerhead is the most common marine turtle along the South Carolina coast, several varieties of endangered sea turtles also swim offshore and sometimes wash up dead on the beach.

The most endangered of all sea turtles is the Kemp's ridley, which nests only on Rancho Nuevo in Mexico. These ridleys spend their early years feeding and growing in rich estuaries along the coast of South Carolina and other eastern states. Some marine biologists suspect the majority of small turtles, shorter than 18 inches, stranded on South Carolina beaches are Kemp's ridleys. The turtle has a white belly and nearly round shell. Younger ridleys are usually black, adults more olive-gray on the carapace or top shell.

The smallest of all sea turtles, the Kemp's grows no larger than 30 inches in shell length and 80 to 100 pounds. In the late 1940s, the turtles formed giant *arribadas* or groups of nesting females numbering some 40,000 at Rancho Nuevo. But 40 years later, only about 500 of the reptiles were coming ashore, thought to be the world's entire population of mature females. Many accidentally drown in shrimp trawls, which harvest heavily in their territory.

The hawksbill sea turtle is the source of tortoise shell for jewelry, a major reason the animal is now on state and federal endangered species lists. Scutes, patterned with brown and yellow, overlap much like shingles on a roof. With its long, narrow head and hawk-like beak, it searches coral reefs for sponges and other food. Adults range from 30 to 36 inches and weigh 100 to 200 pounds.

Leatherback turtles, on both federal and state endangered species lists, are taken for their meat and oil. The largest of sea turtles, the leatherback can reach a shell length of 6 feet and weigh as much as 1,400 pounds. Black with white blotches, the shell has no scutes or plates but instead a rubbery skin with seven hard ridges or keels running the length of the back. The bottom shell is pinkish-white. Although it nests in the tropics, this jellyfish eater ranges as far north as Canada.

Green sea turtles are dark brown with a radiating, or mottled, pattern of dark markings. Older animals are grayish. The relatively small head has a saw-like jaw used as it grazes in pastures of turtle grass. Adults may be 36 to 48 inches and average 300 pounds or more. Listed as an endangered species federally and threatened in South Carolina, the turtle breeds in tropical waters and in Florida. Once called the edible turtle, greens are still taken as food in many countries.

Although measures have been taken by some countries and by groups such as the Convention on International Trade in Endangered Species, turtles continue to be killed deliberately, eggs taken as food and turtles drowned accidentally in fishing gear. Although it is difficult at best to census marine species, counts of nesting females, nests laid and numbers caught in countries that permit harvesting all indicate numbers of these sea turtles have been falling for some time and are continuing to drop.

Cauliflower Mushroom.

Mushrooms —

A mushroom likes nothing better than heat, high humidity and rain. After a summer shower or deluge, small mushrooms will begin popping up in just 24 hours, larger varieties in about three days. But the fleshy cap above ground is only a brief, showy, final stage in the life cycle of a mushroom.

This fruiting body begins as a spore, carried on the wind. A mature mushroom cap produces millions upon millions of spores, measuring only one-three thousandth to one-five thousandth of an inch. Perhaps only a few land in a suitable spot and grow. One variety of mushroom may require a certain type of live tree while another needs dead wood and a third decaying leaves.

When a spore does find the right place and a good supply of moisture, a thin strand or mycelium sprouts. Each mycelium, a few thousandth of an inch in diameter, will provide nutrients for the mushroom-to-be. In time a white, cottony mass of mycelia forms with miles of strands in a single handful of the material. Mycelia store nutrients until moisture spurs the threads to produce a button. Protruding through the soil, the button expands to form a mushroom cap. In the process, the mycelia of many species are depleted, but the fruiting body produces spores and usually decays in just two or three days.

The mycelia of most varieties continue to grow, adding new segments that resemble cane fishing poles. Eventually older sections die but the mycelia keep spreading underground. As a result mushrooms can survive for many years. Taking their food from a living or decaying host, the fungi remain healthy as long as the food and moisture last. And the honey mushroom, which makes its home on a live tree, is supported by nutrients in the wood even after the tree dies.

Although usually hidden, strands of mycelia that look like white or yellow streaks sometimes appear on the damp bottom of fallen leaves. Rhizoids, or compressed strands, sometimes stretch below the base of larger mushrooms and may be seen if the fruit is picked carefully.

Unlike most plants, mushrooms produce no flowers, lack chlorophyll and are not green; the few green varieties are colored by pigments rather than chlorophyll. Primitive reproduction is by spores, which lack the embryo contained in seeds. Mycelia from two different spores may come together and fuse. Two nuclei are joined in each cell and a fruiting body develops, in some species the familiar mushroom cap.

About 6,000 varieties of fleshy mushrooms dot this planet, all of them considered fungi. But fungi also include tiny slimes, mildews, bacteria and rusts.

June through September always brings the greatest flush of mushrooms to coastal South Carolina although a few varieties appear in late fall and even into the winter.

Among the more common mushrooms is the meadow mushroom, or *Agaricus campestris*, which is kin to the domestic mushroom seen in supermarkets. Through summer and early fall, the mushroom crops up in lawns, meadows, golf courses, parks and other open but mowed areas that are somewhat fertile. Growing singly or in groups, caps may measure 2 to 4 inches. As the cap begins to spread, the white gills beneath it turn pinkish and finally brown. Caps and stems are white. At maturity, spores are brown and the mushroom usually takes on a mild scent of anise.

The meadow mushroom superficially resembles some of the very poisonous *Amanita* genus. The gills of these mushrooms remain white and large. Fleshy white or colored *Amanitas* grow in woods by oak trees. The large cup at the base of the stem also distinguishes it from the smooth stemmed meadow mushroom.

Some *Amanitas* are deadly poisonous, among them the destroying angel and the ominous death cap, which grows in South Carolina. The poison of the death cap or *Amanita phalloides*, for which there is no known antidote, attacks liver cells. The cap varies from white to buff to greenish and can prove confusing, enough so that 100 European mushroom devotees died in 1982 from mistakenly eating the death cap. The key to recognizing this poisonous group is the ring that surrounds the top of the stem of each species, including the white, fleshy *Amanita virosa* that appears in the fall.

Amanita vaginata also is abundant in June. Growing in yards and woods, the mushroom stands about 5 inches tall on a long stem with a

Poisonous Amanita Mushroom.

cup at the base of the stem. Caps are grayish or brownish and seldom more than 2 inches in diameter. The edge of the cap is marked with radial striations; gills are white.

The single most deadly mushroom is *Galerina autumnalis*, which contains the same poison as some *Amanitas* but belongs to an entirely different genus. It is uncommon but sometimes grows in the Lowcountry. Also beware the more common, although innocuous-looking, brownie caps that spring up in grassy areas that have been mowed. Sometimes growing in profusion in yards, the light brown *Conocybe tenera* is no more than 1 inch wide and is not fleshy.

At the other extreme is the chanterelle, whose bright orange color, apricot scent and very name sound lovely. In Europe, prized chanterelles are harvested, canned and sold at high prices. The chanterelles of

Chanterelle Mushroom at Cypress Gardens.

the Carolinas, *Cantharellus cibarius*, grow in profusion just after a summer rain under oak trees and in back yards. The wavy, rounded mushroom cap may be funnel-shaped or shallow and convex, measuring 1½ to 4 inches in diameter. Rising through fallen leaves and dotted with soil, the golden-orange cap fades with age.

In yards, colorful *Hygrophorus conicus* sends up yellow stems and conical caps that are reddish to yellowish. The fleshy cap appears waxy and flares open as it blackens during maturity. Because mushrooms can be difficult to identify, the safest tactic is not to eat wild mushrooms and to rely on one or more knowledgeable guides before handling fungi. Squirrels do not offer good guidance. They can safely consume mushrooms that could sicken, if not kill, a human.

A favorite of most mushroom watchers and of children is the fairy ring, which looks as though a magical being has called up a perfect circle of mushrooms. Normally forming each year, a fairy ring continually increases in diameter as the underground mycelium expands. In the Carolina Lowcountry, Morgan's *lepiota* may produce a ring or a semi-circle. The poisonous mushroom has a fleshy cap up to 7 inches in diameter with brown scales. White gills beneath the cap turn green as the mushroom ages.

Although uncommon, the cauliflower fungus or *Sparassis crispa* is one of the most dramatic varieties growing here. The yellowish-beige mushroom looks like a cross between a full-grown head of cauliflower and a mound of intricate coral from the ocean. The elastic flesh is whitish but turns brownish along the many crinkled edges as the mushroom ages. The large head, growing on the ground, most often appears in the mountains among woody remains of conifers. But it sometimes crops up along the coast as early as June.

Among the most colorful Lowcountry mushrooms are the *Russulas*, which begin to appear in early June. Colors range from bright to pale shades of red, purple, yellow and green but cap colors often change with age. One progresses from white to red then, if bruised, to black. The bright rose *Russula* pops up under broad-leafed trees, alone or in small groups. Somewhat less bright is the red or pinkish *Russula emetica* known as "the sickener" because of its poisonous nature. Yellowish spots sometimes appear on the cap, which grows under oaks, but rain turns the cap whitish with only a few spots of pink. The green or cracked variety is yellowish-green and comes up in numerous groups under trees. The less glamorous encrusted *Russula*, often appearing under oaks, is yellow with a slight depression in the center of a crusty-looking cap 3 to 5 inches in diameter. And the charcoal burner, which likes woodland sites, may look quite purple and ranges from blackish to greenish to bluish. As *Russula* caps mature, they flatten and may turn upward, crack or become wavy along the edge.

A similar looking group of mushrooms, *Lactarius* also vary in color. But when cut, fresh caps always exude a latex or milk, which most often is white. One species, *Lactarius hygrophoroides*, is golden-orange and bleeds with a white latex. The light brown *Lactarius volemus*, which also produces a white latex, grows under oaks and deciduous trees in open shade. The *chrysorheus* variety, which prefers shady woods and open shade, has an off-white to pale gray cap that usually is depressed in the center. When picked or wounded, the mushroom produces a white latex that immediately turns bright yellow, a good way to identify this poisonous species.

Hunters have to rise early to find *Pseudocorprinus plicatilis* because the fragile little mushrooms disappear about 10 a.m. on hot days. Less than an inch in diameter, the gray to blue-gray, translucent, thin caps cover small gills, whose spores leave a black mark if touched.

Puffballs are easy to identify because they look just like their names. The gem-studded puffball appears in large numbers and often in dense clusters. They pop up in mowed yards, in open grassy areas and along roads in residential sections. Some of the puffballs, which are covered with tiny warts, remain small but others reach the size of billiard balls.

Puffballs lack gills as do boletes, fungi that disperse spores through pores under their caps. Each pore, or circle, is a tube that emits spores, which ride an air current to a future home. Some boletes show off in bright shades of red and orange, but the leathery surface of the caps is usually brown to tan. The class *Boletus*, which means "sod-like," prefers grassy, mowed areas near pine trees. If broken or cut, some of the mushrooms begin to discolor in just a minute or two.

True to their name, polypores have many pores and tubes. These fungi grow on wood or corky material and usually form overlapping, fan-shaped shelves or clusters on tree trunks or dead wood. Some are perennials, growing in size over the years and sometimes reaching 10 inches in diameter. On occasion a polypore appears to be growing on the ground near a tree, but the fungus undoubtedly has mycelia connecting it to a tree root. Mycelia may even tunnel into the heartwood of a live tree and destroy it. Many polypores, however, have a synergistic or mutually beneficial relationship with the host tree. The mushroom provides certain nutrients to the tree and the tree gives the mushroom moisture.

Other mushrooms serve very different purposes in nature. The saprophytes that live on dead or decaying material reduce that organic matter so bacteria can transform it into soil. Mycorrhizas, which live near trees, mingle their mycelia with the smallest of tree roots. And many a mushroom cap feeds wildlife. Insect larvae often eat their way up stems and into caps, destroying a mushroom that still looks perfect externally. Squirrels show their fondness for the fleshy fungi by breaking off huge caps, nibbling round and round the outer rim until only a bite of the center is left and the squirrel is stuffed. And if the fragile, ethereal cap is not consumed, it soon decays, enriching the soil from which mushrooms spring.

White Ibis waits patiently in nest.

Baby Birds —

Brooded by mother and confined by shell, bird embryos are surprisingly active. Some flap their wings several days before hatching, other varieties peep to parents and the heartbeat of a growing embryo increases when a parent calls. As much as five days before hatching, the chick-to-be raises its head from between its legs and tucks its head under its wing so the bill faces the blunt end of the egg.

Using its bill, the embryo breaks the airspace at that end of the egg and its lungs begin to work. Then the embryo pips or makes a hole in the shell and begins breathing more deeply. The chick may rest another 15 hours or more before continuing a hatching process that may take a small species just a few minutes or a large bird two days.

The chick uses the egg tooth on its upper bill to knock holes in the blunt end of the egg. The egg tooth will fall off a few days after the chick hatches. A hatching muscle, which also will disappear, forms in the back of the head to give strength for hammering on the shell. Shoving its feet against the pointed end of the egg, the chick makes holes in an arc-shaped pattern. Eventually, the chick's pressure pops the blunt end off the weakened shell.

After a nap, precocial young are ready to go. Wood duck hatchlings, for instance, jump from nests as high as 50 feet above the water and begin swimming on their first day. Hatching with eyes open and covered with fluff, precocial chicks include varieties that nest on the ground such at shorebirds, ducks and pheasants. Most of these chicks can feed themselves immediately but remain in a group with a parent. Ducklings stay so near their mother that their down is waterproofed by her oily feathers. Although a duckling swims instinctively and soon after hatching, it can quickly become waterlogged and drown if it doesn't rub against mother's feathers.

Songbirds, woodpeckers, hummingbirds, pigeons, pelicans, cuckoos and others have altricial young, which usually arrive in the outer world without feathers and with eyes closed. Totally helpless, they rely on parents for warmth, food and housecleaning. The mother is quick to eat or remove calcium-rich shell fragments, which she carries away from the nest so they will not attract predators. And she removes or consumes the waste young deposit, often in a gelatinous sac.

Not all species fit readily into the precocial or the altricial group: Oystercatchers, rails, grebes and the like are precocial and follow their parents but are fed by them. Down-covered gulls enter the world with eyes open but stay near the nest for awhile. And species such as herons, ibises and most raptors hatch covered with down but unable to leave the nest for quite some time.

For parents of altricial birds, life is particularly frantic. Since hatchlings cannot control their own temperatures at first, one parent remains on the nest to brood while the other continually searches for food. Eyes open, the hatchling grows down and then feathers on its disproportionately large body and head. Feet and wings begin to develop and the hatchling becomes more aware of its world. Then both parents may leave the nest at least briefly to gather food.

The appetite of hatchlings seems unquenchable. One study found a pair of flycatchers delivered 6,000 feedings, about 30 per hour, to raise a nest of young. Hatchlings often begin begging when they see a parent arrive with food. Some species react as soon as they feel vibrations on the side of the nest, a signal an adult has landed. When a shadow darkens a woodpecker's nest cavity, young squawk, anticipating a parent is outside with groceries and blocking the entrance.

To guide parents' depositing food, hatchlings may have brightly colored mouths of red, pink, orange or yellow, sometimes with elaborate

Open mouths beg for food.

patterns. Mockingbirds and flycatchers, for instance, have unpatterned yellow to orange mouths while sparrows, tanagers, orioles and crows have unmarked pink to red mouths. A cuckoo has 10 white spots on its palate to help parents find the right place for a caterpillar.

Both the color and a hatchling's cries may stimulate parents to keep bringing food. As hatchlings grow older and stronger, they peep all the more loudly, sometimes hollering even when full if a sibling is receiving attention. If food is in short supply, nestlings may compete bitterly and all may starve. Birds such as pelicans and owls lay eggs that hatch a day or even two weeks apart. The oldest hatchlings are the strongest, take most of the food and are likely to survive even if younger siblings do not.

Among songbirds, woodpeckers and the like, hatchlings grow quickly and are soon ready to leave the nest. Bluejays may begin booting their young out in little more than a week. (Many adults already are breeding again and thoughts turn to second nests while the first batch of young are still at home.) While covered with more down than feathers, most altricial fledglings begin peering over the side of the nest and taking their first tottering ventures on the edge of the nest.

With stubby wings and tail, a chubby fledgling first steps onto a branch near its nest. Half falling and half trying its new wings, the young bird winds up on low branches or on the ground. The fledgling may appear abandoned, but parents are keeping close track of their young even if they are scattered in different shrubs. Adults deliver food regularly and, depending on the species, may launch an attack on any predator that comes near. This pre-flight stage is the most risky in the life of a young bird, but songbirds are quick to fly and become fairly independent.

They will, however, beg for handouts as long as parents gullibly provide them. Even when skillful on the wing and as large as their parents, young cardinals continue to flutter and squawk for food. Around a bird feeder, parents may charge a begging adolescent away, insisting it pick up its own seeds. Then moments later the same adult will deliver a beak-full of seed to an intimidated youngster. Parents often show their young where and how to find food so birds that dine at a feeder are likely to introduce a second generation to the spot.

Raptors such as eagles, hawks and owls are far slower to leave the nest. At first they rely on parents to shred prey, but later adults will deliver a whole mouse, bird or other animal for the hatchlings to practice tearing apart and eating. Long after the young have left the nest, parents are still providing all the food and gradually teaching the fledglings how to catch prey. Barred owls may hatch in February yet in June and July young owls may still be with their parents. Adults may station each fledgling in a different tree then go hunting. Left alone, the fledgling makes a forlorn, raspy squeaking sound that rises at the end, the owl equivalent of a baby songbird's peeping for food.

During the fledgling stage, birds may suddenly appear in the middle of a lawn or under a shrub where parents have hidden them. Because young songbirds look so helpless, alone and adorable, the temptation is to save the baby by adopting it. The best course of action, however, is to put the family cat or dog indoors, request that neighbors do the same then check periodically (from a respectful distance) for predators or other activity. And let the parents do what bird parents do best.

Only in extreme circumstances should a person tackle the challenging and too often fruitless task of raising a baby bird.

If a very young bird has fallen from the nest, try to spot the nest and return the hatchling to it. Birds have a very poor sense of smell and will not desert a baby because it has been handled by a human. If the nest is visible but beyond reach, line a small fruit basket with leaves, settle the hatchling in its make-do nest and place or attach the basket to the nest tree. If the nest is not visible, put the youngster in a basket and leave it safely off the ground near the spot the bird was sitting. Parents probably are watching and will take over care of the baby.

Consider hand raising the bird only if both parents have died or if they do not return and the hatchling has virtually no feathers or chance of surviving on its own. It is against the law to keep a migratory bird in captivity; raptors and endangered or threatened species should be turned over to wildlife authorities right away.

Serving as a parent bird requires continual work from sunrise to sunset. A baby bird without feathers must be fed every 20 minutes except during the dark of night.

First provide warmth for any bird that is naked or has only a little down. Choose a small bowl or shoe box to hold the bird. Then place a heating pad, turned on very low, under part of the box. The bird needs an unheated spot to escape if the pad is too hot. Or rig a light bulb above the box for a bit of warmth. Once the hatchling has some feathers, sunshine from a window during the day may suffice but the bird will need its heating pad at night. Only when the bird is completely feathered and resembles an adult should the heat be removed at night.

A basic diet of baby chick starter soaked in water is best for the baby bird. To that add powdered vitamins available at pet shops. Most important is vitamin B-1; a young bird needs about 25 milligrams a day. Seed-eating birds can survive on that diet, but insect eaters such as brown thrashers, woodpeckers and purple martins need equal parts of very lean ground beef mixed with the mash. For fruit eaters such as mockingbirds, add a little apple or banana. As down turns to feathers, young birds are easier to identify. Jays with bright red mouths show blue, cardinals bits of red and mockers have white markings on their gray.

Feeding must be done with care. A bird's trachea or windpipe is an open hole just behind the tongue. Offer food on the end of a Q-tip, popsicle stick or the type of small coffee stirer used at many fast food restaurants. If the hatchling doesn't want to open its beak for a feeding, tap the beak lightly or shake the edge of the box or bowl to imitate the landing of a parent bird with food. When the youngster gapes hungrily, put the food as far back in its throat as possible, which should trigger the instinct to swallow. As long as the patient is eating frantically, keep offering food. If there are siblings, however, the cries of one may keep a competitor begging even when it is full.

Doves and pigeons present special problems since parents regurgitate crop milk for their young. Chick mash or high protein baby cereal and water may be mixed in a blender until smooth. Attach a thin tube to a syringe full of the meal and ease the tube down the bird's throat and into its crop. Be particularly careful of the trachea behind the tongue because the syringe may slip into a lung.

As the bird becomes feathered, feedings may be reduced and eventually a bowl of food left so the hatchling can help itself. When fully feathered, the bird is ready for some food from its natural diet such as wild seed or bird food, wild fruit, insects or whatever the species would normally eat. But continue providing some mash as well. Once eating on its own, the fledgling may be placed in a large cage, hung outdoors in a protected spot. In a few days, the bird should be acting frightened of the hand that used to feed it and should be trying to fly around in the cage. Open the door and let the bird choose when to leave.

The fledgling should learn to recognize and find the kind of natural foods it was given indoors. To ease the transition, however, leave food just outside the cage where the bird can find it easily during the next few weeks. The fledgling may feel so much at home in the yard that the bird stays on to raise its own young, perhaps in the very tree from which it fell the past summer.

Woodcock camouflaged on floor of Francis Marion Forest.

Cecropia Moth on Chinese Privet.

Moths —

Moths may have a bad reputation for eating fine woolens and being dull little winged creatures that flee the light of day. But in reality moths, which like the hot nights of summer best, can be more handsome than butterflies.

As for dining on clothing, moths range from passive creatures that eat wax or fur to winged attackers that cannibalize the larvae of other insects. One scavenger — which fortunately confines itself to Southeast Asia — drinks blood. Another variety wants only tears, fluid from the eyes of man and other large animals. Certain species even prey on live flies. Some of South Carolina's moths enjoy ripe fruit, but most dine on flowers, just as butterflies do.

When it comes to sheer beauty, one of the most colorful is the regal moth, with a 6-inch wingspan of bright orange spotted with yellow and striped with gray. The thick body also is brilliant orange with thin yellowish bands.

Like all moths, the regal passes through three life stages. As large as caviar, regal eggs hatch into voracious caterpillars, which feed on sweet gum, hickory and persimmon. The caterpillar, which may be blue-green or orange or brown, is known as the hickory horned devil because of its black-tipped, orange horns and ferocious appearance.

Also glorious as an adult, the luna moth is lime green with a tiny garnet spot on each wing and a dark red to burgundy stripe along the top of the fore wings. Each hind wing has a very long extension that would put any swallowtail butterfly to shame. The luna pupates in a thin cocoon, usually on the ground. Found only in North America, lunas have been killed by pollutants and pesticides to the point the moths are growing rare.

The rosy maple moth has wings and body of pale sulfur yellow, but forewings are pastel pink at the base and along the outer margin. When at rest with wings flat, the handsome pink is predominant and forms wide stripes along the yellow. This small moth likes deciduous forests and open, brushy areas wherever maples grow. Green with lengthwise white stripes, the caterpillars or green-striped maple worms may strip entire maple trees of foliage.

Moth caterpillars or larvae, usually heavier and more sturdy than butterfly caterpillars, feed on woody or other plant material. A few moth caterpillars eat dried animal matter and a still smaller number are predators. A few, such as corn ear worms, dine on vegetables.

Despite the beauty of many moths, and perhaps because they're seldom seen during their nightly rounds, the animals are often best known as pests. The tomato hornworm moth adores tomato and tobacco leaves during its caterpillar stage while the tobacco hornworm moth caterpillar gobbles up potato leaves as well. Caterpillars of potato tuber moths like foliage, stems and tubers of potatoes, either in the garden or in storage. Eastern tent caterpillars can defoliate entire forests when not molting skins or resting inside the white silken tents the larvae share. The tents of spring are far more obvious than the dull, hairy brown moths that will later emerge.

After feeding heavily, larvae produce silken cocoons in which to pupate, transforming a caterpillar body into a winged beauty. Some varieties hide, without cocoon, in leaf litter while others pupate in an earthen cell or a cavity within a plant stem. Many varieties spend the winter snug inside a cocoon, but a few species overwinter as adults.

Moths, although closely related, are distinct from butterflies. Day flyers, butterflies often are brightly colored, have knobbed antennae and usually hold their wings together vertically above the body while at rest. But most moths are active at night and are more likely to wear darker, duller colors. Some are camouflaged to blend in with tree trunks or even to resemble lichens or bird droppings. Others have clear wings rather than soft, colored scales. Resembling wasps, these moths often are shunned by predatory birds that try to avoid stinging insects.

Antennae of moths vary but often are fringed and thicker than the knobbed antennae of butterflies. When resting, moths hold their wings above as a roof, curled around their bodies or flat against a support. In addition, an adult moth has a heavier, thicker or chunkier thorax and abdomen than a butterfly does.

Seeking nectar in flowers, a moth uses a thin tube or proboscis that may be as long as 4 inches. When the adult first emerges from its cocoon, the mouth parts aren't correctly aligned. Not only must the animal pump fluids into its wings, but it must manipulate its mouth parts to realign what were chewing instruments into a tube that will probe flowers.

One of the more unusual Lowcountry moths is named for the hummingbird and resembles those birds. The body is unusually heavy and spindle-shaped, mostly olive-green with plum to red bands across the abdomen and rear. The moth even has tail-like tufts. The wings, each an inch wide, are plum-red to brownish-black, but scales begin falling after the first flight so portions of the wings are clear. Adding to the confusion, this moth flies by day just as hummingbirds do. It hovers over flowers in full sunlight and makes a buzz with its wings that is softer than the whir of hummingbirds. This moth may have evolved one of the best defenses of all against insectivorous birds: It looks just like a cousin so isn't seized as prey.

Relatively large and strikingly colored, underwing moths frequent forests and woodlands. The moths are known for their hind wings,

Underwing Moth on Chinese Privet.

usually brightly colored with concentric bands of red, yellow or orange. When at rest during the day, the moth conceals its hind wings under drab front wings, which blend in with tree bark on which the moths often rest.

The white-lined sphinx moth has narrow wings and a wingspan of 2½ to 3½ inches. The veins of the dark brown fore wings are beautifully outlined in white while hind wings are mostly pink. Often visiting meadows and gardens, these moths may lay their eggs on portulaca, a favorite food of the bright green caterpillars with yellow heads. The moths buzz like hummingbirds. In fact sphinx moths generally have heavy bodies and strong wings that beat so rapidly that sphinxes are sometimes mistaken for hummingbirds or bees. The white-lined variety usually visits gardens at dusk or after dark, however.

Most sphinx moths have curving wings with an unusual shape and many have a sharp, horn-like projection at the end of the abdomen. The pandora sphinx with a wingspan of up to 4 inches is patterned with olive-green and paler green, suffused in places with pink and gray. The beautifully marked pandora dines on flowers at dusk and before dawn but rarely in total darkness. Like the white-lined and most sphinxes, it is particularly attracted to artificial lights. Its green or reddish-brown caterpillars with white spots and shiny, eyelike buttons feeds on Virginia creeper, wild and cultivated grapes.

So do caterpillars of the Virginia-creeper sphinx, also known as the hog sphinx. A smaller moth, this variety has tan to greenish-gray fore wings with broad dark brown or olive bands. Hind wings are brownish orange. The adult moths forego flowers and instead dine on decaying fruit and fermenting tree sap.

Beautiful silkworm moths wear particularly dramatic markings. But it is best to avoid silkworm caterpillars, which often have setae or barbed hairs that can make human skin itch or fester. The promethea, cecropia, io and polyphemus all thrive in the Carolinas.

The largest silkworm moth in North America, the cecropia has a wingspan of nearly 6 inches. Its speckled gray-brown wings have rusty shading, white crescents and white and red crossbands. Giant silkworm moths have no hearing organs; mouthparts of the short-lived adults are vestigial so they do not feed. The cecropia is not closely related to the true Asiatic silkworm and commercial attempts to use silk from the moth's cocoons have been unsuccessful.

Also vividly marked with eyespots, the polyphemus moth has brownish-yellow or ocher wings, fore wings with an eyespot surrounded by a yellow ring. Hind wings feature an even larger eyespot ringed in yellow then black and finally blue for emphasis. The eyespot on each hind wing is so outstanding that the moth is named for Polyphemus, the giant of Greek myths who had only one eye. Wings, with a span of 3½ to 5½ inches, also bear black and white irregular lines. Caterpillars are bright green with yellow bands and the red and silver tubercles can be painful to man.

The promethea or spicebush silkmoth feeds on spicebush, wild cherry and sassafras as a bluish-green caterpillar. Males and females look quite different and males sometimes fly in the late afternoon while females move about only at night. The wings, body and legs of males are primarily brownish-black and may or may not have spots. Markings include a pale crossband, reddish tip enclosing a prominent eyespot, tan outer margin with wavy dark brown lines and spots. But the body and wings of females are reddish-brown and her markings, similar to the male's, are much more obvious. In size, the moths vary from 2¾ to 4 inches in wingspan.

Handsome io moths, with a wingspan of up to 2¾ inches, have yellow hind wings, each with a reddish-orange band and a dramatic, large central back eyespot. Males wear yellow fore wings while females are reddish-orange. As a green caterpillar with reddish-pink and white stripes, the io has clusters of branching spines that cause a painful stinging. The setae or barbed hairs actually lodge under the skin and fester. The lovely adults, however, are quite harmless to man.

Io Moth.

Another caterpillar to beware is the saddleback, a brilliant green insect with a brown, saddle-like mark edged in white in the middle of its back, positioned as if a smaller insect could climb on for a ride. The body is covered in tufts of bristles, which will sting. The caterpillars often are seen on fruit trees, corn and the kinds of shrubs gardeners plant around their houses, all favorite foods of the voracious larvae. The moth, with a wingspan of slightly more than an inch, is fairly undistinguished. Fore wings are glossy dark brown with black streaks and several white dots. Hind wings are more pale and the heavy body is covered with dark brown scales.

The little eight-spotted forester, with velvety black wings and body, has two large yellow spots on each fore wing and two white spots on each hind wing. The bright orange, hairlike scales on the fore legs give the moth most of its color. Flying by day, adults often are mistaken for butterflies.

Because moths are drawn to light, porch lights, street lights and billboards make prime moth observation spots. It may be difficult to find the larger, more colorful moths on the front porch, however, and many enjoy the relative solitude of the woods. A simple sheet or other white cloth may be strung up by four corners in a wooded area. Place a lantern below the bottom of the sheet to cast a glow against the large expanse of white. Stage a moth-watching party or check the visitors just before sunrise the next morning. Most will settle comfortably on the cloth and stay put until nearly dawn. (The lighted sheet also may attract other nocturnal insects such as beetles, crickets, true bugs, cicadas, leafhoppers, antlions, owlflies, bees, earwigs and wasps.) Moths also will gather to feed on fermented cantaloupe or apple. Place a few pieces on a platform near a light and the moth feeding station should provide good viewing.

Bullfrog stares at camera.

Frogs—

On summer nights, ponds echo with pig-like grunts, train-like snores, banjo-like twangs and deep base wheezes. The bizarre assortment of calls belongs to male frogs and toads, eagerly advertising their claim to a watery spot and their availability to potential mates.

The male inflates his throat, which may be brightly colored and flares like a balloon. Two slits in the mouth allow air to enter the vocal sac, which serves as a sounding board. The animals can even sing underwater by passing air back and forth from the throat sac to the lungs over the vocal cords.

These amphibians are at their vocal best just after a heavy rainfall, which triggers breeding. More enthusiastic varieties even begin chorusing on cloudy days that seem relatively dark and signal rain may be on the way. And a heavy rain after a relative drought can bring such frantic action that frogs and toads literally crawl over one another and shoulder their way through a crowd all bent on reaching the same pond for the same reason.

Covered in moist, bare skin frogs, toads and their close relatives the salamanders are most active on damp days and nights. While the animals spend much of their time in hiding, a rainy evening offers a particularly good time to view them. The amphibians are subject to dehydration or dessication so exposure to dry conditions for any length of time can be fatal. Most live in moist areas or are forced to spend much of their time partially buried in soil under a plant, log, rock or other source of shade. The Southern toad, for instance, often moves into a garden or an outdoor potted plant in the drought of summer. The gardener reliably keeps the soil moist in the pot and the toad can dig its hole and hide under a mound of leaves.

Virtually all frogs and toads lay eggs. The male clutches his mate and fertilizes the eggs as she releases them, most often into the water. Some species lay their eggs in moist, shady sites on land or in nests built above water. To survive, tadpoles must reach the water very soon after hatching. Rain often washes them into a nearby river or pond, but some species carry their hatchlings to the water. A few of the world's nearly 2,700 species of frogs and toads lay eggs that hatch directly into tiny frogs, and one African toad gives birth to live young.

Eggs of many species hatch fairly quickly into tadpoles, which are most visible during the summer. During the tadpole stage, the youngster absorbs the long tail used for swimming and four legs begin to form along what was a streamlined body. Ears develop with a very visible tympanum, a large circle just behind and slightly below the eye.

Frogs and toads rely on an excellent sense of hearing. Females are drawn by the calls of potential mates, males warn away competitors and both sexes holler to signal distress. An eager male, for instance, may mistakenly mount another male, which gives a distress call that ends the courtship abruptly. Some varieties also shriek in terror when seized by a predator or man.

Tadpoles grow into adults and climb out onto land in as little as two weeks in the case of the spadefoot toad. The spadefoot lives in dry conditions such as barrier islands, where ponds may quickly dry up in the summer heat. The bullfrog, on the other hand, spends more than a year in the tadpole stage; females scatter up to 12,000 eggs in different sites to assure at least some survive drought and predators.

The largest of American frogs, bullfrogs measure up to 8 inches and are able to capture and feed on small birds, baby mammals, small snakes and the usual insects so many frogs eat. Thought to live for several years, bullfrogs are brownish-green to yellow above, mottled with darker gray. Undersides are cream to white and may be mottled with gray. The male also sports a yellow throat, which he displays if an intruder nears his chosen calling station. The deep base call sounds something like an order for "Jug o' rum, more rum." The sound may travel more than a quarter mile in the quiet. Nocturnal and less aquatic than some frogs, the animal likes ponds, lakes and quiet streams that are surrounded by plenty of vegetation. If frightened, the frog is likely to flee into the cover of plants.

Bullfrogs are one of the edible varieties most often caught by man. Each year some 200 million frogs are consumed as gourmet food in this country alone, frogs that could consume an estimated 300 tons of insects. When Bangladesh harvested 70 million pair of frogs' legs for export in 1985, serious health problems arose. As mosquitoes and thus malaria increased, so did the use of dangerous pesticides. Pointing to potential ecological disaster, the World Wildlife Fund called on restaurants and food stores to stop selling frogs' legs entirely.

Another type of bullfrog, the pig frog ranges from 3 to 6 inches and is often more brightly colored than the bullfrog proper. The pig frog has a more streamlined body, narrower and pointed snout, black and white stripes on the back of the thighs and body that may be grayish-green to dark brown with dark spots. The porcine frog is named for its explosive, pig-like grunt, which it gives year-round and often while floating. Breeding from spring through summer, pig frogs lay some 10,000 eggs in such favorite habitats as abandoned ricefields or ponds with shallow water and such vegetation as lily pads.

Tadpoles will swim for a year before emerging as adults. Pig frogs often have been taken for their edible legs so grow wary of man. But where the frogs have not been hunted by man, they are generally placid and often let humans approach quite near. Very aquatic, pig frogs float among water hyacinths, cattails and sedges and often feed on crayfish.

Often confused with bullfrogs, river frogs congregate along the Edisto and Ashepoo rivers and live only in the lower portion of South Carolina. Up to 5 inches long, river frogs are dark brown with conspicuous white spots on their jaws and irregular markings on their bellies, which range from gray to almost black. The nocturnal frogs live in swamps near slow-moving rivers and creeks. Their deep, drawn-out call is a train-like, low-pitched snore although the frog also gives a sharp grunt. Breeding in late spring and most of the summer, river frogs remain as tadpoles for about two years and may grow to 5 inches before hopping out onto land. The skins of these newly emerged frogs apparently give off a toxic secretion that makes predators, such as snakes, extremely ill.

The carpenter frog is named for its call, which sounds like a carpenter nailing shingles. The little coastal frog, measuring 2 to 3 inches, chooses permanent ponds in pine woods such as Francis Marion National Forest. Dark but marked with four yellowish stripes, carpenter frogs blend in with sphagnum moss in cypress and gum ponds. The animals also wear the same black and white thigh stripes that accent their relatives, the pig frogs. Because they are shy, carpenters are easier to hear than to see, particularly during the spring and summer breeding season.

Also difficult to spot is the toad-like crawfish frog. The amphibian likes land and frequently moves into dry burrows that crawfish have abandoned. Only extremely heavy rains bring out crawfish frogs, which shun water except during mating. The frog attracts his mate with what would repel a human spouse — a snoring sound. The brownish-gray frog has prominent warts on its back resembling a cobblestone road. The inner legs and groin are brighter with yellow to orange tints.

Like bullfrogs and carpenter frogs, crawfish frogs have teeth in their upper jaws. The teeth, very wide mouth and body up to 3½ inches long enable the amphibian to capture small mammals such as mice and shrews, small birds, lizards, snakes and fellow frogs.

Also known as bronze frogs, green frogs may be either of those colors or brown. A brown to bronze subspecies lives from the Carolinas to

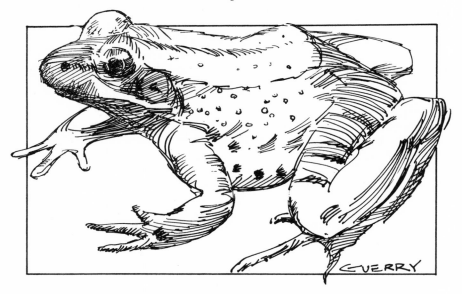

Artist's sketch of Green Frog.

central Florida. The highly aquatic frog often has a spotted back with ridges or folds running about halfway down the back. Below, the frogs are white with darker patterns of lines or spots and the male shows off with a yellow throat. Most often seen and heard as they flee, green frogs usually splash into a pond when a human approaches. The voice of this primarily nocturnal frog is a twanging banjo string, a single note sometimes repeated rapidly several times. Living close to shallow water, swamps, brooks, edges of ponds and lakes, the frog also hides among debris from rotting trees. It takes only a few months for a tadpole to reach adulthood.

Not all frogs spend so much time in the water. Treefrogs are very much at home on branches and, for suction, rely on large toe tips expanded into sticky adhesive pads. Cartilage between the last two bones of each toe enables these frogs to swivel their toes backwards and sideways without moving the sticky pad or breaking the suction. Tree frogs in residential areas often climb window glass to gobble up night-flying insects that are drawn to lights inside a house. All the arboreal frogs are small with slender legs and prefer walking and climbing to jumping. Among South Carolina's summer breeding tree frogs are the squirrel, pine woods, barking, Northern cricket, Southern cricket, pine barrens, bird-voiced, common gray, green and little grass frog.

Particularly handsome is the green tree frog, measuring 1 to 2½ inches of bright green, yellow or greenish-gray. A very distinct light stripe runs along the upper jaw and the side of the body. The frog may also have tiny gold spots edged in black on its back. Breeding from spring into fall, the frogs may mass by the hundreds to give "quank, quank" calls that sound like cowbells from a distance. Often sleeping beneath leaves or in other damp, shady places during the day, these tree frogs usually walk rather than hop. But if frightened, they will take surprising leaps off trees or windows into space.

The plump little barking tree frog may be bright green, yellow, gray or dark brown and is usually spotted if light in color. Yellowish stripes run from the upper jaw along the sides of the body, but the stripes are much less distinct than on the green. Measuring 2 to nearly 3 inches, the frog loudly announces rain with a bark from high in the trees. But its mating call, given from March to August, is a pretty, bellow-like note given near water. The nocturnal frog likes to sleep in secluded spots during the day, spend warm months in treetops and burrow among tree roots or clumps of vegetation during winter or droughts.

The squirrel tree frog is particularly raucous just before a deluge begins. The 1 or 2-inch-long green to brown frog has a white strip along the side of its body. Spending most of its time in trees, it gives territorial calls that sound almost like a barking squirrel. Adults will take to almost any habitat that is moist and offers insects for food. The frogs may hide by day under loose bark, in tree holes, under roof flashing or in ornamental shrubs but at night go searching for prey around outdoor lights.

In pine forests, the pine woods tree frog breeds and calls all summer, particularly if it rains. The gray to reddish-brown frog has light spots on its rear thighs. Singing in a chorus, these frogs resemble a busy office full of typing secretaries; a single caller may sound like the tapping of wooden dowels.

A threatened species, the pine barrens tree frog lives only in widely scattered, isolated pockets of marshy wetlands in sandhills country. Residing in the Carolinas, Florida, Alabama and New Jersey, the frog inhabits only Marlboro to Richland counties in South Carolina. The little frog chooses such special habitat that it has always been uncommon. And it has been endangered by the clearing and draining of evergreen shrub swamps and bogs adjacent to sandhills. The secretive frog is easily overlooked and is being found more regularly in its habitat now than it once was.

A beautiful lime green frog just 1½ inches long, the pine barrens tree frog has dark purplish-brown stripes running from the eyes down the sides. Below, it is white with bright yellow splotches under its limbs. Although resembling the larger green tree frog, the species has an unusual call like the nasal quacking of ducks.

Breeding in spring and summer, males usually call to potential mates from elevated perches in shrub bogs. Groups of eggs hatch in a mere three days and tadpoles become small frogs in 50 to 75 days. Young frogs from eggs laid early in the season can breed the following year. Adults live in small groups usually numbering no more than 10 or 20. Colonies in South Carolina have been found in Cheraw State Park, Sandhills State Forest and Sandhills National Wildlife Refuge.

Last, but far from least, are the true toads, amphibians such as the Southern, oak and spadefoot. Studies in laboratories indicate toads are far more intelligent than frogs, learn more quickly and look before they leap, refusing to jump if the drop seems too far. Squat and plump, toads have rough, warty skin compared to the smooth, damp skin of frogs. While frogs have long legs for jumping, toads have short legs for hopping. Large glands on the neck, just behind the tympanum, secrete a white poison that causes nausea, inflames the mouth and throat, can make the heart beat irregularly and can even kill sensitive animals. A predator usually needs only one such unpleasant lesson and thereafter leaves toads alone.

Breeding in spring and summer, males gather at ponds and sing to draw mates. But during the rest of the year, toads remain on dry land. Far more species live in the Western United States than in the East and several thrive in desert or dry prairie conditions.

The Eastern spadefoot toad, for instance, has been seen hopping around the hot ashes of a newly extinguished brush fire. The nocturnal toad hides away in the protection of its shallow burrow. Usually digging its own burrow, the toad likes sandy, gravelly sites or loose loam in forests, brushy areas or cultivated fields. The spadefoot is named for the spade or sharp-edged tubercle on the hind foot that helps in digging. On damp summer nights, the toad ventures to the mouth of its burrow and may begin calling. The chorus, which carries up to half a mile, sounds like the coarse, low-pitched call of a young crow.

Breeding in spring and summer, the toads lay gelatinous bands of eggs, attached to aquatic plants in temporary ponds. Hatching within two days, tadpoles are ready for adult life in no more than eight weeks. When drought threatens to dry up the pond, the entire metamorphosis from egg to adult can take just two weeks.

If a toad suddenly pops from a garden, beneath a shrub or out of a flower pot, the plump amphibian is most likely a Southern toad, a nocturnal animal very much at home in the suburbs. Spending its day

Southern Toad at Drayton Hall.

in a burrow, it moves onto the lawn or under street lights to feed on insects at night. Breeding from spring through fall, usually in temporary pools and flooded meadows, males make a high-pitched, musical trill in or near the water. During the summer, hundreds of tiny black young may climb from a pond within minutes of one another. Measuring from about 2 to 4½ inches, this adult is brown, reddish or black with many warts that may be surrounded by dark spots. A light stripe may also run down the middle of the back of this species, which is surprisingly tolerant of man.

The smallest of all North American toads, the oak toad has a very distinct white to orange stripe down the middle of its back and four or five pair of dark blotches. A toad of the day, the inch-long animal has a very high-pitched whistle sounding almost like a bird or baby chick. Warm thunderstorms trigger breeding from spring through fall in the pine flatwoods and oak scrub where the toad lives. By day the amphibian hunts for insects in the undergrowth, but after dusk it normally goes into hiding. Only the breeding season brings this toad out at night to chorus and to find a mate.

Orchids —

Sometimes secretive and hidden away, sometimes boldly flamboyant and impossible to ignore, Lowcountry orchids flourish not just in greenhouses but in swamps and ditches, along roadsides and in woods. Known and recognized by too few people, many of the native orchids are every bit as handsome as their cultivated relatives. And the often illusive orchids are relatively easy to find if sought in the right place at the right time.

Of some 30,000 species in the world — half natural and half hybrids — South Carolina has 45 species and two hybrids. Most manufacture their own food and sprout from soil in a surprising range of habitats. However, one variety is an epiphyte or air plant growing on trees while two others are saprophytes that cannot make food and so rely on decaying matter.

Setting orchids apart from other highly evolved plants are the millions of dust-like seeds held in capsules. The seeds contain no endosperm or food reserve to feed the developing embryos. Instead, a soil fungus penetrates each seed and sets up a symbiotic or mutually beneficial relationship. The embryo grows by absorbing waste or by-products secreted by the fungus or formed when the fungus decomposes. In time, it penetrates the roots of the flowering plant and the two live together as long as the orchid survives.

One of the loveliest wild orchids comes into bloom in early summer or late spring. The fragrant grass pink orchids grow in a spike-like cluster of two to 10 flowers, opening one after another on the leafless stalk. A single grass-like leaf helps to identify this wild orchid that is common in low pinelands and bogs.

The grass pink is appropriately named *Calopogon pulchellus*, meaning beautiful beard in Greek, because of the yellow bearded lip petal that stands above the other petals. Like all orchids, the grass pink has three sepals in an outer whorl and three petals forming an inner whorl. In most orchids, the lip petal is larger and more showy than the other two. Only in the *Calopogons* is the lip at

Grass Pink.

the top rather than the bottom of the flower.

A fleshy column projects from the center of the flower. This fusion of the male anther and the female stigma is found only in the orchid world. And orchids, like the grass pink, have very special ways of guaranteeing their flowers will be fertilized. Each species of wild orchid has evolved to attract a single variety of insect, botanists are discovering. Only that one species will enter and pollinate the blossom. The flower and its column are shaped so that the right insect enters and automatically leaves its cargo of pollen on the sticky stigma. As the insect continues its search for nectar, it touches the anther and picks up pollen to take to the next flower.

In the case of the grass pink, the pollinator apparently is attracted by the colorful beard. When the insect lights on the granular, hairy surface of the beard, it drops like an elevator. The insect finds itself against the column and cannot help but deposit a dose of pollen. The insect picks up new pollen but never does find a meal. The orchid has no nectary and thus may assure its pollen is quickly taken to another blossom as the hungry diner goes on hunting.

Although less obvious, the rose pogonia sometimes masses by the hundreds in bogs. Each blossom presents a crested lip, a convenient landing place for insects carrying pollen. The rose pogonia has a slender greenish stem with a single leaf and a single, rose-pink flower less than 2 inches long. A typical orchid flower in appearance, the June blossom features a large lip petal fringed and bearded in the center with short, yellowish bristles. The 3 to 24-inch-tall plant lives in wet open woods, meadows, swamps and sphagnum bogs. The related rosebud pogonia, at the edge of savannahs, has a long, narrow lip and spreading sepals.

Also in savannahs, the spreading pogonia blooms in early June. The flower holds its slender, reddish-purple sepals back from magenta to white petals. The bluish-green plant has a frosted look, resembling the white coating on a plum. This large-flowered and particularly lovely pogonia often grows near pitcher plants in bogs and needs the same extremely acid soil. Not often seen, the orchid will quickly die if its home becomes dry. But under favorable conditions, the plants spread quickly and form clumps.

Related to the pogonias, the rosebud orchid of wet or dry grasslands, pine barrens and thickets needs very acid soil. Its summertime flowers are pink and tubular with three very long, narrow, spreading brownish or purplish-green sepals atop a long stalk.

Bogs and savannahs are the best place to search for summer orchids, particularly the beautiful members of the genus *Habenaria*, which appear one after another in a variety of colors.

In June, the snowy orchid unfurls. From a distance, the plant appears to have one large bloom, but in fact the flower stalk is lined with small blossoms. An entire bog of the orchids often bursts into bloom at the same time, giving the site a snowy look so brilliant that it is almost blue-white.

From July through September, four other members of the genus *Habenaria* are flowering: the white fringed, yellow fringed, yellow fringeless and crested fringed orchid. All may live separately or mixed together in bogs and savannahs; Highway 41 in the Francis Marion National Forest is one good place to look for the plants.

The yellow fringed orchid is outstanding with many deep orange to bright yellow flowers clustered atop a leafy stem. Blossoms are drooping with deeply fringed lip petals. The very showy orchid is eye-catching in wet, sandy woods, open woods, thickets and dry meadows. The white fringed forms an elongated, dense or sparse cluster of pure white flowers with deeply fringed, long lip petals that closely resemble the flowers of the yellow fringed. The two summer bloomers may be the most entrancing of all the orchids in the state. When they live near one another, insects often cross-pollinate the two, producing a hybrid with cream colored flowers.

The yellow fringeless and the crested fringed are very similar, but the fringeless is extremely rare. It has a smooth lip

Yellow Fringed Orchid.

and saffron colored flowers rather than the fringed lip and orange flowers donning the crested. Cylindrical in shape, mature flower heads on the fringeless look almost like small torches brightening savannahs.

The water-spider orchid, a *Habenaria* which blooms in early June, lives on floating mats of vegetation in freshwater ponds. Blooming sporadically almost all year, the orchid prefers the edge of ponds, ditches, freshwater marshes and river edges. The creeping orchid twines its roots around debris and the roots of marsh plants. The yellow-green flowers are almost the color of the plant and so are easy to miss. But the orchid is common in abandoned ricefields along the Cooper River and in the Goose Creek Reservoir.

Although common, the Southern rein orchid is not often seen because it hides away in wet woods, in swamp forests, along coastal rivers and especially in reclaimed ricefields. It often grows on tussocks, thick with competing plants that help disguise the orchid. The yellow-green flowers and green foliage also make this *Habenaria* inconspicuous, yet the orchid thrives along almost every coastal river system in South Carolina.

A spike of white flowers with deeply fringed lips tops green fringed orchids from late May to early July. Although one of the most common orchids in the Northeast, the inconspicuous orchid is rare near the coast. Specimens of this and other rare orchids have been transplanted to the Bluff Plantation Wildlife Sanctuary near Moncks Corner in an attempt to increase Lowcountry populations.

Another summer orchid, the crane fly, is so named not because that fly pollinates the flowers but because the straggly, flimsy, long-spurred blossoms are thought to resemble crane flies on the wing. The orchid begins its unusual growth cycle in autumn as leaves in the forest fall and sunlight reaches the ground. From a series of underground corms, a single leaf rises just to the top of debris covering the forest floor. The leaf lasts until May then withers and vanishes. Not a trace of blossom is seen until mid-summer when a slender, leafless flower stalk appears.

Late in July blooms erupt on green fly orchids, perched on the branches of trees growing in very damp or wet places. Named for the insect that pollinates it, the plant is the only epiphytic orchid in South Carolina. (Most tropical and subtropical orchids are epiphytes, but South Carolina's orchids are largely terrestrial.) Although the roots of the green fly ramble over branches, a thickened, absorbent tissue called velamen helps the orchid absorb its food primarily from the atmosphere. The green fly is found only in Southern swamps such as Francis Beidler Forest, the sanctuary in Four Holes Swamp near Harleyville. The little flowers, cream colored with a slight tinge of green, are delicate and typical orchid shape. A flower spike about 3 inches long springs from the base of the single, spatula-shaped, dark green leaf.

Coastal South Carolina also has three saprophytic orchids, lacking chlorophyll and so unable to manufacture food. Instead, the three coral-roots pull the nutrients they need from decaying organic matter in the soil. A soil fungus supplies water and helps these pale plants obtain food. The crested coral-root, which is widely scattered across the state but less common along the coast, has golden flowers in late July. Stems, ranging from flesh color to purplish, rise in dense groups from branching, underground tubers that resemble coral.

A second variety blooms in spring and a third in fall. The autumn coral-root, which grows in scattered coastal sites but more often in the mountains, wears a white wavy lip with bright purple spots. The plant remains completely underground for years gathering strength to bloom. It exhausts itself flowering and fruiting and rarely blooms again.

In mixed hardwood forests, the green adder's mouth orchid commonly produces its racemes in July and August. Small flowers begin opening on the bottom of the stem, but the top flowers may not pop until three months later. During the rest of the year, the plant is a single, glossy green leaf. Also in the summer, the less common Florida adder's mouth begins producing equally inconspicuous blossoms that open slowly on a flower spike. The Florida variety is often overlooked but usually grows in grassy, transitional areas between swamp forests and deciduous forests. The orchid may be buried in sedges and grasses or, farther south, may grow almost as an epiphyte on cypress knees and floating logs.

The three birds orchid of late summer has clusters of lovely flowers vaguely resembling a flying bird. The two upper petals form a pink hood over the white lip petal, which is rounded with a crinkled margin. Each blossom unfurls at night and lasts only one day. One often is open while a second is in bud and a third withered, giving the orchid its name. The orchid is found in the mixed hardwood forest of I'On Swamp in the Francis Marion but typically prefers mountain retreats. After sending out a fragile stem and flowers, an underground tuber may remain dormant for several years.

Unlike many orchids, the downy rattlesnake plantain has very attractive leaves, striped almost like a snake. Superstition holds that the

Leaves of Downy Rattlesnake Plantain.

leaves should be chewed or cut then applied to a rattlesnake bite to save the life of the victim. In July, a downy stalk produces a spike of fuzzy, greenish-white flowers. The rosette of leaves then withers, but the dried, bare spike may remain standing into the next spring. Below the ground, the rhizome continues to grow longer each year, producing new roots below and new rosettes of leaves above. The plant is sometimes found in deciduous forests near the coast but prefers the mountains, where it forms dense colonies.

As fall settles in and late summer orchids continue to blossom, the fragrant nodding ladies' tresses, shadow witch and autumn coral-root also burst into bloom. Flowers may last late into the fall while the spring coral-root and Southern twayblade begin early in the year. Despite the delicate appearance of flowers and the devoted care cultivated varieties seem to demand, hardy

Ladies' Tresses.

wild orchids will bloom in the South Carolina Lowcountry 11 months out of the year.

Jellyfish —

A jellyfish stranded on the beach may be an innocuous, lifeless lump worthy only of a child's curiosity. Put that same jellyfish in the sea, however, and it may cause a major panic. Lurking half hidden in the water or speeding about by jet propulsion with tentacles streaming behind, one jelly can clear the ocean. Swimmers flee, fearing everything from an itchy rash to painful blisters to respiratory failure and death.

By and large, jellyfish are misunderstood creatures, given a bad reputation by the poison of a handful. Most of South Carolina's 50 species are totally harmless and almost too small to notice. These members of the *Scyphozoa* class do not set out to sting man. They would rather save their ammunition for hunting dinner. Most painful encounters come when man accidentally brushes against tentacles or prods an otherwise docile jellyfish.

The safest rule is to know the few potentially harmful species of jellyfish, animals that occur year-round along Carolina beaches but are most abundant in summer. Appearing from spring into fall, varieties to beware include the infamous Portugese man-of-war, the sea nettle and the sea wasp. The oceanic jelly and the lion's mane may cause milder reactions.

The man-of-war, whose stings can send adults to the hospital, is actually a colony of individuals. A gas-filled blue float up to 10 inches long rides above the water as a warning. Drifting below are slender tentacles, some of which may reach more than 60 feet. Tentacles have blue, beadlike stinging cells that remain intact and can sting even after the man-of-war has died and dried on a beach. These polyps contain one of the most powerful poisons known in the marine world and can cause severe burns and blisters. Also dangling from the float are polyps of blue, tubular feeding parts with mouths at the end. A third type of polyp has treelike, branching gonads, colored salmon-pink at maturity. Men-of-war are most plentiful in or near the Gulf Stream. But they can change the shape of their floats to catch a prevailing wind or may simply drift with ocean currents and wind up in shallow water.

More often encountered along South Carolina beaches, the sea nettle also is venomous. In estuaries and along the coast, sea nettles float near the surface of the water year-round but are most common during the warm months. Severe stings have hospitalized a few people and encounters can be painful. But rarely do nettles cause more than an itchy irritation. Usually less than 6 inches in diameter, the animal is a typical bell or mushroom shaped jellyfish. Pink with radiating red stripes, the bell is dotted with five warts. The tube through which the nettle feeds looks like four long, ruffled, lacy lips that hang well below

PORTUGUESE
MAN·OF·WAR

SEA
NETTLE

Two poisonous types of jellyfish found in South Carolina waters.

the sides of the bell. And 40 long, yellow tentacles alternate with marginal sense organs.

Some sea wasps are highly venomous and the Australian variety is dangerous to man. South Carolina's two species seldom cause problems, but it is safest to avoid these wasps, also known as box jellies because of their cube shape. The *Chiropsalmus quadrumanus* variety is clear, 4 to 5 inches high and 5 to 6 inches wide with several tentacles at each corner of the umbrella. The animal has stung Gulf Coast residents badly enough to require medical attention but appears less troublesome in the Carolinas.

The other variety, *Tamoya haplonema*, is nearly as tall but only 2 to 3 inches in diameter. Each of the four tentacles has a paddlelike base and a strong filament. This speedy jellyfish usually stays near the bottom.

Seldom seen near shore, the oceanic jelly remains in the open sea, where it may float past boaters. Adults are rarely more than 3 inches in diameter with a brownish or brownish-yellow umbrella. The arms are the same color as the body while the tentacles and gonads are pink to purple. This bioluminescent jellyfish can bother man, but its sting is milder than that of the sea nettle.

Because it is most often seen in the South during winter and early spring, the lion's mane seldom tangles with bathers. But it can produce a mild, usually harmless sting. The largest jelly in the world, the lion's mane has a broad, flattish bell and numerous combination mouth-arms. Below the umbrella with its eight primary lobes are eight clusters of tentacles. South of Cape Hatteras, the lion's mane is most often pinkish and seldom larger than 5 inches. Elsewhere the color ranges into orange, red or purple and in the Gulf of Maine, this jelly is known to reach at least 8 feet.

If stung by any jellyfish, carefully remove the tentacles and flood the area with alcohol to prevent any additional discharge of poison. To ease the discomfort, jellyfish victims turn to such treatments as meat tenderizer, tannic acid, sodium bicarbonate, boric acid solution, soap and vinegar. Consult a physician immediately in case of more serious reactions, which can include shock, cardiac or respiratory arrest.

Stings (or worse) are caused by nematocysts, the thread bladders known only among *Cnidaria*, including jellyfish, sea anemones, corals, hydras and hydroids. All jellyfish have the microscopic bladders, but they usually are not strong enough to bother man. The egg-shaped capsules are imbedded in cells, each having a bristle or trigger on its surface. A long tube coils inside the nematocyst. When prey or predator touches the trigger, the tube shoots out and sinks into the object, be it dinner or a hungry fish. A tiny bit of poison is injected through this thread. Because a nematocyst can only be used once, jellyfish are constantly producing new ones.

Science has divided nematocysts into 17 types, but all are of bascially three sorts. Poisonous kinds penetrate the victim. Others lasso or spiral around projections on prey while sticky nematocysts entangle prey and cling. Jellyfish explode nematocysts into small animals to paralyze and trap the potential meal. It sticks to the tentacles and they in turn pull the food toward the mouth.

While the common umbrella shape of jellyfish is well known, the animals may have as many as nine life stages, most bearing little resemblance to the adult. Life begins as a fertilized egg, which develops into a microscopic, free-swimming larva shaped like a cigar. After several days, the larva attaches itself to a rock or shell and slowly becomes a flower-like polyp with tentacles. Feeding on microscopic organisms, the polyp grows to ⅛ inch then multiplies by producing buds. These may separate from the parent or may form cysts, which hatch into tiny new polyps.

If conditions are favorable, the polyp develops constrictions until it looks almost like a stack of saucers. Then each saucer becomes a minute jellyfish, which is released into the water. In just a few weeks, the ¼-inch larval jellyfish or ephyra grows into a medusa.

After the tiny jellyfish are released, a small part of the remaining stack of saucers can grow tentacles and return to the polyp stage. A few weeks later, the polyp is producing more jellyfish. Although an adult jelly may live only two or three months, the attached polyp stage is really perennial and could conceivably live forever.

Through many of their life stages, jellyfish are harmless to man. And most of the jellyfish floating or pulsating through the Carolina seas cause man little if any misery even as adults. Among those large enough to be visible are the jellyball, mushroom jelly and moon jelly, all common during warmer months.

The best known of some 200 species of true jellyfish worldwide, the moon jelly has a flat, colorless umbrella. A fringe of very small tentacles droops from the margin. Growing to 3 inches in height and 16 inches in width, the saucer-shaped moon jelly is translucent and whitish. The animal has a short, stout feeding tube that expands as four long arms with frilly margins. The distinctive reproductive organs are round or horseshoe-shaped, yellowish or pink or violet in females, whitish in immatures and yellow to yellow-brown or rose in males. Most often seen in summer or autumn, moon jellies usually float near the surface just offshore. During high tides or storms, the medusas often wash up on beaches. The sting of a moon jelly may sometimes cause a slight rash that may itch for several hours or may not be noticeable.

The jellyball, whose numbers vary greatly from one year to another, can hinder shrimp trawlers and other fishermen by clogging and damaging nets. The very firm jelly deteriorates slowly on shore and so the harmless jellyfish may dot the beach. The most common jellyfish here, it has an 8- to 10-inch-wide umbrella with a brownish border. Most along the coast and near mouths of estuaries, jellyballs have no finger-like appendages on the underside.

The mushroom jelly, which is often mistaken for the jellyball, has projections beneath the lower surface. The umbrella is flatter, the jelly less firm and there is no brown band. Often reaching 10 to 12 inches in diameter, mushroom jellies may grow to 20 inches or more. The umbrella is translucent or yellowish, the frilly underparts brown. And while the jellyball appears sporadically year-round, the mushroom jelly comes out most often in spring and winter.

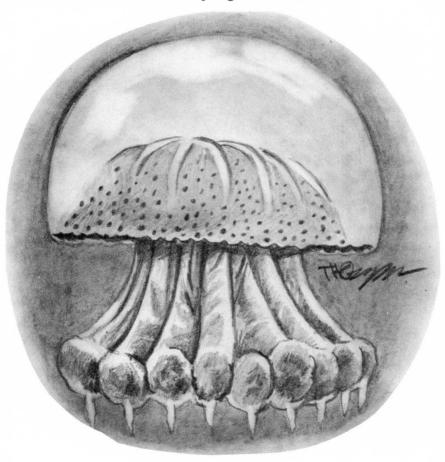

Mushroom Jelly.

Pelicans—

Soaring on a wingspan of 7 feet, Eastern brown pelicans are the most spectacular fishermen of the Southeastern coast. A day at the beach never seems quite complete without the graceful glides and dramatic dives of pelicans searching for food.

Only a few pelicans spend the winter along the South Carolina coast. But in late March and early April, the birds begin returning from Florida to Lowcountry rookeries. Each male chooses his nest site and aggressively defends it against what can be intense competition. The highest, most desirable area is usually the center of a sand spit that sprouts only grasses. The more experienced birds stake out those areas first, leaving younger pelicans to lower sections that could be over-washed by high tides.

A male may spend days enticing a female to his small chunk of territory, where he alternately is hostile to males and submissive toward females. Thought to be mute as adults, pelicans cannot rely on song as most birds do. Instead a male signals a potential mate by repeatedly moving his head sideways in a figure eight. At the same time he displays his gular pouch, which can hold 17 pints of water. If a female becomes interested, the male begins a more exaggerated series of posturings to prove he can both protect the nest site and be gentle to his mate.

Although the birds are positively somber in their courtship, they wear a golden glow on their white feathers. The tips of the mandibles or beak have turned red as has the area around each blue eye. When courting grows more intense, the birds bow, with neck arching away from the body and bill pointing down and slightly back. Wings, held a slight distance from the body, jerk and the birds make a guttural hiss in the trachea.

Once the pair have reached their agreement and mated, the male may present the female with the first bit of nesting material, but she will carry out most or all the construction. In Florida, where the webbed-footed birds nest in trees, the male offers a stick and the female begins building a platform that will serve as the bottom of the nest. But in South Carolina, the birds nest on the ground and the female twines a nest of grasses. Initially standing a foot or higher, the nest is nearly trampled to the ground over weeks of landing, taking off and delivering food to young.

The 4-foot-long birds mate daily while building their nest and establish a set routine of tending the nest, a duty both share. The male also sits stolidly beside the female as she prepares to lay her first egg. She settles on the nest the night before and refuses to eat; her partner, too, largely stops eating until the egg arrives. The couple then return to fishing and dining until a second and usually a third egg are laid at two-day intervals.

Incubation takes about 30 days, the female doing most of the sitting but the male standing beside her. Young hatch on different days. If fish are in short supply that summer, the oldest and strongest probably will have enough food to survive while the younger birds may perish.

A newly hatched pelican is one of nature's most unattractive babies. Born bare and with eyes closed, the youngster has an ill-shapen body,

Young Pelicans at Cape Romain National Wildlife Refuge.

a head distorted by two large eyesockets and a wrinkled fold of pouch. Reddish in color, the hatchling will barely move during his first day. On the second day, his eyes open and his skin turns blue. The next day, the lumpy gray body with sticks of wings still can barely lift his head or rise to his feet. Parents bring fish and regurgitate into the nest for each chick.

In about 10 days, a trace of down sprouts and the bird can reach into his parent's pouch for food. Adults trade parental duties. One goes fishing and the other remains at the nest. The adult may stand with wings extended to shade the young from sun that could blister and kill in an hour. At three weeks, the hatchlings are covered in white down and begin venturing short distances from the nest. Full of squawking and quite ready to strike out at an intruder, the young grow more independent each day and by five weeks are carousing with other pelicans their own age. These boisterous groups may race through nests, trample newly hatched young and squash untended eggs. As a result, watchful adults may beak an errant youngster and send him sprawling.

Near 10 weeks, young have their full juvenile coloring — brown backs, heads and wings but white bellies. Only as mature birds, at age 3 or 4 years, do pelicans take on a brown belly and white head. By that age most of the fledglings are gathering where land and water meet in a dense congregation that seems to be waiting for something to happen. At 11 to 12 weeks it does. Parents stop feeding their young and in effect leave them to learn the ways of the wild. The birds have been receiving 30 to 40 percent of their body weight in food every day. Overweight with baby fat, the fledglings are about 3 pounds heavier than adults. Fat collected in the lower neck and upper chest must nourish each young bird as he figures out how to fly and fish.

Relying only on instinct or what he might see adults accomplish at a distance, a pelican discovers how to spot a fish or a school and capture dinner. The bird must estimate his own weight and speed, the speed of the fish, its depth, its true location disguised by refraction and the point at which bill and fish should meet. Beginning a dive from 10, 20 or occasionally 50 feet above the water, the pelican folds his wings halfway back, holds his feet forward and tucks his neck back. As his descent and speed increase, the ungainly looking bird becomes streamlined with feet under tail, wings flattened tight back and neck stretching forward.

When bill tip touches water, the pelican opens his mandibles and collects pints of water. Feeding on such fish as menhaden, silversides and mullet, usually within 2 feet of the surface, the bird is thought to aim for one specific fish rather than to dive randomly into a school. Under water, the pelican turns so that he can surface facing into the wind. After draining water from his pouch, the pelican maneuvers the fish and swallows it headfirst so the gills will not cut his throat.

Rookeries such as Marsh Island in Cape Romain National Wildlife Refuge fledge an average of only 1.1 or 1.2 pelicans from a nest of three eggs. Some of those fledglings will not catch on to fishing and eventually will starve. Still other young birds will not head south in time so will die from starvation and exposure.

Despite such problems caused by nature, pelicans are doing fairly well in the Southeast now. The U.S. Department of the Interior removed Atlantic Coast pelicans from the federal endangered species list in the spring of 1985. They remained an endangered species in Gulf Coast states, California, Mexico, Central and South America. South Carolina kept the birds on the state threatened species list because erosion often jeopardizes nests and rookeries.

At the turn of the century, pelicans were widely hunted for their feathers and scores of thousands were killed in Florida alone. Although protected from shooting, populations later were ravaged by DDT, the same pesticide that destroyed the eggs of bald eagles and ospreys. DDT accumulated in the tissue of fish and built up in the flesh of fish-eating pelicans. Residues thinned eggshells and reproduction fell drastically.

Throughout the late 1960s and early 1970s, pelicans were rare in many of their former haunts. The birds disappeared in Texas and nearly vanished in Louisiana, where they are the state bird. A species that had been on earth 20 to 30 million years appeared headed for extinction. But pelicans still were attempting to breed in Florida and South Carolina. The nadir of nesting in South Carolina came in 1970 when only 945 young fledged.

Restricted in this country in 1972, DDT stopped flooding the environment. Although DDT and other pesticide residues lingered, pelicans began showing the first signs of recovery. Populations have risen steadily and healthy birds have even been restocked into such states as Louisiana and Texas.

The species still faces threats such as habitat loss due to development, sewage pollution leading to infection and death, overfishing, foul weather and disease. Although studies have shown pelicans take very few fish species that are commercially caught, fishermen have accused the birds of competition and on occasion have deliberately maimed them. Pelicans also drown after becoming entangled in monofilament line, the nondegradable line now popular with sport fishermen. Because the birds are fairly slow in lifting off from the water, some have been run down and killed by boaters.

In South Carolina, erosion seems to be the greatest threat. Bird Key, at the mouth of Stono River off Folly Beach, was the largest brown pelican rookery in the Eastern United States in the early 1980s. More than 2,600 nests were counted there in 1980, more than 3,200 in 1982. But erosion began eating away at the low-lying sandy stretch. In 1983, severe weather and high waves had destroyed so many pelican eggs that Bird Key fledged only a quarter of its usual number of pelicans.

While dredging nearby, the Army Corps of Engineers placed spoil on the island and pelican reproduction rose. However high tides and storms continued to take nests, at least 800 in the summer of 1985 when

Brown Pelican rests atop post in Shem Creek.

only 1,564 pair of birds bred there. Spoil was added again the next year to build up the island. When disastrously high tides hit that summer, Bird Key lost only 100 of its 3,065 nests. After the water receded, some 600 pairs of pelicans from around the state regrouped and renested there.

Pelicans had been breeding on only one other site in the state, Marsh Island. The island in Cape Romain hosted more than 3,200 nests in 1985, but erosion was taking its toll. Only 1,775 pair arrived the next summer and 400 of their nests washed away.

As one island shrinks, however, others grow. Historically pelicans have bounced from one spot to another as the sea has built up then torn down sand banks. In 1985, for the first time, pelicans tried Bird Island in Bulls Bay and Egg Bank in St. Helena Sound. The following year pelicans also took to White Banks and began loafing, although not nesting, on Deveaux Bank near Edisto. Immature pelicans had been using Bird Island as a bachelor colony, but adults built 255 successful nests there the first year. Nearly 400 of the almost 500 nests laid there in 1986 survived high tides to fledge young.

A pelican rookery was first reported in St. Helena Sound in 1904 and that site, referred to periodically through 1943, is thought to be Egg Bank. In the 1930s, pelicans began moving from that elevated sandbar to Deveaux Bank and in the late 1940s Egg Bank washed away entirely. Deveaux Bank rose above high tide for the first time in 1921; the growing isle hosted nesting pelicans, gulls and terns from at least 1949 to 1979 when Hurricane David washed over the island and left pelicans searching desperately for nesting sites.

In 1985, pelicans built 260 nests on the newly emerged Egg Bank. And more than 10,000 royal terns nested there, probably making it the largest royal tern colony on the South Carolina coast. Jamming a small strip of high ground on Egg Bank, pelicans lost some of their nests during a storm that year and virtually all 183 nests to high tides in 1986. But dunes are building and could provide more nesting room in the future.

In 1986, record high tides took nearly 1,000 of the state's 5,839 pelican nests. Nearly 800 pair renested successfully and raised their young as summer moved into fall. Such late fledglings often fail to master fishing and die of starvation or exposure during their first winter. Young normally begin fledging in July and parents start heading south, leaving the good fishing grounds for inexperienced youngsters. By late August, juveniles outnumber adults in South Carolina and may begin appearing off the coast of Jacksonville.

Pelicans continue to depart throughout the fall and early winter, particularly when a northeaster sweeps through. Those lingering into December may flock south overnight if the temperature drops. Cold sends fish deep into the water, below the level pelicans can dive. From January into March, many sun along the east coast of Florida while others hang out off the coast of Cuba. Some of North Carolina's nesting pelicans, which now number in the hundreds, spend the winter in South Carolina.

Although a rare site and probably an accidental straggler, a white pelican occasionally flies into South Carolina. This western species, which sometimes winters in Florida, has been seen in downtown Charleston lakes, around Mount Pleasant docks and on Charleston County pelican rookeries. But sightings are of a lone bird, which never finds a mate. The magnificent 5-foot-long white pelican has a wingspan of 8 to 9 feet, black wing tips, an unmistakable pelican pouch and a bill of yellow.

Alligators at Charles Towne Landing.

Alligators —

Despite the noisy pretense, tough hide and belligerent reputation, alligator courtship is a gentle affair. After emerging from winter dens and basking in the sun for a few weeks, both males and females begin bellowing their intent. In May the roaring may sound from freshwater, saltwater or brackish marshes as well as rivers, ponds and lakes.

Before bellowing, the alligator makes subsonic sounds that rise to the surface as bubbles, sounds potential mates may hear underwater. If interested, a male and a female swim toward one another slowly, touching heads and necks lightly to prove they feel romantic rather than hungry for a meal. The male caresses the female and then the pair begin to press each other under water. The action gradually becomes more forceful until the pair unite.

In June, the female begins building her nest. She most often chooses a secluded area near water, usually a small creek, canal or overgrown shallow pond. Nearly three-quarters of the alligators living near the South Carolina coast nest in diked areas, many of them managed as waterfowl habitat. Most of the other alligators select remnants of diked areas such as former ricefields.

The female carries mouthfuls of soil and vegetation to the site then uses her body, hind legs and powerful tail to shape the material into a cone. The elliptical base is usually about 6 feet in diameter and about 20 inches high. Because alligator embryos can drown if submerged, females normally build their nests at least a foot above water. Being nocturnal, alligators do most of their construction as well as hunting at night.

If she began piling up her nest in early June, she may even abandon her first site. At the least, she works at a leisurely pace and may not lay her eggs for three weeks. By late June or early July, females are slapping nests together almost frantically and eggs are deposited almost as soon as the cone is ready.

In the center of the nest, the gator digs a cavity for 15 to 60 eggs, on average about 44. Studies of South Carolina alligators show larger females produce larger eggs and more of them than smaller females. Females usually are larger than 7 feet when they begin breeding; males mature at 7 to 9 feet. Sheer bulk apparently is the key. Emerging from a winter den in the mud or from the bottom of a river, alligators spend the spring sunning to raise their body temperatures. Only when their temperatures are high enough can the reproductive cycle start. Alligators less than 6 feet are slender, too light to sustain the necessary temperature. But above 6 feet, alligators begin putting on weighty bulk and can maintain their temperatures even during cloudy days, cool nights and rainstorms that will chill a young alligator.

Females appear to nest a bit earlier during warm springs, but rainfall and length of days also are important and drought can delay nesting. Usually laying from mid-June until mid-July, an alligator often oversees or actively guards her nest. The mother gator hides a little distance away but appears and climbs up on the nest if danger approaches. She may hiss a warning or, mouth open and teeth showing, she may charge an intruder. Biologists studying alligators have captured and temporarily restrained a very aggressive female if she charged over her nest and chased them. After being confined a time or two, however, even the most protective mother alligator becames shy, scientists have found.

In contrast, most reptiles lay their eggs and abandon their nests. But like other reptile eggs, gator eggs are incubated by the sun rather than by the mother. While baby turtles can climb from sandy nests unaided, alligators apparently need their mother's help. In South Carolina, most alligators hatch in the first week of September although hatching con-

tinues from the third week in August to the third week in September.
A 2-ounce alligator first pips its egg with a small egg tooth on the end
of its snout. Working its way out of the shell, the youngster begins
making sounds to draw its mother. In most cases she responds and
opens the nest. If for some reason she does not return, only a few
hatchlings usually can struggle out of the nest. Most will die.

Usually opening the nest at night, the mother alligator takes her
young to nearby water, most often a small canal or sometimes shallow
water with dense vegetation. If they hatch near brackish water, young
alligators seek out the freshest water available. Large adults can tol-
erate fairly high levels of salt for a time but excavate a hole or den
where freshwater will collect. Hatchlings also gather in such gator
holes.

If hatchlings cannot find adequately fresh water, they perish, a potential problem if the summer has been dry or water in diked areas
has been drawn down. But if the summer is too wet, if high storm tides
or a hurricane flood a nest, gator eggs drown. In 1981, for instance, the
high tides caused by tropical storm Dennis flooded coastal areas and
half the alligator nests studied that year failed to hatch young. Attracted by the calls of young just before or after they hatch, raccoons
may take hatchlings or eggs a few at a time. Predators will keep
returning to feast until they have consumed the entire nest.

In the end, slightly less than half the eggs laid survive to emerge as
hatchlings. The pod, or group of hatchlings, will remain near the nest
for a year or even longer. Their mother often dens near the site and
may even share the area with her young.

The youngsters begin feeding themselves immediately. On a diet of
insects, small fish and frogs, hatchlings will grow about 6 inches a year.
(In warmer climates such as Florida, alligators grow twice that fast.)
It takes South Carolina females 16 to 20 years to reach maturity. The
larger the alligator grows, the larger prey it can tackle. More than any
other species in the Carolinas, the alligator can and does eat an incredible array of animals. At various sizes and stages, the predators
and scavengers will dine on snakes, turtles, water birds, small
mammals, fish, shellfish, carrion, raccoons, dogs, deer, horses and
occasionally other alligators.

Hunting at night, an alligator feeds only when its body temperature
is warm enough to digest food. A gator basks in the spring sun for some
time before capturing a meal and stops eating in the fall long before
denning up. And if sunning on a warm winter day, the reptile will not
eat. If it should feed while its temperature was low, the meal would
spoil in its stomach and the alligator die.

Despite their fearsome reputation, alligators are not always on the
prowl for food. A single meal can last an adult a full year when prey
is short. In droughts, for instance, large adults will congregate around
a shrinking pond of freshwater and peacefully coexist without any food

and without killing one another. In fact alligators, which waste little energy, eat only 10 percent of the food a warm-blooded animal would consume. Whether an alligator is starved or force fed large amounts of food, the animal will maintain a constant blood sugar. An alligator can slow its metabolism and breathing at will, enabling the animal to lie for hours on the bottom of a river.

Although not famed for their brilliance, alligators are among the most intelligent of all reptiles. In laboratory or test situations, gators can learn quite rapidly.

They also have a remarkable homing ability, as the animals have proved time and again. When removed from a populous area, such as a golf course, an unwanted gator can easily find its way home. The animal prefers a water route and will follow a waterway that heads in the right direction. But a gator also will cross dry land to get home. Studies in South Carolina show females are more eager than males, which may dally on their way home. Youngsters less than 5 feet long may adopt the new spot while a mature alligator will head back to his home territory. One 8-foot female made a 17-mile journey in five days. When biologists retrapped and moved the alligator once again, she returned in just two days or, rather, two nights of swimming and crawling. Another female, outfitted with a transmitter and tracked, needed only 13 days to make a 25-mile trip back to her territory.

In other ways, however, alligators are relatively simple animals with rudimentary body systems. The animals do not react to pain. If the heart is removed, the alligator will continue to move and live for a time. Even if the brain is fatally injured, where another animal would die on the spot an alligator will swim away.

Supremely well adapted to their semi-aquatic life, the animals essentially have not changed in 180 million years, since the days dinosaurs ruled the earth. Over time alligators have evolved resistance to disease. A large alligator is undisputed king of the marsh or swamp. No animal but man is likely to challenge that fact.

Man has proved to be the only substantial threat to alligators. European settlers undoubtedly began hunting alligators but took relatively few. During the Civil War, significant numbers were killed for meat and leather. As weapons improved and demand for hides grew, tens of millions of alligators were killed between 1800 and 1910. When the outboard motor became available, even more gators were taken in ever more remote places. With the Depression came increased hunting even though gators were decreasing. After World War II, oil exploration and development brought new pressures throughout the alligator's range; resort as well as residential developments in South Carolina began taking over favorite alligator habitat.

In sheer numbers, alligators dropped to their lowest ebb in the late 1950s and early 1960s. Some of the same problems, particularly hunting and trapping, were taking a disastrous toll on related crocodilians around the world. By the year 2000, some experts fear, the alligator will be the only crocodilian still alive.

Indeed the alligator has made a remarkable comeback. In South Carolina, a law prohibiting night shooting was adopted in 1955; although designed to protect deer, the legislation also reduced alligator hunting. A 1962 law, which reduced poaching, required trappers to be licensed and hides to be tagged. The federal government took its first step with the Endangered Species Protection Act of 1966 then added more protection in 1970 with an amendment to the Lacey Act and in 1973 with the Endangered Species Act. Both the state and federal governments classified alligators as endangered inland and threatened along the coast.

Large Gator eyes photographer.

South Carolina's alligators did not rebound as quickly as those in Florida, Louisiana and Texas, where warmer winters enable gators to grow and mature more quickly. In Louisiana, for instance, 68 percent of female alligators 6 feet or longer nest each year compared to 33 percent in South Carolina. Only about one South Carolina gator in 50 nests in a year. And while Florida has nearly 8 million acres of prime alligator habitat and Louisiana has 5.5 million, South Carolina has 200,000 acres or less.

More than a million alligators are now thought to thrive in the Southeast. The U.S. Department of the Interior has reclassified alligators in parts of Florida, Louisiana and Texas, opening the way for limited trapping seasons or removal of alligators classified as a nuisance. In 1986 Interior proposed reclassifying the alligator in all the Southeastern states, from North Carolina to Oklahoma. The new listing would be "threatened by similarity of appearance," acklowledging the animal has recovered but assuring that monitoring will continue.

In 1986, South Carolina adopted a strictly controlled program to trap nuisance alligators along the coast; gators inland of Highway 17 remained classified as endangered and are not included in the program, however. That year the population was thought to be 67,000 to 80,000 alligators, double the population of a decade before.

As the number of gators has increased, so have nuisance complaints. Charleston and Berkeley counties alone recorded 173 complaints the year before the new program was approved. Complaints come primarily from resort and residential areas developed in prime gator habitat, areas that often draw newcomers who are unaccustomed to seeing alligators. Complaints run the gamut from young 1-foot alligators to the state's record, a 13-foot, 2-inch gator. While even a very small alligator sends a chill down the backbone of some people, an alligator measuring 5 feet usually weighs only 35 pounds or less and is still a youngster. Man is not on the alligator's menu and gators generally are not aggressive to humans.

What will make a gator aggressive, however, is tossing the animal marshmallows, hot dogs or other food. Such hand-fed alligators quickly come to associate man with food and will even chase a retreating human in hopes of finding a store-bought meal. To prevent such problems, South Carolina has outlawed the feeding of alligators.

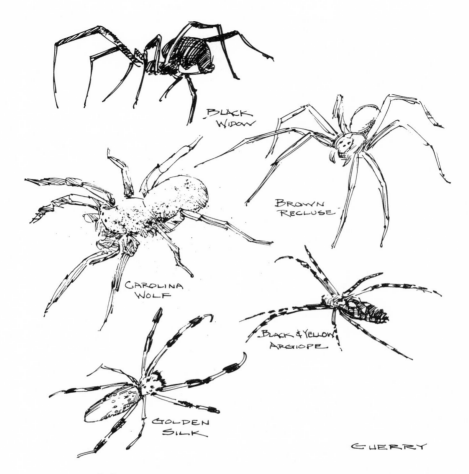

A few of South Carolina's many spiders.

Spiders —

Arachnids may be dismissed as creepy crawlies, respected for their masterful constructions, feared for their poison, admired for their beautiful web patterns, appreciated for their consumption of bothersome insects or loathed for the clutter they leave in quiet corners. Love them or hate them, spiders are out in force each summer. To anyone who walks through the woods, works in the yard or keeps a clean house, spiders are a fact of life.

South Carolina can claim 326 species of spiders and another 164 may live in the state. The little arthropods never have been surveyed in detail and biologists estimate 500 species may actually crawl, jump, spin, hide and balloon (with the help of a silken parachute) around the state. More than 35,000 species have been identified around the world and scientists think even more species remain to be found.

At one extreme, the large Carolina wolf spider races after and attacks its prey while the fishing spider can grab tadpoles and small fish. Brightly colored crab spiders blend in with flowers and wait for a butterfly or moth meal to come to them. The infamous black widow and brown recluse are known for their powerful poison, but they kill fewer people in North America each year than bee and wasp stings do.

Golden silk spiders build huge, strong webs that can easily span trees and surprise an unsuspecting hiker or horseback rider. Yet the trap-door spider spends all its time underground and spins only a small web, which holds a hinged door at the entrance to its tunnel. The bola spider may emit pheromones to attract moths, its favorite dish. It tosses a sticky ball and line at a passing insect then pulls dinner in with the string.

Non-enthusiasts may think of spiders and all insects as bugs, but in fact spiders are arachnids rather than insects. Both groups belong to the Arthropod phylum, the largest in the animal kingdom. Insects have three body parts and six legs while spiders have eight legs and two body parts. The latter, in fact, are more closely related to scorpions, horseshoe crabs and ticks than to insects, which have antennae and crushing mandibles that spiders lack.

Being carnivores, all spiders produce a powerful, fast-acting venom that paralyzes prey almost immediately, before it can thrash about and damage a web. Dinner remains paralyzed but alive until the spider is ready to dine. Able to digest their own poison with immunity, spiders inject venom through fangs at the tip of their chelicerae, just below the eight simple eyes most spiders have. The front portion of the spider's body or cephalothorax includes the head, thorax, chelicerae and poison glands, glands so large that spiders cannot swallow solid food. Instead, they inject digestive juices into their prey and drink a liquid meal. Later the arachnid often cuts loose the dried remains, which explains why debris collects beneath a web.

Spiders are probably best known for their webs despite the fact many species spin no web at all. Males often make no webs or at most construct an insignificant web in the corner of a female's elaborate home. The small male may look more like a baby spider, living on the fringes of its mother's web and dining on her leftovers. Or sometimes a male moves into an abandoned web and feeds on whatever food was left behind.

Constructing a web, a spider draws silk through its spinnerets from silk glands at the base of the abdomen or rear body portion. Most females have six finger-like spinnerets, at the end of which may be 100 or more spinning tubes. Silk from those tubes is said to be stronger than a comparably thick strand of steel.

Spiders can make different types of silk for different uses such as building webs, wrapping prey, holding eggs or sperm and ballooning over the countryside in the wind. Silk for webs is even made in a separate gland from silk for egg sacs. Web silk may contain minute drops of very sticky material that helps to hold prey until the spider can strike and immobilize the animal. Some spiders also are equipped with special claws enabling them to travel over their own webbing without getting caught.

Between the mouth and the first pair of legs, adult males have a set of pedipalps resembling false legs with boxing gloves on the end. Before he ever ventures near a female, the male usually spins a special web into which he deposits a drop of sperm. The pedipalp will carry the fluid from the web to the female or egg sac.

When it comes to sex and the single spider, the male must search out a female with considerable care — black widows are not alone in devouring their suitors. Little jumping spider and large wolf spider males wave their forelegs in intricate patterns when approaching a female. Some orb weaver males pull on the female's web in a precise way. The vibrations announce a suitor rather than prey is entering the web. Sometimes much smaller than the female, the male may sneak into the web while his potential partner is dining; some safety-conscious males even present an insect meal to assure their welcome. Some varieties race across the female's web, do their deed and abruptly jump to the ground and out of harm's way. A sac spider male seeks out and captures a young female, wraps her in silk and waits until she matures. Then the male frees his partner and mates with her. Perhaps the safest tactic of all, some species simply fertilize an egg case the female may have left on a twig, in leaves or in her web.

Some females give birth to live young but most lay eggs, anywhere from three in the case of a jumping spider to nearly 1,500 for a large fishing spider. The egg sac may be thin or elaborate, a cocoon with a substantial outer covering and a soft center around the eggs. Most adult spiders die in the winter cold, but the next generation survives in the egg sac. When the tiny spiderlings emerge the next spring, they are completely on their own. Not knowing how to hunt and catch meals, many starve. Being cannibalistic before and after leaving the egg sac, other young die at the chelicerae of their brothers.

Given a breezy day, young may disperse from their mother's web by spinning small parachutes of gauze. Particularly common in fall, this ballooning or drifting in the wind has helped spiders spread over an extremely large range. Because many species do well in a wide variety of habitats, almost any place a youngster lands will make a good home.

Spiderlings may not resemble their mother but instead take on adult color and marking as they grow and repeatedly molt. For instance the poisonous black widow spider is orange, brown and white as a spiderling. With each molt, it gains more black until, as an adult, the female will be shiny black with a red hourglass below on her almost spherical abdomen. A member of the comb-footed spider family, the black widow male has white and red markings on his sides. Just an eighth of an inch long, one-third the size of the female, the harmless male does not bite man.

Black widows hide in piles of brush or other debris, under fallen branches, in brick or cement piles, in moist dark areas in and around buildings, in pumphouses, even under furniture and outhouse seats. Webs are an irregular mesh with a funnel-shaped retreat at one end. The female usually hangs upside down in her web. Living three years or longer, she is quite likely to kill and consume the male. With just one mating, she can store sperm and continue producing egg sacs as a widow. A good mother, she rarely leaves her web and stays close to her pale brown, pear-shaped egg sac. She bites defensively if the eggs are threatened or she is disturbed. She wraps her prey in viscid silk before injecting a neurotoxic venom that is poisonous to humans.

If bitten, a person usually feels pain and stiffness quite soon in his muscles, particularly around the abdomen. Perspiration, nausea, fever and high blood pressure may also set in. The victim rarely dies but may suffer fatal convulsions that cause asphyxia, insufficient oxygen in the blood.

Far more toxic is the venom of the brown recluse, a spider probably introduced into South Carolina and now spreading. The complex venom of this spider works slowly, the bite usually being painless at first and later causing a small, red, swollen spot. In time the skin around the bite may become blue-gray. An ulcer begins to form as fever, chills, nausea and vomiting often set in. Several days later, the victim may go into convulsions as infection and fever spread rapidly. Dead skin and crust slough off the bite to reveal a gaping wound that may reach to the bone, take months to heal or even require amputation. Systemic reaction to the bite may cause death.

Unlike other spiders, members of the brown spider family have six rather than eight eyes. Also known as the violin spider, the brown recluse is orange-yellow with a dark violin pattern on the front segment of the body. Legs are grayish to dark brown but orange-yellow at the base. The abdomen is grayish to dark brown. Males are a quarter inch long, females slightly larger. In Arkansas and Georgia, part of the spider's native range, the recluse has been found hiding under bark and rocky ledges. But in South Carolina, confirmed sightings have been indoors in storage rooms, under rolls of insulation, in ceiling light fixtures and in outbuildings. Old boxes, stored papers, shoes, clothing, folded towels and furniture are other favorite spots of the reclusive spider.

Biting when it is disturbed, the brown recluse forms a loose web of irregular strands. Eggs overwinter in a loose sac suspended in the web and the mother guards her eggs until she dies.

Other spiders pose less of a threat to man. But the large wolf spider, which looks ferocious, has potent venom that can make children sick. Wolf spiders are sometimes hairy, generally dark and mottled so they are well camouflaged in dead leaves and other debris. There the arachnids lurk, waiting to chase potential meals. Some wolves dig holes to serve as homes or hideaways while others, perhaps confident of their size and prowess, have no retreat at all.

When it comes to webs, the orb weavers are among the most talented. Engineers have even studied their gossamer homes and picked up tips for bridge construction. Orb weavers such as the black-and-yellow argiope, the golden silk, the crablike spiny and the arrow-shaped micrathena first make a tag line that radiates outward. Relying on wind, gravity and climbing, the spider moves from point to point stringing the first silken lines. The orb weavers build concentric circles around a hub with lines running out like spokes of a wheel. Lines are placed with care, not so far apart that insects can slip through but not so close that wind may rip the webbing.

The argiope, often called a garden spider, reinforces the center of its orb web with a heavy zigzag of silk. Bright yellow and red or yellow and black, the large female rests head down in the middle of the web. Unlike many varieties, the male argiope builds his own small web with its own zigzag in the outskirts of his mate's den.

The golden silk spider, named for its gold body and legs, builds a hefty web in the woods and may pop up in the path of passing hikers, horseback riders or even fliers. On occasion a small bird has tried to zip through one of the webs and been found later with its wings bound in sticky silk. Or, too heavy for the web to hold, the bird may fall to the ground and have a difficult time freeing its wings. The female spider repairs her web each day and may have to replace up to half the web at a time...especially if a bird has struck it.

Each group of web-spinning spiders weaves a characteristic pattern that identifies one from another. Among them are cobwebs, sheet webs, funnel webs and the more grandiose orb webs.

Trapdoor spiders spin tiny webs, a hinge of silk that holds a door over the spider's tunnel. When prey wanders by overhead, the trapdoor opens, and the spider jumps on its meal. True jumping spiders, in contrast, don't build webs but hop around on their short, clubby legs and catapult onto victims.

Fall

Three Bonaparte's Gulls and a Ring-Billed Gull (center).

Migration—

Long before the arrival of autumn weather, migration draws birds south along the Carolina coast. Spring nesters may spend a brief four months here and, once young are independent, head home to places such as the Caribbean Basin. Slightly more than half the 650 bird species nesting north of Mexico go south in the fall, usually to Central America but sometimes to South America.

Terns may start flocking by in late July, but the first flush of migration begins in mid-August. Shorebirds are moving through in mid-September as winter ducks arrive. Hawk migration peaks later that month, warblers in early October. Sparrows are flying through about the first of November and by mid-November numbers of shorebirds and ocean-going or pelagic birds may appear.

Fall is the best of seasons for the Lowcountry birder. Migrants tend to take a coastal route south in fall but prefer the mountains for spring trips north. Feathered masses often come through on Northwestern fronts, which force the birds to fly at relatively low levels and sometimes bring casualties at towers. Fall brings not only more birds than spring migration but also surprises, Western birds and other unusual species considered rare if not accidental. Between the summer birds leaving, the winter residents arriving and the travellers passing through, Lowcountry birding becomes an adventure from mid-August through November.

Adding to the unpredictability is the nature of birds in fall. They've fallen silent, abandoning their glorious spring songs for unimpressive chipping calls often made by loose flocks of songbirds migrating at night. Females, and more especially males, have lost their bright spring plumage and wear the somber, less identifiable shades of winter. Many may be molting, showing a range of colors and marks. And the young of the year are often decked out in juvenile plumage, perhaps resembling their mothers but often unlike either parent.

Juveniles also help to make coastal migration so interesting in fall. Known as coastal effect, young birds on their first migration often are pulled toward the shore. Ornithologists have only recently discovered coastal effect, which some still consider a theory and others a documentable fact. Coastal banding stations operated in the fall by the Charleston Museum net about 90 young birds for each 10 adults. Inexperience and bad weather are thought to send young birds toward the shore while mature birds fly farther inland, where food and landing spots are more plentiful. Or adults take a more efficient trip directly over the sea from North to Central or South America.

Exhausted birds are sometimes pushed far out to sea by storms and may seek any refuge they can find. A passing ship may pick up hundreds of hungry, weary songbirds or a single large hawk. Predators such as peregrine falcons have been known to dine on warblers and other small stowaways. A sympathetic crew may put out food for smaller seed and berry eating birds, but insect eaters often have a difficult time finding food on board and may perish. Stopping for more than a respite, birds frequently remain on board and ride a ship into ports such as Charleston. Birds disembark when their ship docks or land comes into view. On occasion a bird may even hitch a ride from Europe or the East to the Carolinas and successfully take up residence in its new land.

Migration is triggered by the shrinking amount of daylight, which causes hormonal changes in feathered bodies. That, in turn, brings metabolic changes. Birds feel restless and gain fatty food reserves for the trip ahead. The blackpoll warbler, for instance, spends three or four days flying 2,000 to 3,000 miles primarily over open ocean. Greenish in winter plumage, the warbler normally weighs 11 grams or about two-fifths of an ounce. But studies have shown blackpoll warblers double their weight before migrating. When offered all the worms it wanted to guzzle, one little fellow topped the scales at 29 grams and was too heavy to lift off the ground until it dieted.

Food is the primary driving force in fall migration. A cold spell may suddenly seal off a food supply in the north or freeze ground that birds had been probing for food, so large flocks will rush south all at once. With the growing popularity of feeding stations, some birds have abandoned migration and become year-round residents in what was their summer range. Annual winter surveys in New England are documenting the spread of such birds as cardinals, mockingbirds and tufted titmice.

For some birds, however, lingering into a cold winter without adequate food can prove fatal. Ruby-throated hummingbirds should leave the Carolinas in September for Mexico and Panama, but some may stay until October or December. To encourage hummers to leave when they should, nectar feeders may be taken down in mid-September. If a feeder is left up all winter, occasionally a rufous hummingbird may appear, but it is a casual to rare visitor in South Carolina.

A cold front, with a current of air that birds can easily ride south, may encourage a wave of migrants. And once a cold spell hits the Northeast, feathered creatures race toward their winter homes with all the frenzy of birds heading toward breeding sites in spring. But earlier in the autumn, migration is more leisurely in pace and in numbers. A songbird may take the trip by itself or with small, informal groups. Some species wander through over a period of weeks with individuals stopping to feed and rest.

Kicking the migration season off are black terns, which also breed along the coastal Carolinas. The birds may visit briefly from late July into September. Such rare summer residents as noddy, bridled and sooty terns depart for points south in September as do greater shear-waters, relatively common summer residents . From August into Sep-tember, look for migrating whimbrels and such winter shorebirds as marbled godwits. Arrivals in late September include Wilson's phalaropes, gadwalls, American avocets and American wigeons. In October, sanderlings may be migrating through, black-bellied and pip-ing plovers arriving for the winter, ruddy turnstones and semipalmated plovers temporarily increasing as migrants join local populations. Most common during migration, red knots may begin passing through in early fall but later will settle and spend the winter.

Western Sandpipers live here year-around but migrate in fall.

Throughout September, unusual shorebirds often stop to rest along the Carolina coast. Buff-breasted sandpipers may appear or American golden plovers may be blown off course by easterly winds. Rare visi-tors to the Carolinas, these plovers nest in the eastern Arctic but head to Labrador and Newfoundland in late summer to fatten up on fruit. Then they depart on a 2,500-mile trek to the northern coast of South America. Finally the birds take yet another major flight across the Amazon Basin to their principal wintering grounds on the pampas of Argentina, Patagonia and Tierra del Fuego.

Also in September, winter duck residents such as teal, black ducks and shovelers begin arriving and there is a major increase in mallards, whose winter populations in South Carolina are second only to year-round wood ducks. As September progresses into October, blue-winged teals sometimes gather by the thousands in mashes and ponds. Also on the move in late September are redheads, gadwalls and sometimes American wigeons, but wigeon may not show until early November. In all the unpredictabilities of fall migration, ducks seem particularly variable. Late October usually marks the arrival of the American scoter, greater and lesser scaup and pintails.

Between early October and early November, migrating ducks peak in South Carolina. Some of the birds move on in November to Florida and Cuba. But the final flood of ducks will not pile in until the winter's first major cold front strikes the Great Lakes and the Ohio River Valley.

Duck migration began drawing more than a little interest in the mid 1980s as populations plunged to the lowest ever recorded by U.S. Fish and Wildlife Service breeding duck surveys. In 1985, for instance, mallards and pintails were at an all-time low. Only about 62 million ducks headed south that fall, compared to 100 million ducks Fish and Wildlife hopes to see each year.

Nesting problems repeatedly struck in the prairie pothole region of Canada, where some 70 percent of North America's waterfowl hatch. Lack of rain, increased farming and modern techniques have destroyed many of the places ducks once bred as well as food on which nesting birds relied. Use of lead shot, poisonous to red-blooded creatures, killed not only ducks hit by bullets but birds that picked up shot with grit needed for digestion. Annual winter duck surveys in South Carolina brought record low counts of 73,000 birds compared to 550,000 ducks 20 years before.

By Labor Day, numbers of land birds are building as migrants temporarily join summer or year-round populations. Blackbirds increase as do Eastern kingbirds, white-eyed vireos and red-eyed vireos, the last a summer resident that usually stays until early November. The time is right to begin looking for varieties seen only during migration such as bobolinks, abundant transients from early September to early December.

In mid or late September, numbers of prairie warblers and yellow-throated warblers, both common permanent residents, swell as black-and-white warblers arrive for the winter. Warblers, which begin moving through in mid-September and peak in early October, are a highlight of fall migration although the birds wear less brilliant plumage than in spring. Breeding varieties such as the prothonotary warbler and the rarer Swainson's begin leaving in August and throughout September. Blackpoll, magnolia, Cape May and yellow warblers as well as redstarts, a type of wood warbler, are common transients beginning in September.

That month and the next may offer such rare migrants as Tennessee, Canada, blue-winged, chestnut-sided, golden-winged, bay-breasted, Wilson's and cerulean warblers. Black-throated blues are most easily seen during October migration although a few may spend the winter in the southeastern corner of South Carolina. And warblers such as the Connecticut sometimes put in surprise visits during September. So may the Kirtland's, a rare warbler that breeds only in north-central Michigan and may pass through to wintering grounds in the Bahamas. Orange-crowned may arrive for the winter during September while yellow-rumped wait for October.

Red-Tailed Hawk.

Hawks begin travelling through about mid-September and continue for a month. These raptors may migrate in small or large congregations of several hundred hawks of several species. Soaring with ease, these hawks usually travel at such high altitudes that only silhouettes may be visible through binoculars. But even silhouettes are distinctive. Front beaches and marshes are good spots to look for hawks, which often follow the coast as they move south. Among them are kestrels, merlins, ospreys and peregrine falcons. Both the falcon and the merlin are unusual winter visitors; kestrels spend the entire year upcountry but visit the coast only during migration and in winter. Other hawks migrating through include sharp-shinned, Cooper's, marsh, red-tailed and red-shouldered. Like peregrine falcons, Cooper's hawks suffered from pesticides and vanished from part of their former territory.

Bald eagles also begin arriving in October. Pairs that mate for life return to their territories and begin refurbishing nests.

October is the time to look for migrating swallows, which may flock through or stop to feed in groups of thousands. Cliff and bank swallows, both considered transients below the South Carolina fall line, are easiest to see during fall migration. The season also brings wintering tree swallows to join year-round barn swallows.

By mid-October sparrows, among the last land birds to migrate, arrive and vastly increase the number and variety of sparrows seen during the summer. Swamp, song and chipping sparrows are among the first to settle in. Coming along are such common winter sparrows as Savannah, sharp-tailed, white-throated and vesper. Less common winter residents include grasshopper, Henslow's, LeConte's, clay-colored, white-crowned and fox sparrows.

Sapsuckers appear in September, swelling the woodpecker roster to its full winter rank. Eastern phoebes fly in about the same time and hermit thrushes check in no earlier than mid-October for their winter's stay. Ruby as well as golden-crowned kinglets should be finding their cold-weather homes by mid-November as should brown creepers, a fairly common winter resident.

By mid-November, such shorebirds as purple sandpipers, great black-backed gulls and Bonaparte's gulls are due. And so are gannets, common and red-throated loons and great cormorants, all four exotic looking water birds. Gannets normally feed far out to sea but, like some varieties of shearwaters, may be blown near shore during fall migration or during winter storms. Scoters and scaups may not appear until mid-November, but numbers will increase until mixed flocks of thousands are visible in the winter ocean off spots like Folly Beach.

As if pushing the migration season, woodcocks don't arrive until late November with the largest influx the first two weeks in December. That very month, the more precocious males will begin putting on spectacular courtship displays. Most often at sundown and dawn, a woodcock will strut along the ground then suddenly spiral upward as high as 200 feet. Suddenly his body goes limp and falls like a leaf, giving a musical three-syllable whistle as he descends.

Owls also begin courting and singing when other species are long through nesting. Throughout the fall and winter, year-round screech, barred, great horned and barn owls are hooting. A few winter visitors also are migrating in, among them short-eared owls. Snowy, burrowing, long-eared and saw-whet owls are all uncommon residents during the cold months. And still more rare is a glimpse of these nocturnal winter visitors.

Elderberries are a favorite of birds.

Wildflowers —

With the first hint of fall in the air, wildflowers come to life. As the blistering summer droned on, plants all but stopped blossoming. When evenings cool and days shorten, however, a whole new wealth of flowers appears including asters, sunflowers and goldenrods. Purple and golden flowers predominate in this season, which almost rivals spring in the variety of wildflowers that erupt.

There is method to the apparent madness of plants that bloom as winter approaches rather than in spring, when the long summer ahead offers time for seeds to mature. The majority of fall bloomers are perennials which are later to pop up in spring. Growing more slowly than annuals, perennials may find less competition in the fall, when plants can blossom in openings and along rights of way that may have been cut during the summer. Each individual flower also may attract pollinating insects more easily in the fall — autumn means more insects yet fewer flowers than spring.

Insects probably are the reason yellows and purples outnumber the pinks, oranges, reds and whites of other seasons. Insects can readily pick out yellow and purple shades, some of which emit ultraviolet light. Seeing white as blue-green and not seeing red at all, bees view flowers very differently than man does. These insects respond to ultraviolet light invisible to man and so discern patterns known as nectar guides or landing strips that lead the bees to pollen. Active well into the fall, and sometimes even on very mild winter days, bees sometimes are caught by the chill of approaching evening. The insects may snuggle down on a blossom and spend the night there only to warm up and resume their pollen gathering the next morning.

Fall wildflowers also attract butterflies, newly emerged adults that developed from eggs laid by a spring generation. Spiders lurk on flowers in hopes of catching a visiting insect. In short, fall flowers become stages, presenting dramas as pollinators arrive, then spiders and even birds gather to feed on the insects.

Forty different species of goldenrod bloom in South Carolina. Al-

Goldenrod pollen often is erroneously blamed for hayfever.

though hayfever sufferers sometimes blame the blossoms for sneezing and misery, the pollen has proven too heavy to blow in the wind and to bother nostrils. Ragweed, which appears after the earliest goldenrods, is the real culprit. A native that grows wild only in North America, goldenrod is taken for granted on this side of the Atlantic yet the British prize the import as a garden showpiece.

Around the Carolina Lowcountry, look for sweet goldenrod, with leaves smelling like licorice, and seaside goldenrod living near the coast. The earliest of fall goldenrods, in flower by early September, is *Solidago odora* or sweet goldenrod. It bears crowded, cylindrical, yellow flower clusters on plants in dry, open woods and pine barens such as the Francis Marion National Forest. Growing 2 to 3 feet tall, the plants have linear leaves that alternate on stems. When crushed, the leaves smell like licorice, a sure way to tell this goldenrod from other varieties. An entirely unrelated plant, false goldenrod has blossoms resembling heads of true goldenrod that refused to open fully.

Swamps in the Carolinas have a fall surprise, which looks like the yellow jessamine of spring. Unlike the state flower, the rare swamp or Rankin's yellow jessamine has no scent and blooms only during the fall.

At least two dozen different species of sunflowers bloom through fall until frost in South Carolina. The first to pop is the very rare cucumber-leaved sunflower, which begins opening in May but is still going strong in September. Such sunflowers as the well-known black-eyed Susan and sneezeweed, which has drooping golden petals, continue their late summer bloom. Joining them are rayless, swamp and oxeye daisy sunflowers as well as Jerusalem artichoke. The oxeye is the common white and yellow daisy of fields and roadsides. The Jerusalem artichoke, whose tubers were cultivated by the Indians, makes dramatic displays 5 to 10 feet tall; the large golden flowers, up to 3 inches wide, resemble those of a black-eyed Susan but have yellow centers. The swamp sunflower hides away in moist roadside ditches.

In the world of asters, also members of the sunflower family, the earliest variety in South Carolina begins blooming in the Piedmont in late July. But by fall it is outshown by others such as camphorweed, a weedy variety growing in the sandy soil of waste places and roadsides. Resembling small daisies, the yellow flower heads are half to three-quarters of an inch wide and stand on hairy stems 1 to 3 feet tall. Growing along roadsides and fields, the plant has a lean, thin look. Alternate, oblong leaves are long and stalked but become smaller with wavy edges near the top of stems. The plant has been spreading northward, in part because grazing livestock do not like its flavor so leave it untouched to bloom and seed.

Camphorweed is just one species of the genus *Heterotheca*. Several different related varieties bloom in fall with yellow, aster-like flowers. They mature into white, fuzzy balls that resemble seed heads of dandelions. A cousin of camphorweed, silver grass has small yellow flowers. The long stems on which the half-inch flowers rise are silver on one side, green on the other.

Heads of tiny white flowers dot the *Melanthea* species of aster, usually abundant in early October. More unusual asters such as Maryland golden, cottony golden and grass-leaved golden flower in fall as does the uncommon pink climbing aster, which thrives in very damp conditions and even standing water. Much like a vine, the plant rambles up willows and is most often seen in Berkeley County.

Pea-like flowers also abound in fall, among them bladderpod. Despite the unattractive name, bladderpod plants have delicate leaflets and lovely, yellow flowers. By late September, the tall plants are beginning to show their pods as well as their flowers along roadsides; the 2-inch-long pods, dangling from outstretched branches, will inflate and turn bronze as fall progresses.

Several varieties of *Lespedeza* produce pea-like blossoms beginning in September. Most of the flowers wear shades of purple on tall plants with leaves divided into three leaflets. Tiny, pea-like, pink flowers surround the green stems of smartweed, a *Polygonum* in the legume family. Flower clusters are long enough to be showy on several varieties that bloom in swamps as well as moist waste places. Pink knotweed, with flower clusters up to 2½ inches long, sprouts blooms that songbirds particularly enjoy. Another *Polygonum*, white knotweed, has flower clusters 2 to 3 inches long on large, bushy plants 3 to 7 feet high.

As the name suggests, butterfly pea produces pea-like flowers of pink to lavender with white, protruding throats. The solitary, showy, 2-inch blossoms dot vining stems that sometimes grow erect in dry soil, open woods and thickets. Flowers close each night and open in the morning. Another member of the pea family, groundnut or *Apios* blooms along roadsides in fall. The flowers of this climbing vine are small but so handsome that people have transplanted it into home gardens. The rich, maroonish-brown blossoms are pea-like and form a compact, almost circular head that rises from leaf axils. Delicate leaflets line central leaf stalks; the potato-like tuber below provided food for Indians and Pilgrims. The plant prefers rich soil and moist, low sites such as ditches.

Another early fall vine is *Clematis* or virgin's bower, which likes rich, moist roadsides and stream banks. Inch-wide white flowers have four or five petal-like sepals but lack true petals. More noticeable in these clustered flowers are the numerous, long stamens and pistils. Female flowers, on separate plants from male blossoms, have feathery tails or plumes and sterile stamens. The vine lacks tendrils but supports itself on twisted stems that wrap around other plants.

Keeping to the yellow and purple theme of fall, spotted horsemint has yellow blossoms dotted with purple. Purple sepals form the bottom of the flower, a variety of bee balm and one of the prettiest and most unusual wildflowers of the Lowcountry. This true mint grows in sandy areas. Another mint, obedient plant has a square stem typical of mints. The plant is decked out in spike-like clusters of paired flowers, each up to an inch long; clusters are up to 8 inches tall. Spotted with purple, the collective petals or corolla has two lips while the calyx or group of sepals has five pointed teeth. Sometimes called false dragonhead, the snapdragon-like plant grows in moist thickets and swamps.

Mist flowers look like ageratums escaped from the garden and taking over ditches and moist areas. The compact, flat heads of tiny blue blossoms appear fuzzy up close and brilliant blue at a distance. Joe-Pye weed resembles a purple mass of fuzz atop stems reaching 2 to 6 feet. The flat-topped clusters of flowers spread 4 to 6 inches. According to folklore, an Indian named Joe Pye used the weed to cure fevers. American colonists turned to it in cases of typhus.

Mist Flower.

Another purplish blossom of early fall is gerardia with relatively pale, pinkish-purple, inch-long, bell-shaped flowers ending in five fused petals. The light throats are spotted on these inch-long flowers that protrude from the axils of opposite, linear leaves. Growing in moist soils, this member of the snapdragon family stands 1 to 4 feet high and has thin leaves 1 inch or longer. The plant likes moist areas and ditches.

Also in moist areas and ditches, *Liatris* or blazing star has tall stems only sparsely covered with inch-wide clusters of pink-lavender flowers. They have extremely long stamens trailing from flower heads like the trains of blazing stars. Again in ditches, look for the tiny purple flowers of stinkweed. The plant smells innocent enough if left alone, but if picked, the plant lives up to its name.

Blue curls are a true delight of early fall. Four long, blue-purple stamens extend from the center of the half-inch flower and distinctly curl down. Above is an upper lip with four lobes, below a single lobe, all curving away from the central curls of the stamens.

The dark purple blossoms of a fall *Rhexia* look much like its spring relative, the pink meadow beauty. Four petals with eight prominent stamens will soon fade and turn into little urn-shaped fruits, a nice harvest for dried arrangements.

Well into October, great lobelia plants standing 1 to 4 feet tall show off bright blue flowers. Forming a lengthy cluster on the leafy stem, the inch-long flowers in axils of leafy bracts have two lips, the lower one striped with white. The sepals are hairy with five pointed lobes. This member of the bluebell family is the blue counterpart of the summer's cardinal flower and a larger version of lavender lobelia; the great variety grows in rich, lowland woods, meadows and swamps.

Delicate sea lavender blooms in marshes rather late in the fall. Stems forming a very open, branching cluster are dotted on one side only with ⅛-inch flowers. The perennial often grows with other broad-leaved marsh plants; competition from those plants and growing conditions in general determine the size and vigor of the highly variable sea lavender. Leaves may be 2 to 10 inches, plants 1 to 2 feet.

Another delicate blossom is the dull white or purplish flower of pennywort, sometimes called dollarweed, growing in moist hardwoods and thickets. The low, fleshy plant produces paired, roundish leaves and takes its genus name from *obolos*, the Greek word meaning small coin. Usually in groups of three, the blossoms form in axils of purplish, bract-like upper leaves.

Plants that bloomed earlier in the year are laden with ripe fruit in fall. Heavy heads of elderberries may be shiny and black in early August. Along roadsides and moist areas, elderberry plants with divided, toothed leaves grow 3 to 13 feet tall. Plants may bend nearly to the ground with the weight of the tiny fruit, a favorite of birds and other wildlife. Thriving in sun or shade, elderberries are prolific and increasingly popular. Nurseries now offer new hybrids and young plants may be carefully transplanted from the wild in spring.

Muscadine grapes also draw birds in August and September. In woods and thickets, the toothed, heart-shaped leaves may be seen vining their way around roadside plants.

Rose hips or berries from fertilized roses turn red in autumn. The hips are touted for their high vitamin C content and are often listed as an ingredient in vitamin tablets. Covered with short hairs, winged sumac berries color to a reddish-brown panicle of fruit. The plant, which grows 3 to 30 feet tall, is the only safe member of an otherwise poisonous family, *Rhus*. Among the dangerous relatives is poison sumac, which has white berries. Leaves of the winged sumac have 13 sections rather than the three of poison ivy. And a wing runs along the midrib of each leaf between leaflets.

Cocos or cocoa palm fruit also brightens in August. Often growing near beaches, cocos palms have leaflets all along the leaf blade. Larger palmetto trees, in contrast, have feathery leaves only at the end of stalks. The very sweet, fragrant, elongated golden-orange berries of cocos palms draw a host of hungry birds, squirrels and insects.

Bright purple French Mulberries.

French mulberry, which had undistinguished little blossoms in August, puts on a show with bright purple berries in fall. Clusters of small, round fruit surround stems at intervals. Less brilliant is the yellowish, ball-like fruit on Chinaberries, which will cling to the trees into winter. More than half an inch in diameter, the rounded fruit becomes slightly wrinkled as it ages. One of the hardiest members of the mahogany family, this native of southern Asia has poisonous fruit whose stones are sometimes made into beads. Introduced to American yards as exotics, Chinaberries long ago escaped into the wild.

Myrtle trees, a wild species often adopted into yards, put on waxy purple berries. Birds dine on the fruit during fall and winter to build up a layer of fat, insulation against the cold. The bayberry scent of the fruit also attracts man. Colonists boiled the berries in water, collected the wax that rose to the surface and made it into bayberry candles.

Pokeweeds produce poisonous, purple-black berries that droop in clusters around a red stem. Colonists used the berry juice as a dye and songs have even been written about poke salad. Both berries and roots are poisonous and even leaves should not be trusted once pink appears on these plants of the open woods, damp thickets, clearings and roadsides.

Gray Squirrel at Palmetto Islands County Park.

Squirrels —

The first signs of fall bring new vigor to the pace of squirrels. The sheer abundance of nuts and seeds inspires a burst of enthusiasm and activity, feasting and storing. Squirrels, in a sense, have their cake and eat it too — they not only gorge on such delights as acorns and dogwood berries but also bury food for the winter ahead.

In the mild Carolina climate, squirrels remain active year-round although they may spend the coldest winter days snoozing in a cozy den. The animals routinely search for food during the winter and nuts generally are abundant well into winter or early spring, which brings the first flush of edible shoots. Perhaps pampered by such a smorgasbord, squirrels often appear wasteful. A single bite seems all an acorn is worth and a prize garden tomato warrants only one nibble before the diner casts it aside and moves on to other taste treats.

But in fall, instinct takes over and even Lowcountry squirrels begin hoarding. That means collecting nuts or mast from oaks, beeches, magnolias, gums, dogwoods, hickories, pecans and other trees. During warmer months, squirrels also feed on flowers, buds or mushrooms and few suburban squirrels will turn down birdseed.

After choosing a meal to save, a squirrel often turns the food over and over and licks it. Then he scampers off to dig a shallow hole, bury the nut, tamp down the soil with front and hind feet and cover it with leaves or debris. A squirrel may inter nuts all over the yard, yet if the winter proves lean, he will find one of his morsels when he needs it.

Squirrels were credited with having great memories. But studies with captive gray squirrels have now shown that smell, not memory, guides the animal to his food. Gray squirrels have a very keen sense of smell, good hearing and a large field of vision. The same may be true of the nocturnal flying squirrel and the less common fox squirrel. All three are very much at home throughout South Carolina. Red squirrels have been spotted in the state but only in the highest mountain sections.

Throughout the South, the mammals undoubtedly plant at least some of the new tree seedlings that sprout each year. Farther north, where winters are less fruitful, studies have shown that squirrels recover the majority of nuts they bury. A squirrel will even watch a neighbor bury a nut then will unearth it and conceal it in another spot. Months later a third animal may feed on the same stolen nut.

The fall harvest and storage activity comes just as female squirrels have finished raising their second litter of the year. The gray squirrel breeds in late January and again in early June, often a riotous courtship. Couples chase one another from branch to branch, ground to tree or in spirals around a tree trunk. Some biologists are convinced the female does not ovulate without such a romp.

The race may end abruptly, sometimes punctuated by the squirrel's characteristic bark of "que, que, que" and a flick of the tail that is thought to acknowledge a friend or acquaintance. At other times the boisterous run evolves into a gentle interlude as a pair slowly crawls over each other. During copulation, the male secrets a wax plug, which prevents the female from breeding again. During the 44 days she carries her young, the female first begins to shun the company of other squirrels and later chases others from the tree she chooses for her den.

During the warm months, squirrels are often content to sleep in a hastily built leaf nest. But for raising young, a female usually prefers a natural tree cavity, an abandoned woodpecker hole or even a man-made nesting box. If she finds nothing suitable, she will build an open nest that provides far less protection. Soaring overhead, red-tailed hawks can easily spot and pick off adults as well as youngsters in such exposed nests.

Helpless newborn are less than 5 inches long and weigh half an ounce. After a week of their mother's milk, the young double their weight and during their second week grow fur. Their ears open and first teeth appear at 1 month but eyes do not open until 5 weeks. By then the young

Feeding time for three adopted Gray Squirrels.

are 10-inch, 4-ounce bundles of fur, eager to chew anything they can find from insects to one another.

Meanwhile, the mother squirrel may have moved her family to a second or even a third nest, an attempt to avoid fleas that can infest nest cavities. With her teeth, she picks up each youngster by the belly; the baby grabs hold with his feet around her head or neck.

At about 6 or 7 weeks, young squirrels begin venturing from the nest to feed on insects, leaves and buds. But the mother continues nursing until her young are 9 to 10 weeks. At 2 months, teeth can handle adult food such as nuts and acorns. By 3 months, young are on their own and their mother is carrying her second litter of the year, which will be born in mid-July or early August.

That second litter sometimes falls victim to hurricanes or other late summer storms. If the mother is well, she usually will reclaim a youngster that tumbles from the nest. But if the mother has been killed, a baby squirrel may be up for adoption. A nest may be fashioned from towels or rags atop a heating pad turned on low or a hot water bottle. Or suspend a 60-watt lightbulb above the nest until the squirrel is fully furred and eyes are open. Once the squirrel is warm, feeding can begin.

Try three egg yolks, a little evaporated milk and a little whole milk mixed together and strained. Baby squirrels will take the food from an eye dropper or a syringe, larger squirrels from a pet nurser or baby bottle. Equipment should be sterilized between feedings and the formula should be warm not cold. Young need feeding round-the-clock, very small ones every hour and larger ones every two to four hours. At home in the nest, the mother squirrel stimulates her young to eliminate. So before each feeding, adopting parents must do the same. Place the youngster on a towel or cotton moistened with warm water; stroke the genital and anal areas until the animal has done his duty.

Once the dark eyes open, offer a small bowl of high-protein baby cereal mixed with formula. Then gradually introduce solid food such as rolled oats, fruit, sunflower seeds and shelled pecans.

When the youngster is weaned at about 3 months, he may move to a cage outdoors. Introduce him to the ground but let him spend most of his time in the protection of the cage. A few days later, begin keeping the cage door open so the squirrel can leave of his own accord. Food should be put out for the squirrel as he learns what is edible in the wild and meets the competition of resident squirrels. Adult males often issue challenges, chase the newcomer and may drive him away to establish his own territory elsewhere.

During aerial acrobatics, the gray squirrel's flattened, bushy tail with silver-tipped hairs helps him maintain balance. The tail doubles as a shelter from rain, a fur coat on cold nights and even a parachute if the animal falls. The squirrel also communicates with his tail, sometimes signalling dominance, submission or willingness to breed. Where home ranges overlap, each squirrel recognizes the other and knows his place in the social order. The dominant animal will crouch slightly, reach toward the submissive squirrel with one or both forepaws then spring toward him. On the ground, the dominant squirrel will run toward a fellow with tail almost flat.

An extremely busy squirrel, the gray is most active from dawn until about 9 a.m. and again late in the afternoon. One of the noisiest and most gregarious of squirrels, he also can be shy, wary and elusive when he chooses to be. All the squirrel species become increasingly wary as the hunting season progresses from mid-October until March.

Measuring 17 to nearly 20 inches and weighing 1 to 1½ pounds, this squirrel is gray above with buff underfur that shows primarily on head, shoulders, back and feet. Underparts are paler gray. Sizable albino colonies thrive in South Carolina and the Charleston area has a white race that is not albino.

Grays are seen far more often in South Carolina than flying squirrels, but these nocturnal residents of hardwood forests and yards are also quite common. The first or perhaps the only hint of these gliders may be the thump as a 9-inch-long squirrel lands on the roof at night. Listen for a scolding similar to that of gray squirrels, a squeaking, churring or twittering.

Since flying squirrels adore bird food, check feeders regularly at night to see if a squirrel appears. If so, he is likely to return about the same time almost every night. The tamest of the Carolina squirrels, flyers are reddish-brown or grayish-brown with pure white underparts and a blackish border separating the two colors on each side. The squirrels with the huge, dark eyes have a patagium or loose flap of furry skin from the wrist of each foreleg to the ankle of each hind leg.

Females may defend a small home range but males do not. The animals sleep the day away in tree cavities or woodpecker holes and will nest there or in bird boxes. On occasion, one will use a leaf nest or take over the former nest of a gray squirrel. The squirrels raise two litters, each slightly later than the gray. If an orphan is found, he may be raised the same way as a gray squirrel.

At 6 weeks, the young are more than three-quarters grown and make their first short glides. Although urged by his mother, a youngster apparently needs no lessons. He simply jumps with all four legs spread and patagium stretched. By raising or lowering a leg, he can change directions, but the gliding path is always a gradual descent. Using air currents and his flat, rudder-like tail, the squirrel has been known to zip 150 feet, but a 50 or 60-foot glide is routine.

Before landing on a tree trunk, the squirrel swings tail and head up to reduce his speed and soften his landing. He usually races around the tree and runs up the trunk with ease then he often glides again and again until he reaches his destination. That goal may well be a meal of such favorite foods as nuts, tree buds, fruit and berries, insects, mushrooms and on occasion bird eggs or birds. Like gray squirrels, flyers gather and store nuts for the winter, often in cavities and crevices. The squirrels remain active year-round but, being gregarious, may den together during the cold of winter.

Less common in South Carolina is the fox squirrel, whose numbers appear to have declined in recent years. Populations now are consistently low and erratically scattered. North America's largest tree squirrel is most often seen at places such as the Isle of Palms (particularly the golf course area), Bull's Island, Brookgreen Gardens north of Litchfield Beach, Litchfield Country Club Golf Course and the golf course at Murrell's Inlet.

Spending much of his time on the ground, the fox squirrel is larger and heavier than the gray and can handle pine cones that would baffle a gray. Yet foxes do not appear to compete well with grays, which dominate more favorable habitat and almost never share sites with foxes. Grays are very energetic, alert, always on the move and quick to scurry up a tree at any sign of danger. Foxes react to danger rather slowly and try to escape by running along the open ground. So fox squirrels are more visible and vulnerable to such predators as bobcats, foxes, red-tailed hawks and great-horned owls.

In addition, foxes appear to breed only once a year, probably in January. They use leaf nests even during the dead of winter and may not locate a tree den in which to raise young. As a result, many may fall prey to climbing snakes, raccoons and opossums. South Carolina's lengthy squirrel-hunting season does not distinguish between gray and fox squirrels and the more unusual variety is often taken as a trophy.

Foxes live in pine and old-growth, pine-hardwood forests with open understories, sites that increasingly are being cut then planted with short-lived timber. Soils are poor in those older forests and food less abundant, but the fox's slower pace conserves energy and enables him to survive in that habitat. Foxes are active at all hours of the day and particularly during warm days in January, when the mammals are probably seeking mates.

As squirrels go, the fox is an impressive animal, measuring from 18 to nearly 28 inches, almost half of which is a very bushy tail. The fox's color varies but in South Carolina is usually silver-gray, gray with a black mask around the forehead and eyes or predominantly black. The black version is especially handsome with a white nose, white ears and white or gray feet. At least some gray foxes may be youngsters that will grow black fur later.

Pampas Grass at Middleton Place.

Plant Harvests —

Fall brings out the instinct to harvest. The plant world is laden with edibles so wild creatures are gleaning. Ants, bees and other insects are foraging, squirrels are tucking nuts away, birds are eating seeds and fruit, putting on weight for migration or the winter ahead. Whether it is a primeval urge coming out in man or simply all the signs of nature, humans also feel that autumnal call. The backyard vegetable garden is only one obvious place to pick produce. Nature offers a bounty of material in fall to decorate the house for many months if not years.

A key to remember is preservation, preserving not just a stem for an arrangement but wild species in general. Fresh flowers may be pressed and dried in spring and summer, of course, but that dooms the seeds. By fall, flower heads have dried on their own and seeds probably have been shed. Just to be certain, however, give pods and flowers a shake to release lingering seeds in the spot the plant grows. Pick in a site the species is abundant. Because many wildflowers are annuals, only the seeds will ensure that the plants reappear for next spring's blooms. Choose only common plants. Cones from a loblolly pine or magnolia tree, cattails, dried heads of goldenrod and sunflowers all are good candidates.

Cattails, for instance, normally grow in congregations. One single plant can produce 35 new ones in a growing season. Over the years, one plant and its progeny will fill three acres of pond. With such reproductive ability, a few cattails may be harvested just after they release their golden pollen. Cattails are among the first plants ready for picking. In June the tails begin turning brown and casting their pollen to the wind, sometimes as much as 175 million pollen grains from a single tail. Cut the small tails soon after, in June or early July. By late summer and fall, the tails may look prime, but they will soon explode into a pom of tan fluff. Even if the head looks solid, the dry, warm heat of a house in winter can trigger a messy surprise. To help keep the cattails intact, coat the brown head liberally with hairspray.

June is not too early to pick dock and needle rush, which is flowering in damp places early that month. Dock produces lime green or reddish, whorled seedheads that deepen to dark red. Drying on the shrub or by hanging, the branching stems of dock stand out atop plants 2 feet or taller in old fields and roadsides. In early June, when the rest of the countryside is lush green, dock is turning a rich brown. Harvest can wait until later summer or fall since dock is durable in the field.

Needle rush with its sharp, thin, needle-like leaves produces a cluster of flowers in June that dry on plants growing in damp areas. A little later blooms appear on soft rush with its grass-like stems and more showy clusters of seed-like flowers. Soft rush grows in swamps and damp open ground.

In early fall, begin looking for seed heads of such plants as spartina grass, standing well above reeds and often at the edge of former ricefields. Pampas grass has larger, lusher, off-white plumes in the wild and also in yards. Plume grass is in all its glory along pine barrens in October. Resembling purple to pinkish-gray pampas grass, the feathery heads unleash their seeds not long after they open. If the plume is still closed, the warmth indoors will unfurl it; if fully open when picked, it may send seed flying in a heated house.

If a common grass is plentiful at a site, so a few plumes can be spared, heads may be picked and dried before they go to seed. Hang the grass upside down to air dry then douse with hairspray to assure plumes stay intact.

Famed for its contribution to the basket world, sweetgrass blooms in late September or early October with pinkish-purple blossoms resembling cotton candy. The grass is increasingly difficult to find so plumes should be left in place to cast their seeds. Foxtail grass produces much shorter stalks, topped with rusty-red tufts that imitate a fox's tale. The bristles will stick to this grass so after picking, give each stem a good shake to release all seeds. Panic grass, which has tiny flowers similar to baby's breath, grows in a variety of places. But the nicest of some 90 to 100 species is found in marshes.

Various grass-like sedges bloom from summer into early fall in wet sites. The long, narrow leaves of salt-marsh bulrush appear in brackish marshes; reddish-tan spikelets top three-sided stems. The long, straight, poker-like spikes are most durable if picked when half developed. The spikelet of white flowers on white-topped sedge is far less showy than the five or six long, drooping white bracts with green tips. The bracts look almost like large daisies atop trianglar stems, growing 8 inches to 2 feet high in brackish swamps, marshes or moist pinelands.

At the beach, sea oats shine golden in the fall sun. But resist the tempting display because the oats are protected by law and must not be picked. The oats prove invaluable in preserving fragile beach dunes

Sea Oats at Edisto Beach.

against erosion; the plants hold shifting sand underground with their roots and above ground with their blades. In addition, a host of birds including grackles rely on the oats as food. Seeds not consumed will fall to sprout the next year.

Popcorn berries begin popping open on trees in October. Growing wild along streams and rivers, popcorn or Chinese tallow trees are often cultivated in yards as well. Dressed in lovely yellow leaves each fall, the trees produce clusters of white, waxy, popcorn-like seeds in husks. As soon as the husks turn black and begin to part, pick the branches for use at Christmas or any season of the year. This Lowcountry favorite is quickly ruined by rain. Dampness causes a gray mold on the pristine white. Even if dark husks are partially closed, they will continue to dry, open and eventually fall indoors.

Pecans, hickory nuts, black walnuts and acorns begin to drop very noisily in October. Sweetgum balls release a dusting of seed. The intricate spheres, covered with points and holes, are almost golden when they first fall, darker later in the season when squirrels may have nibbled off the points. Cones from such pines as the loblolly and the less common longleaf also are naturals for decorating. If splotched with sticky pitch, wash the cones in detergent and scrub with a stiff brush then dry in the sun or indoors in artificial heat.

Also watch for trees such as sycamores, whose fruits dry readily. The inch-wide balls hang on long stalks, each composed of many narrow nutlets with hair tufts. The fruit matures in autumn and drops in winter from trees growing in the wet soil of stream banks, flood plains and the edges of lakes and swamps. Winged sumac berries turn a velvety purple-red in fall. Rounded fruit forms dense clusters that will linger through the winter if critters do not consume the berries on these large shrubs and small trees. The reddish shade of the showy clusters endures and makes a good contrast to the more somber browns of other dried materials.

Magnolia pods are among the most handsome of all wild produce in autumn. From October into November, the oblong, cone-like pods open to disclose bright red fruit. Each berry protrudes from a rust-colored case, making an elaborate display. Later in the fall, the fruit will drop or be gobbled up by wildlife, leaving a dark brown cone 3 or 4 inches long with slits intricately scoring the surface.

Interesting pods grow on a number of trees including eucalyptus, catalpa, acacia, honey locust, mimosa, ailanthus and black locust. The black locust has a pod 3 to 4 inches long, dark brown outside but white inside. Honey locust pods can stretch to 16 inches; the glossy brown, slender pods twist and curl into particularly unusual shapes. Acacia pods, growing up to 10 inches, also curl and change colors; if picked while immature, the pods remain green. Ailanthus or tree of heaven, which can grow through cracks in city pavement, produces bright clusters of red-orange seed pods that will retain their color when dried. Each pod is shaped like an airplane propeller with a seed in the middle. Eucalyptus or red gum, more often grown in yards than in the wilds of the Lowcountry, has upright clusters of bell-shaped seed cases. Pencil thin catalpa pods may reach 18 inches and endure into winter.

Wisteria vines become laden with velvety, soft green to beige pods. If allowed to dry on the vine and release their seeds, the pods often curl attractively to expose a smooth, white interior. Trumpet vines or trumpet creepers have red-orange flowers that by fall have turned into satiny, dark brown, bean-shaped pods about 5 inches long.

Look for plants such as bladderpod, whose delicate leaflets and yellow flowers in early fall announce pods to follow. About 2 inches long, the seed capsules dangle on plants growing 6 or 8 feet tall along roadsides. Later in the fall, the pods will swell and turn a handsome bronze color; pods on the outstretched branches are best cut on dry days. Because the pods are poisonous, they should only be used in arrangements children and pets will not investigate.

In fields and along roadsides, rattlebox plants also produce inflated pods up to 2 inches long. In late summer, the plants have yellow, pea-like blossoms, but by late fall pods have dried and wind rattles the seeds inside.

Lovely little pods top delicate branches of meadow beauty, which grows 1 or 2 feet high in damp sites and woods. In spring, the meadow beauty bore pink flowers, that dropped their petals to show intricate, urn-shaped pods that flare at the top. Thoreau compared the shape of the smooth, light brown pods to cream pitchers. In October or November, upend the pods and shake to remove all seeds.

In gardens, look for spikes of pods on such flowers as hosta, delphinium, larkspur and snapdragon. Bean-shaped pods on sweet peas will remain green after picking. Oriental poppies have oval cups of seeds on slender stems while tulips produce light tan, oval seed cases in three sections. Siberian iris has oval pods that dry to a tan color. The oval seed pods of most lilies are worth collecting and the large, showy pods of lotus plants growing in lily ponds are so handsome that they routinely are sold in shops as decorations. Letting cultivated plants go to seed at the end of the season not only produces pods to pick but may draw hungry birds or, if a plant is not a hybrid, viable seeds for the next spring.

In the vegetable garden, let some okra form interesting pods that brighten as they mature and finally turn into long, ridged, tan capsules.

In fields, search for summer flowers that have dried naturally and so need no special treatment. Fresh flowers, in contrast, demand pressing, hanging upside down in an airy spot, submerging in silica gel or burying in simpler materials such as sand, borax, cornstarch or corn meal. Nature-dried flowers may not have the bright colors of fresh flowers but have taken on delicate beige, tan or brown shades and, of course, have already shed their seeds.

Relatively easy to find are the centers of daisy-like blossoms including black-eyed Susan, field and oxeye daisies, sneezeweed, coreopsis and Jerusalem artichoke. Also drying nicely in the field are yarrow, thistle, sumac, boneset or Joe-Pye weed and goldenrod. The last blooms throughout the fall so may be harvested, pale brown and dotted with white softness, late in the season or even into the winter.

Common mullein produces a tightly-packed spike of yellow flowers on a woolly stem that captures far more attention than the plant itself. A sturdy pole of small, intricate seed cases, the very straight flower head of this biennial may reach 2 to 6 feet. The related moth mullein also sends up a long stalk of bloom, but flowers and thus pods are scattered along the stem. Both varieties are preserved well on the plant or may be cut and laid flat to stiffen. The later in the season the spike is picked, the darker it will dry.

Other fall flowers that dry well in the wild are yellow asters, yellow *Heterotheca* such as camphorweed and blue mist flowers that look like the tight heads of garden ageratum. The perennial false indigo produces a spike of ovals that are black when dried. Wild sennas don very hairy brown pods that are long, thin, flat, curved and jointed, pods that hint the senna is a member of the pea family.

Wild lupines form lovely dried spikes of peapod-like seedheads. Look for plants 8 to 24 inches tall in dry open woods and fields. The mallows that bloomed with white flowers in summer put on pale, silver-gray seedheads that resemble closed stars.

Yarrow, which looks like a coarser version of Queen Anne's lace, dries beautifully in the field. Or pick flower heads no more than three-quarters open then suspend them upside down in a dry, dark, airy room.

From the yard or garden come already dried flowers or pods of Chinese lantern, clematis, columbine, delphinium, hollyhock, honesty, and sea lavender, also known as statice. All may be dried by hanging as well. Such flowers as pinks, spiraea and Sweet William do better if dried upright.

Try hang drying the brilliant orange heads of butterfly weed flowers, celosia, clover flowers, globe amaranth and garden hydrangeas or wild oak hydrangeas.

Fruit has its own demands. Choose well-laden branches of pyracantha, other berries or rose hips. Mix one part glycerine with two parts very hot water. Pour into a bottle and shake thoroughly. Or mix automobile anti-freeze with an equal amount of hot water and shake to blend thoroughly. At least 2 inches of stem should be in the preservative; rose hips and pyracantha should be allowed to drink for about three weeks. The same preservatives and procedure may be used to treat such plants as mistletoe, dock, cypress including cones, ivy with berries and many foliage plants. To prevent shrivelling, spray preserved berries with hairspray.

If bees have done their duty and wildlife hasn't dined too heavily, yucca or Spanish bayonet plants can produce very dramatic clusters of fruit. Drying to a tan color, each squash-like fruit is an oblong capsule that often narrows near the middle. The tall flower spike is packed with many flowers and can mature into a spectacular dried piece. More often, however, only a few fruits survive and so may be best harvested and used as individuals in bowls of assorted nuts, pods, cones, seeds and other fall bounty.

Bats —

As Halloween nears, thoughts turn to an often forgotten mammal, the bat. His nocturnal habits, secretive lifestyle, vampire myths and assorted old wives' tales make bats a fitting symbol for Halloween's hauntings and frights. But most fearsome bat notions are bad raps. The world's only flying mammal is a helpful, sometimes delightful furry creature with considerable talent.

Bats need not only better public relations but also preservation. Throughout the world, populations are declining quickly and some species already are extinct. In this country, five bats are on the endangered species list and the Indiana bat is also on the South Carolina endangered species list. The late Robert H. Coleman, a professor at the College of Charleston, first noticed a sharp decline in bats along the South Carolina fall line in 1947. Where he once saw 1,000 in an afternoon, he was rarely spotting more than one or two.

Like most bats in this country, South Carolina's residents are insect eaters and extremely sensitive to some insecticides. Not only is prey reduced by pesticides, but bats consume poisoned insects and may accumulate toxins. In the Southwest, Central and South America where bats often roost in caves, thousands of the animals have been exterminated at a time because they were feared or thought to carry disease. Even Americans who enjoy exploring caves are thought to have run retiring bats out of their lodgings so often that colonies dispersed. In some poor countries such as Thailand, bats are eaten. In a single month, 10 poachers will kill more than 10,000 large nectar and fruit-eating bats, some with wingspans wider than a man's extended arms. Bat blood mixed with liquor also is thought to be an aphrodisiac and to relieve back pain. Very small bats, including the world's smallest mammal weighing less than a penny, have been been killed and sold as souvenirs in Asia or used as decorations.

Assuming fruit-eating bats are competition, some fruit farmers have either killed or lobbied for destruction of the mammals. Studies have instead shown fruit-eaters dine on very ripe or fallen fruit that would not be marketed. More importantly the bats pollinate and spread the seeds of more than 130 kinds of plants, particularly in tropical rain forests where up to half the species of mammal residents are bats. The animals pollinate such crops as peaches, bananas, mangoes, avocados, dates, figs, the cactus used in making tequila and trees cut to build furniture. The night flyers are famous for their guano, rich droppings that produce fertilizer sometimes at the rate of nearly 210 tons a year from a single cave. During the Civil War, guano was even used as a source of sodium nitrate for gunpowder.

Most bats in this country are insectivores, consuming hundreds of thousands of tons of destructive insects annually. A large cave of bats may feed on a quarter million pounds of insects a night.

While these very clean, well-groomed mammals can carry rabies, biologists now estimate less than one half of 1 percent of bats ever contract it. Bats, whose faces sometimes resemble those of dogs, appear to be the only animal that can survive the viral disease. Worldwide only a handful of people have died from rabid bat bites, and in this country, only 10 people in 40 years have died from any bat related diseases. On occasion, however, a bat may bite when handled so it is best not to touch the animals or to wear very thick gloves as protection against the tiny, sharp teeth.

As for the tale that bats land on human heads and get hopelessly tangled in hair, bats have absolutely no interest in such adventures. Occasionally a wild bat might swoop down toward a person, but only in search of a mosquito or other insect. Kept in captivity by scientists, some species have proven quite affectionate and individuals will readily fly to a recognized human friend.

Two tropical varieties of bat do feed on blood, specifically the blood of livestock, but neither bat lives in North America. A chemical in the saliva keeps blood from clotting so the bats lap up their meal. The true vampire bat weighs only an ounce and can take in just a tablespoon of liquid. These vampires were discovered about 400 years after legends spread about Transylvania's human vampires. The bat was named for the ghoul and not vice versa. Only in this century have human vampires consistently been portrayed as bats. Other cultures, however, view bats quite differently. In the Orient, for instance, bats are a symbol of good luck, long life and happiness so the Chinese often use bats in their art work and on exports.

The world's 900 species of bats, dating back 50 to 60 million years, probably evolved from shrew-like animals that lived in trees. The front limbs of these primitive shrews evolved into wings and bats developed a number of special adaptations making the mammals well suited for their special style of life.

The webbed wings are stretched between four elongated fingers. A short, clawed thumb is free of the wing and if the four fingers were equally short, the wing would be useless. The wing membranes, often transparent and without fur, beat as often as 20 times a second. Some species fly as gracefully as swifts and may even join those soaring birds at dusk. Others are far more awkward, but many can fly long distances as witnessed by those that migrate 1,000 miles each fall to escape winter cold. On the other hand, bats are comfortable walking, climbing or swinging from one tree branch to the next with wings held against their bodies.

During daytime slumber, or when contentedly full at night, bats hang upside down with wings folded. Clinging with one hind foot, a bat can use the other to groom his fur or even clean his teeth. Hind legs are attached to the hip opposite those of other mammals so the knees point backward but the bottom of the foot faces forward.

Having small eyes and relatively poor vision, bats rely on echolocation that is much like sonar. As he flies, a bat emits 30 to 60 squeaks per second, a continuous series of supersonic sounds emerging through the nose or partially open mouth. The pitch, intensity and timing of these sound waves varies from one species to another and guides each in the best possible way. A fruit-eating bat, flying through a dense jungle canopy, whispers such low intensity sounds that only leaves and branches nearest the bat bleep back. Insect-eaters flying high in the open air emit high intensity sounds that travel much farther, sounds that would totally entangle a jungle bat in echoes, information and tree limbs.

Muscles in the ear, which often contains a projection called the tragus, contract and relax, blocking out sounds as the bat makes them but picking up the returning sound waves. The brain of a bat, very similar to man's, is small and devoted almost entirely to sound. Apparently the mammals can deciper echoes as to size, location and movement of nearby objects and so can find meals.

The search for food usually begins at dark. But as dusk approaches bats become restless and the movement of a single bat in an attic, tree hollow or cave will waken the others. At dark bats emerge from their colonies and solitary bats crawl from tree branches, loose bark, rock crevices or even window shutters.

The first stop is often a pond, stream or other body of water to dip the lower jaw for a drink on the wing. Dining is usually on the wing as well, once a young bat is weaned from mother's milk.

A bat catches a meal in his wing tip and transfers the insect to his wing membrane or the interfemoral membrane between his legs. Getting the food from membrane to mouth sometimes sends a bat into a mid-air somersault. Some varieties can also catch insects in their mouths. And if a very large insect is captured, a bat will land to eat it. In other parts of the world, some varieties prefer smaller bats, fish, mice, lizards or nectar and may take a meal back to the roost.

Fall is a particularly busy season for bats. They mate in the fall and are either migrating or searching for a place to spend the cold months ahead. Courtship includes whining, screeching, shared grooming and licking. Among species that hibernate rather than migrate, females store sperm through the winter and fertilization takes place in spring. (Scientists are studying bats to learn more about artificial insemination and birth control.) When just one bat wakes from hibernation, his stirrings rouse the others. All the females in the colony ovulate at virtually the same time and most give birth to one or two young at the same time. Unlike perhaps every other mammal, baby bats arrive feet first. Not yet experts at clinging, at least some young usually fall to the ground and perish during their first days.

Some South Carolina bats head south in the fall to places where insects are abundant. But many find a snug place to slumber through the winter. Adults consume enough food each fall to deposit a layer of fat one-third their weight. Preferring to hibernate at 41 degrees, bats will die if the temperature in their winter quarters drops below freezing. But if the den is too warm, their metabolism may increase, burning their stored fat and causing starvation. In the Lowcountry, warmer winter evenings give bats a chance to forage and the animals will pour out to search for a mid-winter feast.

The cosmopolitan mammals may live in the wilderness or in the heart of cities. In fact, one of the best places to see bats is downtown Charleston where they routinely hide away in attics and church towers but emerge to hunt insects around street lights.

Bats in the belfry, or in the house, can become an odoriferous, sometimes noisy problem. In addition to scurrying around on foot, bats make harsh, shrill chirps and screeches during the mating season or when upset. To discourage these visitors, wait until they depart for a night of feeding or on fall migration. Then install wire screen inside ventilators and other openings in the attic to block their return.

The Brazilian free-tailed bat is the most common resident in the city of Charleston while the red bat chooses less populated areas and forests. Other varieties often seen in the Lowcountry include the silver-haired, Eastern pipistrelle, big brown, hoary, big-eared, Northern yellow and evening bat. Species that spend at least part of the year in the state include the little brown *myotis,* Keen's *myotis* and the Seminole bat.

The Brazilian free-tailed will migrate nearly 1,000 miles from Southwestern states to Mexico, but in South Carolina the 3½ to 4½-inch-long bat remains active year-round. Named for a tail that hangs free of the interfemoral membrane, this species has dark brown or dark gray fur that is whitish at the base. The free tail generally flies all night at speeds of 10 to 15 miles per hour and dines on such favorites as moths, ants, beetles and leafhoppers captured in the interfemoral membrane. Each night this bat eats up to a third of his half-ounce weight in insects. Some 100 million free tails are thought to reside in this country and such a population could consume 200 million tons of insects. While some varieties live 20 years or more, this free tail usually survives 13 to 18 years. Hawks, owls and man are his chief enemies.

The red bat wears a bright red coat, males being particularly colorful. A solitary bat of the woodlands, he lives in the Lowcountry year-round but is seen upcountry primarily, if not exclusively, during warmer months. The bat roosts alone or in small groups in trees and shrubs, where his color camouflages him as a dry leaf.

Similar in appearance is the Seminole bat, which has much darker fur slightly frosted with white. Roosting in trees, bark, leaves and Spanish moss, the Seminole is active all during the year and is most often seen in the Charleston/Berkeley/Dorchester county area.

Living in trees, silver-haired bats have brownish fur washed with white on the back. In spring and summer, females gather into maternity roosts away from males.

The little Eastern pipistrelle, relatively common throughout the state, spends days in caves, hollow trees, rock crevices, leaves and buildings. The erratic flyer has hair that is dark at the base, yellow in the middle and brown at the tip, giving the bat a grizzled yellow look from above, yellow-brown below.

The largest in South Carolina, the hoary bat has wings sometimes spanning more than 13 inches. Fur is a combination of browns, yellows and deep reds with waves of white over the back giving a frosty appearance. The bat appears most often along the coast during winter but breeds in the north.

The evening bat, in contrast, spends the whole year in South Carolina, where he roosts in trees, in buildings and under bridges. The evening bat, like the big brown bat, has brownish fur that is slightly lighter on the abdomen. The latter is thought to roost in caves, hollow trees or houses and to remain relatively active during the winter.

The big-eared bat lives up to his name and also has a thick, wart-like lump between his eyes and nostrils. The long, woolly fur is blackish at the base and yellowish-brown at the tip on upper parts but white at the tip on chest and belly. The bat likes to roost in trees and buildings and can hover almost like a hummingbird.

The Northern yellow bat is predictably yellowish-brown. The bat is not well known in South Carolina but has been found in Charleston and Barnwell counties on the edge of woods.

The two members of the *Myotis* genus are rarely seen in South Carolina, but each species may congregate in caves, mine shafts and similar spots during the winter. The silky hair of the little brown is olive or yellowish-brown above and gray below. Ears, wings and tail membranes are dark brown with almost no hair. The Keen's is similar, but the fur is less glossy and more buff colored. The bat probably lives only in mountainous parts of the state.

Spartina Grass edges former rice field at Middleton Place.

Color—

By mid-September, the lush green of summer has faded. In marshes, spartina grass turns yellow as do sycamores, the first tree to color in the Lowcountry and a harbinger of fall. Soon popcorn or Chinese tallow trees take on a pure yellow.

In mid-October, the mountains present the most intense autumn hues of the Carolinas. The midlands brighten next and less vividly. Lowcountry foliage, usually coloring in early November, is often dismissed as dull yet some years leaves wear brilliant reds and yellows. Temperature, moisture, amount and strength of sunlight, tree health and site all determine how colorful leaves will be so the drama of fall may vary considerably from one year to the next and even one tree to another.

Foliage usually is most handsome when days are bright and cool and nights cold but above freezing. Drought subdues leaves as do warm nights. Yet a mild autumn may produce a glorious display if a cold snap strikes before leaves wither. The Lowcountry fall may peak in early December and colorfully argue with Christmas lights.

During spring and summer, leaves look green because chlorophyll is so abundant that it masks the other colors naturally found in many leaves. Chlorophylls contained in minute structures called plastids use energy from the sun, water and carbon dioxide to manufacture simple sugars. Much as carbohydrates in fruit and vegetables give man strength, carbohydrates found in plant sugars fuel the growth of trees.

Stomas, or pores, allow needed air to move into a leaf. Palisade cells on the upper surface of leaves receive rays from the sun while a transparent waxy layer within the leaf admits sunlight but prevents water from evaporating. With every tiny part doing its job, leaves produce plenty of food and ship it to the tree through veins. Also supporting each leaf, veins carry water from the tree to the leaf.

While manufacturing food, plants are breaking down and using chlorophyll. During the growing season, a plant or tree can replace chlorophyll so abundantly that leaves remain green. But fall brings changes both inside and outside flora. Veins are closed off as a layer of cork cells forms at the base of each leaf. The leaf can take up less water and minerals so chlorophyll decreases. Slowly carotenoid pigments, hiding in plastids, begin to outshine green chlorophyll and leaves take on a yellow, brown, orange or golden tone.

An entirely different group of pigments produces the reds and purples of autumn foliage. These anthocyanins begin to develop late in the summer in the sap of leaf cells. During summer, phosphates break down the sugars made by chlorophyll. In fall phosphate, other chemicals and nutrients move from leaves into the stem of the plant or tree. This changes the way a plant handles its sugar and causes leaves to produce anthocyanins. Light also fuels the formation of these pigments; the more intense the light, the brighter the red of leaves. The acidity of soil also plays a role. The same species of tree may have bright red leaves in very acid soil, purple in less acidic soil and lavender if acid is low.

More subtle signs of anthocyanins and carotenoids appear in other seasons. When young leaves unfurl from buds in early spring, the edges of some may be temporarily tinged with anthocyanins. Carotenoids are sometimes so abundant during spring or summer that a tree takes on a yellow-green cast.

Anthocyanins provide the familiar colors in cranberries, strawberries, cherries, red apples, blueberries, plums and purple grapes. Each fall the pigments also color wild fruits on dogwood, holly and prickly pear cactus, the last gradually turning red in autumn then purple and eventually almost black.

Credit goes to these pigments for red dogwood leaves, poison ivy, sumac, Hercules' walking stick, sweetgums, tupelos, black gums, persimmons, oaks and sourwoods. Black gums often turn orangy-red while sweetgums lean toward purplish-red and sumac a bright, pure red.

Carotenoids give their hue to carrots, corn, egg yolks, rutabagas, daffodils, buttercups and even canaries. The yellow pigments transform sycamores, grape vines, hickory trees, elms, tulip trees, redbuds, sassafras, popcorn trees and ginkgos. Across the country,

Ginkgo leaves turn a brilliant yellow in fall.

ashes, yellow poplars, aspens, birches, black cherries, cottonwoods and alders all wear carotenoid shades.

Varying from pinkish to red, purple and yellow, maples may contain either or both types of pigment. Only when the two combine do leaves glow firey red, bronze or deep orange. Bright orange is the color of persimmons while some maples and elms may take on yellow-orange hues. And as fall progresses the green of pyracantha berries flames into yellow, gold and finally brilliant orange.

As deciduous trees and assorted berries are taking on their fall colors, evergreens are fading. Magnolias, live oaks and palmettos are losing their luster and the richness of their summer green. Like their colorful, deciduous cousins, pines and other evergreens react to a drop in chlorophyll so begin to look dull. Live oaks will not regain their true green until late the following spring, when trees put on a flush of new growth and drop a portion of their old foliage.

Wild Turkeys feeding in Francis Marion National Forest.

Turkeys —

As a domestic turkey is starring on the Thanksgiving table, wild turkeys are gobbling acorns in the Carolina woods. The Eastern wild turkey may be related to its commercially raised counterpart, but there is little resemblance beyond the name and similar shape.

The farmyard turkey is a pale version of the wild bird in every way. Turkeys raised for the table have white tail tips and upper tail coverts or are entirely white while the wild variety has chestnut tail tips and coverts with its bright metallic bronze plumage. The wild bird also has a bluer bare head and a beard of hair-like tufts on the breast, much more obvious in males than females. The entire body is more slender and streamlined than that of the domestic, which is bred for its large breast.

The table variety would have about as much chance of making it in the woods as a parakeet would. Domestic turkeys are known for their lack of smarts. When rain falls, a tame turkey will stand there watching the water rise until the bird drowns. Or when frightened, farmyard turkeys will pile up in one end of a pen and suffocate. Spanish explorers discovered these domestic birds in Mexico and introduced them to Europe. European colonists in turn brought them to this country. Inbred generation after generation, the bird has lost its wild wiles and gained mild, tender flesh quite different from the more flavorful but tough and stringy meat of the wild bird. Moving no more than a few inches in a lifetime, turkeys raised exclusively for the dinner table have shorter legs, so weak they hardly support the heavy body and massive breast.

To survive, a wild turkey has to run rapidly, fly very well and evade such predators as foxes, raccoons, wildcats and hogs. And *Meleagris gallopavo* is no dummy although a wild bird may seem a little slow of wit when he falls for a hunter's gobble. What may look like stupidity may only be curiosity on the part of an adult or naivete on the part of a young turkey. If he lives long enough, he is likely to grow very wary. Many a turkey watcher will assert these birds are illusive, talented at avoiding man unless they choose to be seen. They are wily enough, for instance, to roost over water and thus outfox nocturnal enemies.

The wild turkey faces innumerable risks almost from the moment a hen lays her eggs on the ground, easy pickings for predators. About 50 percent of turkey nests are lost during the 28 days of incubation. In South Carolina, many turkeys choose sites on the edge of fields and roads so timber-cutting equipment and farm machinery take a toll. Shortly after laying her eggs in mid-April, a hen will abandon her nest of eight to 12 eggs if a hiker passes by let alone heavy vehicles. She usually seeks a spot near or under shrubby cover or against a fallen log or the foot of a tree. The hen sparsely lines the shallow hollow with vegetation or dead leaves she finds nearby. The polygamous male, which has a harem of several hens, is not involved in building the nest, incubating eggs or feeding nestlings.

Of the eggs that hatch, 50 percent will be lost to bad weather including rain, which can give hatchlings a fatal chill. The mother may be killed or her young poults may be taken by such predators as crows, skunks, raccoons or dogs. Covered with down when they hatch, the young quickly become active and can even leave the nest if necessary. The hen keeps her poults under her for the first two weeks of their life; although hatchlings can feed themselves, their mother broods and guards them. To distract people or predators, however, she feins a broken wing and races away from her poults. Between 2 and 4 weeks of age, they learn to fly and can take to tree limbs when danger approaches. Young will roost in a tree with their mother and remain with her until late fall.

About the time people are carving their Thanksgiving turkeys, wild turkeys as well as quail are going through the fall shuffle. The young of one hen may wander off with another female while the first mother picks up a following from other nearby hens. As a result, a female may have young of two different sizes, some young gobblers being considerably larger than she. In fall, groups of young sometimes gather and readily move to a new range 10 miles or more away. This movement provides a genetic mix, which is thought to help keep turkey reproduction high. Hens occasionally lay as many as 20 eggs in a single clutch, but eight to 12 is more usual.

Meanwhile, mature gobblers also are gathering into flocks. Apparently the birds find or sense safety in numbers. In spring, however, longer days trigger receptors in a turkey's eyes, hormones flow and gobbler groups split apart. Each male tries to attract hens, which separate from their brood groups and may join together temporarily. Hens respond to male gobbling and the breeding season may stretch from March into late June.

Male turkeys measure 48 to 50 inches, females about 36 inches. The favorite food undoubtedly is acorns; but turkeys also dine in fall on beechnuts, cherries, grain, wax myrtle berries, some poison ivy and dogwood berries. Spring meals include such tender greens as grain and grass plants. Wild males are said to reach 40 pounds, but valid records rarely are higher than 22 pounds. In fact the average turkey lives a little less than two years. If a turkey reaches adulthood and learns about predators, however, he has a good chance of surviving three to five years or longer.

Benjamin Franklin's candidate for this country's national bird once thrived in 39 states. Numbers dropped seriously in the 1930s and continued to decline until about 1960 as turkeys disappeared from 18 states. Despite poaching, some survived on South Carolina plantations along the coastal plain. The Francis Marion National Forest became the state's major refuge for turkeys and one of the last strongholds in the nation.

In the late 1930s, the country had an estimated 20,000 to 30,000 turkeys, but the count is now estimated well above 2.5 million. While research, management and habitat improvement have helped, turkeys have rebounded in large part due to live trapping and stocking wild birds. The National Wild Turkey Federation in Edgefield, S.C., and various state game departments have placed turkeys throughout their former range and even in new areas. During the early days of restocking programs, the national forest supplied many of the birds sent to other parts of the Carolinas and to other states. In 1951 South Carolina began live trapping and moving turkeys to the central and western Piedmont, where the birds flourished. In 1977 a state-wide turkey stocking program was launched. Wild turkeys have now become established in every state but Alaska and now reside in virtually every part of each state in which the birds would be likely to survive.

Today the king of game birds is doing well in such diverse areas as Ohio woodlots, Pennsylvania sites disturbed by man, a large downtown

St. Louis park, 10,000-foot Montana mountains, eastern Oklahoma, Hawaii and even West Germany. (The German population is thriving and spreading toward the Rhine Valley. Being fond of fruit, turkeys may run amok in the vineyards of wine country one day.) Turkeys are proving themselves very adaptable as long as they are given some protection in the woods and against poaching.

Through stocking, the Piedmont has gained turkeys, but the Low-country and Midlands are losing birds as turkey habitat falls to development. Another threat comes from pen-raised birds, which landowners want to introduce for hunting. Pen-raised birds are less savvy than wild birds, can muddy the wild turkey gene pool and may carry diseases that can rapidly wipe out populations of wild birds. Undercover investigations, court suits and research all are being called into play to prevent disaster.

The turkey tale may be repeating itself now in other South Carolina game birds. Populations of bobwhites and woodcocks both have fallen recently and biologists are trying to learn the status and the problems of both birds before numbers fall seriously low.

Bobwhites began to decline in the mid-1960s and the pace escalated in the 1970s. The major problem is modern farming, the disappearance of favorite habitat such as fence rows. So-called unclean farms offered seed-bearing brush with plenty of food and hiding spots. (In return adults and particularly youngsters gobbled up grasshoppers, boll weevils, army and tobacco worms, cutworms, potato and cucumber and squash beetles that farmers now battle with pesticides.) Today's clean farming methods clear away cover and food. About 80 percent of the bobwhites or bobwhite quails hatched in South Carolina die within a year and only about 20 percent live long enough to reproduce. Many starve, unable to find food in late winter. Plantations and game management areas are now planting crops such as bicolor lespedeza to provide winter meals for bobwhites.

The woodcock population in the Eastern United States fell by 45 to 50 percent from the mid-1960s to the mid-1980s. Changes in woodcock habitat in South Carolina and in breeding grounds may have brought about the decline, but hunting also has been blamed. Dining primarily on earthworms, the birds also suffer if the ground freezes and their probing bills cannot unearth dinner. Studies are underway to learn more about the dramatic drop in populations of this shy woodland bird. Nesting throughout the Northeast and into Canada, woodcocks gather in South Carolina for the winter. The first of these late migrants arrive about Thanksgiving.

Deer—

In fall a change comes over gentle-eyed deer. Bucks posture, fight or threaten with their antlers. Does become fertile in October and emerge from a summer spent guarding their fawns. Breeding reaches

White-Tailed Buck.

a peak late that month and in early November. Not only will a buck charge a human who crosses his path, but a female may become dangerous during this season of hot tempers and high spirits.

Toward the end of summer, shorter days alter hormone levels and testosterone increases in bucks. Antlers, growing since April, stop. Composed of bony keratin much like human fingernails, antlers are covered in velvet with a leathery membrane beneath. Even at rest during the fall, adult bucks and yearling males rub their antlers against trees to remove the coating. In the process, neck muscles swell, retaining water and making the neck of even an 18-month-old, 100-pound buck look enormous.

White-tailed deer, *Odocoileus virginianus*, carry their antlers into January, February or occasionally early March then rake off old antlers on a tree or kick them loose with a hind foot. The small bloody spot that remains will heal in a couple of weeks and almost immediately new antlers will appear. The final size of the antlers is determined not only by age but by diet and genetics. A yearling buck standing 3 to 3½ feet at the shoulder may have branched antlers with as many as six or eight points in the Lowcountry, 10 or 12 in the Piedmont. But a two-point buck with a single tine on each antler is more common. A wealth of food apparently spurs heavier antler growth in males and may bring does into estrus at just 8 months. Does suffering a hormone imbalance also grow antlers.

Until recent times, bucks probably used their antlers for protection, to fight off cougars, wolves and other predators that have all but vanished from South Carolina. But deer still find a use for their racks, which may spread as wide as 3 feet. Young deer have mock battles, jostling with each other more in play than seriousness. When a bit older, a buck will fight his way up the social order of the deer world. Once a buck with a wide, massive rack has established a niche on or near the top of the order, he only needs to reaffirm his standing. Known as presenting the antlers, a buck will lower his head ritualistically and show his antlers to an intruder or a buck interested in one of his females.

Bucks that spend the winter in a harmonious group become intolerant of one another in fall and establish territories of about one square mile. A doe's home range is just a quarter that size. While territories tend to overlap, a buck will defend his land, particularly if a younger buck intrudes or a doe is in season. A male usually mates with several does but occasionally has only one partner. Antler presentations usually prevent a battle, but bucks will fight and on rare occasion inextricably entangle their antlers. Such locked horns usually doom the pair to death, but even an accidental puncture in the face or neck may lead to infection and kill a deer.

Equipped with a keen sense of hearing, sight and smell, deer also communicate with scent. While rubbing his antlers, a buck usually touches his forehead glands on nearby brush and deposits scent that alerts other males and females. Both sexes also have powerful scent glands on legs and feet that help mark territory.

White tails also communicate with assorted snorts and blatting. To issue a threat, a deer stomps his front feet and a buck may wave his antlers for emphasis. Snorts and stamping warn other deer of danger, as does the flash of white when a deer raises his tail and runs. This white flag apparently signals fawns to follow or adult companions to flee as a group, making attack by a predator more difficult. The most common hoofed wild animal in North America, white-tailed deer can reach speeds of 35 miles per hour and are good swimmers.

The fall rut may continue into early January in the Carolinas, enabling very young does to breed and bear a single fawn. Most does carry a pair of fawns for 28 weeks, throughout the lean winter months when the usual reddish-brown coat turns a grayish-brown. Farther north, where snow locks land for the winter, deer may have difficulty finding food and occasionally may bog down, belly deep and immobile in the snow. Bucks, does and their young herd together sometimes by the hundreds in deer yards. But along coastal Carolina, a doe often keeps company only with her young. Deer can find browse fairly easily all winter although the search for greenery, acorns, other nuts and twigs may bring deer out of the woods and into yards. Lusher seasons offer fall fruit and a spring smorgasbord of tender shoots on sweet gum, maple, oak, mistletoe and poison ivy. Yellow jessamine, honeysuckle and cat's paws are particular treats for deer, which feed largely at dawn and dusk but also by night and day.

Young are born primarily from May through July. As labor begins, the doe becomes restless, alternately lying down, standing up and lying down again. After as little as 10 minutes or as much as an hour, the forefeet of the fawn appear then the head. Very well developed and weighing 5 to 6 pounds, fawns try to stand almost immediately. The doe thoroughly checks her newborn and vigorously washes them with her tongue, which sends them sprawling. Because the fawns are so unsteady on their feet, their mother may even lie down to give her young their first drink of very rich milk, fortified with almost three times the fat and protein of cow's milk. About an hour after birth, fawns are walking so their mother leads them to a safer, protected spot.

Dotted with about 300 white spots, the tawny-red fawns are difficult to see and wear far less scent than their mother. For their protection, the doe spends most of the next two weeks away from her young. Feeding in relative darkness and bedding down in a concealed spot by day, a new mother returns to nurse and tend her fawns eight or 10 times each 24 hours. She also keeps an eye out for predators and will arrive, sharp hooves flying, if she senses danger to her young.

Sometimes bleeting when left alone, a fawn may attract attention from human passers-by, who assume the youngster is abandoned. He simply is waiting for mother's next visit and is not at all in need of a new home. A little fawn raised in captivity grows into a large adult that is dangerous during breeding season, needs at least half an acre of land to range and is ill equipped to tackle life if released to the wild. A fawn should not even be touched because the doe, with her fine sense of smell, can detect human odor and may temporarily or permanently desert her baby.

Captive White-Tailed Fawns are startled by photographer.

When about 2 weeks old, fawns stop napping and begin following mother. Although youngsters nurse often for nearly two months and are not weaned for three months, fawns are trying grasses and twigs at just 2 or 3 weeks. But on occasion a yearling will barge in to nurse side by side with newborn brothers and sisters. Family groups of mothers and female fawns often stay together for a year while young males usually are pushed around by their elders and forced to stay mobile. Adults and yearling bucks will form groups of five or more during spring and summer as females guide their young.

In areas where hunting is not allowed, deer will live 10 to 12 years or longer. After a decade, teeth begin to wear out so the animals develop internal problems. In the Lowcountry, the average white tail lives 1½ to 2½ years with a yearling buck of 18 months weighing about 100 pounds and standing 3 to 3½ feet at the shoulder. Older bucks weigh in at 200 to 300 pounds, does at 150 to 250. Having 250,000 to 500,000 deer, South Carolina has set a very liberal hunting season, some years the most liberal in the nation.

Widely hunted and rousted from some former haunts by development, deer appeared to be headed for trouble early this century. The mammals had disappeared in much of their range, particularly the Northeast and Midwest, and were the equivalent of an endangered species. Populations were helped dramatically by hunting restrictions, restocking and game management programs. Deer remained relatively plentiful in the Lowcountry's Francis Marion National Forest and the forest helped restock the Piedmont, where numbers had fallen extremely low. Among other things, management programs have planted fields of deer food. Changes in agriculture also benefitted deer as have modern timber practices, cutting stands more often and opening forest floors where browse will grow.

Now deer are found in almost every habitat in South Carolina, virtually from parking lots to seaside. The Carolinas and mid-Atlantic states have more deer than ever before and the white tail is considered the most plentiful game animal in the East.

In addition to the white-tailed deer of the mainland, South Carolina has three subspecies, which developed because of geographic isolation. One lives only on Hilton Head, a second on Bull's Island and a third on Hunting Island. The three are distinguished by their body size, skeletal size and color; because diet affects size, color is the major difference. In the Florida Keys, another subspecies is on the endangered species list. A dwarf deer weighing 50 pounds or less, the Key Deer is now making a comeback in a refuge established to protect it.

Winter

Holly Berries are a favorite Yule decoration.

Decorations—

When it comes to the plant symbols of Christmas, South Carolina has them all in wild abundance. Festive red berries cover several varieties of native holly plants, pine trees crop up everywhere and seductive mistletoe forms large clumps overhead.

The host trees of mistletoe conveniently shed their leaves a few weeks before the Yule season so the invasive plants that hid all summer suddenly pop into view on bare branches. The bushy, green plant seems particularly at home on oaks but will grow on almost any deciduous tree. Mistletoe prefers moist or even swampy spots and requires sunny locations. Tree leaves provide shade during the heat of summer and light shines down in winter.

Appearing as dense spheres or airy bunches with irregular shapes, mistletoe is sometimes labeled a parasite. But in fact, *Phoradendron serotinum* takes only minerals from its host and can make its own sugar and starch through photosynthesis. Roots reach well into the bark of a tree limb to anchor mistletoe and provide daily mineral supplements.

The plant has thick, leathery, dark green leaves from 5 inches long to less than 1 inch. The wedge or egg-shaped leaves grow opposite one another on flexible, smooth, green stems. Although more familiar than the foliage, the white berries are borne only by female plants, which bloom in September or October. Female flowers, no more than one-eighth of an inch wide, lack petals and have a three-lobed calyx or outer whorl of protective leaves. Growing on separate plants, male flowers merely serve to pollinate the females, giving rise to clusters of round berries less than a quarter inch wide.

Each berry is coated with a sticky material, poisonous to man but apparently safe for birds. Cedar waxwings and bluebirds relish the fruit, particularly in winter when fresh fruit is hard to come by. Mistletoe berries form in early winter and last into spring if birds fail to do them justice. The pulp dries and hardens almost like glue. If a bird dines on the fruit then cleans his beak on a tree branch, tiny mistletoe seeds cling to the future host. A sucker then pushes its way into the bark and the young plant is anchored for life. Or birds may digest the fruit and leave droppings containing seeds on branches.

To preserve mistletoe (or other evergreen leaves) for the holiday season, mix equal parts of water and glycerin, usually available at flower shops and pharmacies. Let freshly cut branches drink the liquid for several days.

The Yule favorite known as American or Christmas holly thrives in Lowcountry woods, usually in such vast spreads that the holly virtually forms a forest. Prickly leaves, dull green above but yellow-green below, remain year-round on trees that may reach 40 to 70 feet. Only female holly trees produce the round, red fruit, which very rarely is orange or yellow. Although the berries are bitter, they become an important winter food for many mammals, game birds and such songbirds as mockers. This holly prefers moist to wet but well-drained soil in woodlands and rich bottom lands. Growing well in mixed hardwood forests or in the sun, the holly is plentiful along rivers which flood with silt each spring such as the Santee and Cooper.

In sandy, moist soil, the native holly is yaupon. Shiny berries, lining the twigs of these branching shrubs and small trees, usually turn red in fall or early winter, well after the Christmas holly has colored. The evergreen leaves are small, shiny, wavy-toothed and elliptical. Primarily a coastal species, yaupon was a favorite Yule decoration for early settlers in the Lowcountry. Also known as cassena and Christmas-berry, yaupon bears the Latin name *Ilex vomitoria*; indeed American Indians steeped the caffeine-laden leaves and used the tea to induce vomiting.

Also called Christmas-berry, dahoon is formally known as *Ilex cassine*. The coastal evergreen shrub, or small tree, likes wet soils along streams and swamps, sometimes sandy banks or brackish sites. The shiny, leathery, dark-green leaves usually lack teeth and spines. The shiny, round, red fruit sprouts profusely and makes this native a popular ornamental. The closely related myrtle dahoon or myrtle-leaf holly is similar but has smaller leaves and grows primarily along ponds and swamps in sandy soils that are poor or acid.

Inland in the Carolinas, possumhaw or swamp holly takes over. A deciduous shrub or small tree, the plant has wavy-toothed leaves. The abundant small, red berries become most conspicuous in winter, as they cling on leafless gray twigs. Mammals, such as raccoons and opossums, as well as songbirds and game birds eat this holly and its relatives.

Mountain winterberry or mountain holly also is found in the Carolinas where the elevation is 200 to 6,000 feet and soils are moist. Berries are bright orange-red, less frequently red or yellow. The winterberry is sometimes classified as a variety of Carolina holly, which spreads through most Southeastern states but is not often seen in South Carolina. A plant of well-drained soils in upland forests, this holly has elliptical, sometimes round, red, translucent berries.

Also donning red berries in winter, *Smilax walteri* is a member of the lily family. The evergreen, woody vine with curling tendrils has thin, egg-shaped, leathery leaves that lack spines and may be mottled with lighter green. Red berries grow directly on the stems of this vine that sprawls over bushes.

Holly fern, which looks like American holly, has glossy green leaflets that may be toothed. These evergreen ferns of bottom lands and rich, hardwood forests have leaflets shaped like Christmas stockings when viewed horizontally or like Santa's sleigh when seen vertically.

Of the Carolina pines, the handsome longleaf once predominated but the trees were heavily cut for turpentine manufacture and naval stores. In their place stand loblollies, today's primary source of commercial Southern pine.

Longleaf pines produce groups of three needles measuring 8 to 18 inches. Usually more than 11 inches, the needles are the largest of any Eastern pine just as the narrowly conical or cylindrical cones, at 6 to 10 inches, are the biggest cones of any Eastern pine. The longleaf does well in sandy soils in the Lowcountry and Sandhills.

Ranging from 5 to 10 inches long, the needles of loblolly pines usually form clusters of three, sometimes two. Attached to extremely short stalks, cylindrical cones up to 5 inches long open and release seeds but remain attached to branches. Throughout most of South Carolina, the loblolly thrives on poorly drained flood plains, well-drained hilly uplands and almost every habitat in between. Pure stands of the pine often take over abandoned farm sites and the fast-growing species is widely planted for use as pulpwood and lumber.

Another Southern yellow pine, shortleaf pine, grows throughout the Carolinas except near the South Carolina coast. The tree usually has two needles to a bundle, needles measuring from nearly 3 to 4½ inches. Cones of 1½ to 2½ inches are conical or narrowly egg-shaped with small prickles.

Slash and spruce pines barely extend into Southeastern South Carolina. Slash pines have clusters of two or three needles 7 to 10 inches

Slash Pine cones (left) and Loblolly cones.

long and produce narrowly egg-shaped cones up to 6 inches long. Spruce pines have two-needle bundles up to 4 inches long with reddish-brown cones that are conical or narrowly egg-shaped.

Nearly round to egg-shaped cones in the Lowcountry and Midlands belong to pond or pocosin pines. Shaped like cups before they open, the shiny yellow cones remain closed on trees for years. Measuring 5 to 8 inches, the needles form bundles of three. The favorite habitat of the evergreen is shallow bays, ponds or swamps as suggested by the Indian word pocosin, meaning pond or bog.

Another conifer, redcedar has sharp, three-sided, scale-like needles growing in pairs and lining up in four rows along four-sided twigs. Sometimes cut and used as Christmas trees, these evergreens sprout small, blue berries with a whitish bloom. Attractive as Yule decor, the winter berries are even more appealing to opossums and some 50 different species of birds. The Southern redcedar thrives in the Lowcountry, particularly in sandy soil near the beach. The Eastern redcedar grows throughout the Carolinas except along the coast and has slightly larger berries. The Eastern variety does well in sites ranging from dry uplands to flood plains, swamps and abandoned fields.

Blue berries also dot the waxmyrtle, another Carolina plant used for holiday decorations. If immersed in hot water, a pound of fruit will produce about 4 ounces of wax, which in colonial times was made into bayberry-scented candles. Like the other Christmas-time berries, waxmyrtle nutlets are scoffed up by birds: The calories produce a layer of insulating fat to help birds fight off the winter cold. Leathery waxmyrtle leaves are wedge-shaped, spotted with resin and sometimes toothed toward the tip. The shrub or tree, which may grow to 30 feet, lives in sandy soil.

In addition to such obvious choices, many of South Carolina's wild plants have become traditional holiday decorations. Redbay, which often lives near waxmyrtles, is bound into spicy wreaths that smell like bay leaves. Other naturals for wreath making are grape vines, honeysuckle, Carolina jessamine, wisteria, smilax and even Spanish moss strands.

Pyracantha berries.

Particularly in the Lowcountry, popcorn berries from Chinese tallow trees find their way to wreaths, arrangements and Yule trees. The Chinese used to boil the white, popcorn-like kernels and skim off the wax to make candles. Popcorn trees prefer sunny, relatively damp, sandy sites along the coast, streams and rivers.

The full range of seeds, nuts, berries, balls and pods on trees or shrubs blend in with natural Christmas decor. Even in the yard the bright orange berries of pyracantha and clusters of red nandina berries take on a holiday look, a fitting decoration for the house or one that will be appreciated and gobbled up by wildlife before winter comes to an end.

Once the holidays have passed, consider recycling some of the decorations nature provided. Birds will discover holly or other berries scattered near the feeder. And the entire Christmas tree can serve as a temporary haven. Tie the Yule tree to a support or bury the base in the ground. Add some snacks such as suet, homemade balls of suet and seed or suet and raisins, fruit, popcorn, bits of bread and other bakery goodies. Or give birds a Christmas present by decorating a live tree in the yard with munchables.

Eagles—

In the depths of winter, Southern bald eagles are hunkering on nests 100 feet or more above the ground. An endangered species as well as the national emblem, bald eagles have been gradually increasing in South Carolina; nesting and fledging rates have risen perhaps slowly but steadily in the last decade. And the bald eagle is becoming a less rare site along the coastal plain from fall through spring.

Mature Bald Eagle.

As early as September, bald eagles begin returning from the North to their home territories, their lifelong mates and their mammoth nests. A pair of eagles remain loyal to each other and to their territory unless, or until, one of the birds dies. The survivor will then accept only a novice bird, a young eagle that has never bred. The new couple may start their own nest, most often high in a live pine tree, or may take over the mass of sticks, branches, bark and debris the older bird built.

But first the eagles court with dramatic dives, flips, wheels and turns. The pair sometimes lock talons, one bird above the other, and fly or free fall together. Each year the couple repair or add to their nest, which often measures 6 feet across and 6 to 8 feet deep. Over the years, nests have grown to 15 feet in height, 9 feet in width and 4,000 pounds. The pair line the aerie with moss, grass, weeds and, for some reason known only to the eagles, a single evergreen branch. Interior decorations include such bizarre items as tennis balls, light bulbs, shoes, bottles and candles. If an extremely large aerie topples a tree, or if the nest tree is destroyed, the pair often will turn to a tall tree nearby. The birds prefer nesting within a mile of lakes, diked waterways or other bodies of water, apparently making fish meals convenient. An eagle normally establishes his territory and nests in the general area where he or his mate hatched.

The female usually lays two surprisingly small eggs between late November and early January. More experienced birds commonly nest earlier. Not maturing and attaining the fully white head and tail of adults until about age 5, younger birds are less likely to produce eggs or fledglings right away. A new pair may spend their first nesting season selecting a territory and getting to know each other. The second winter they may begin working on a nest, but often they lay no eggs until their third year together.

The female and the male take turns keeping the eggs warm for 35 days. The male also may supply his incubating mate with fish he has caught near the surface of the water. The raptor keeps a tight grip on his catch with the help of tiny spikes beneath his sharp talons. Eagles also dive on rafts of coots or gallinules and on injured ducks. In time the repeated attacks exhaust one of the less fit waterbirds. No longer able to submerge below the 6-inch reach of the eagle, the smaller bird proves defenseless. The raptors also take small mammals occasionally and scavenge on dead fish, particularly near hydroelectric plants. Rivers with diked areas nearby and inland reservoirs below hydroelectric plants are the best places to see South Carolina eagles from September into May.

Downy nestlings are gray initially but later sprout drab brown down. Young put on their dark juvenile feathers at about 5 weeks, are full-grown and leave the nest at 10 to 12 weeks. The fledging flight is anything but auspicious. Although eagle chicks cling to the side of the nest and practice flapping several days before takeoff, the birds manage little more than a downward drift with a crash landing. For several days, the young may not be able to lift off the ground so parents guard them. For up to six more weeks, the adults will continue catching prey for and feeding their young. Once an eagle has learned to fish and become independent, the bird may live for more than 30 years. But many never do master the art of hunting or die at an early age from collisions or other traumatic injury.

In late spring or early summer, young and adults head north, from South Carolina toward Chesapeake Bay and sometimes as far as Canada. One eagle hatched in South Carolina, the first equipped with a transmitter then tracked by satellite, wandered from Pennsylvania to Florida, through eight states before returning to South Carolina for the winter. While nesters may linger in South Carolina through spring, juveniles and adults from other parts of the country may be visiting throughout the year, giving South Carolina bald eagles year-round.

Measuring about 32 inches in length, adults have a wingspan of 6 to

Young Bald Eagle has dark feathers on head.

7 feet and soar with wings at right angles to body. At 7 to 10 pounds, eagles are thought capable of carrying their own weight. The keen-sighted bird can see prey three miles away as he flies at speeds of 60 miles per hour or more. Although the largest raptor in South Carolina, Southern bald eagles are smaller than relatives breeding in the North.

The body is a uniform dark brown, bill and eyes and feet yellow, tail white. The term bald eagle refers to a white, not a bare, neck and head. The formal name *Haliaeetus leucocephalus* means white-headed sea eagle. Immatures, in contrast, vary considerably but are blackish-brown mottled with white and have dark bills and eyes.

Young bald eagles are sometimes confused with golden eagles, rare winter visitors in most of South Carolina but rare permanent residents in the mountains of the Northwestern part of the state. Basically a Western bird, the golden is an endangered species in the state and may never again be widely seen in the Eastern United States. Measuring up to 41 inches in length and having a wingspan up to 7 feet, the adult is dark brown with light tawny steaks on his head and neck. Immatures are similar but have white at the base of the tail. This very powerful predator takes prairie dogs, gophers, rats and young domestic animals in the West but assorted mammals, game and nongame birds in the East. Able to seize young lambs, goats, calves, mountain sheep, larger geese and turkeys, the golden can heft prey weighing more than 12 pounds. As a result, the species has been widely shot or otherwise killed.

Now listed as an endangered species federally and in almost every state where he lives, the bald eagle is still shot on occasion in South Carolina and elsewhere, despite the protection of federal and state laws. Bald eagles also have lost when competing with man for the coastal habitat both value. Yet another threat came in the 1950s — the widespread use of DDT and other long-lived pesticides proved disastrous to eagles and many other predatory birds. Pesticides flowed from fields into rivers, built up in fish and accumulated even more in eagles dining on fish. Eggshells grew so thin that reproduction was near zero.

At one time more than 100 pairs of eagles nested in South Carolina, probably representing 200 adult birds and 100 immatures. By the late 1960s, the state could claim about a dozen pair. Use of DDT was banned in 1972, related pesticides soon after. Eagle nesting habitat was pre-served, laws were passed to protect the birds and programs educated people not to kill eagles.

In 1975, the federal Fish and Wildlife Service declared no bald eagles at all nested in South Carolina. That same year South Carolina became the first state in the Southeast to hire a nongame biologist and the first state in the nation to write a cooperative agreement with the federal government to begin nongame research. The research on eagles found a dozen nesting pair by the winter of 1977; six pair managed to produce young, a total of nine hatchlings that year.

The population stabilized in 1980 and numbers have risen each year since. Active nest sites increased to 17 in 1980, 28 in 1984 and 35 in 1986. Nesting success jumped from 50 percent to as high as 85 percent and eagles consistently have been establishing new territories as well as reclaiming long deserted territories of former residents. About 100 eagles now are tallied in mid-winter surveys in South Carolina, up from 57 in 1983.

Today shooting still remains the greatest single cause of eagle death in the state although trapping, poisons and pesticides also take lives. Lead has become a growing concern. Lead shot wounds ducks, which also gobble shot as grit from the bottom of ponds. Sometimes proving fatal to ducks, lead builds up in waterfowl and concentrates even higher in eagles feeding on wounded or sick birds.

The lower 48 states are thought to have about 2,000 bald eagles now, Alaska 30,000 and Canada 50,000.

Shells litter Edisto Beach.

Shelling—

The winter beach takes on a clean feeling. The crisp air, biting edge of waves and cold winds seem to scour the sand fresh. But in reality, the ocean is pouring its wealth onto the shore in winter. Shells are more plentiful than at any other time of the year, and a beach walk may turn into a rewarding adventure.

Winter weather raises a ruckus on the ocean bottom; northern and eastern winds cause waves that tear at the ocean floor and may expose mollusks that had buried in the sand. After predators strip the animals from shells, waves go to work tumbling the empty casings and eventually washing them onto the beach. Tides are unusually high when the moon is full so shells are tossed far up on the shore. Then winter brings below normal minus tides that disclose parts of the beach normally submerged. At no other time of year do shellers have such a wide expanse of sand to explore.

The best shelling begins an hour or two before dead low tide and continues for a short time after. Receding waves bring to light new shells with each retreat. As temporary ponds collect water, small animals or live shells are trapped in the pools and rivulets drain into the ocean. Several distinct rows of shells and other debris show where high, low and extremely high tides have left their cargo.

Check seaweed or grass for shells or examine the thin lanes of tiny shells and rubble for some of the handsomest finds. Look behind sand dunes. Peak tides may breach the dunes and leave goodies hidden in grass. Walk down the beach on the outgoing tide along an upper stretch of shells then back along the water at dead low tide for an entirely different scene.

Near the water keep an eye out for convoluted trails, depressions that show a living shell is travelling just beneath the surface. Like a puzzle, the lines twist, turn, meander, backtrack but eventually stop. Beneath trail's end could be the mollusk itself. Some varieties, such as fragile angel wings, dig so speedily that they are almost impossible to catch. Others are slow moving, even more lethargic in the winter cold. Carefully scoop sand aside for a rare look at a living mollusk.

Although some serious shellers might want to keep a handsome live shell, try to resist the temptation. A live shell taken today will mean fewer shells on the beach next year. Instead turn the shell over, examine the protruding animal and then place the shell, animal down, in the water so it can bury itself once again.

Knobbed whelks, often the easiest live shells to find, may leave more than just a trail. The light-colored shell, variously streaked and splotched with grays, browns and golds, wears a series of thick spines along its outer whorl or circle. Reaching 4 to 9 inches in length as adults, these tough, durable, spindle-shaped shells have knobs as much as half an inch long. Hiding just under the surface of the sand, the snail normally keeps its siphon above the sand and in the water. But as the tide rolls out, each wave removes a little more sand and may reveal the top knob or the tubelike channel from which the siphon rose.

The shell will prove to be elongated with a long, narrow canal flaring beneath the knobs. When trekking along the ocean floor, the eyes and antennae appear at the thin end of the canal while the larger portion of the shell provides the power from behind. When found in the sand, however, the head and internal organs — many of the same organs man has — will be tucked inside the protective shell. Only the dense, strong, very muscular foot will protrude from the opening or aperture. The pinkish foot of the snail, hard and tough to the touch, bears a flat, horn-like operculum. If disturbed or threatened, the animal pulls its foot into the shell and seals the aperture tight with the operculum, turning the shell into a fortress.

Less commonly found on the beach are related channeled whelks, which also appear live but buried in sand during the winter. The tubelike siphon, which makes a triangular pattern in the sand, may be the only clue that the off-white, pear-shaped whelk is resting below. Where the knobbed whelk has thick spines, the channeled whelk has a spire of smooth, angular rings, each making a precise right angle at the base of the next whorl. Reaching 3½ to 7½ inches, the whelk feeds on fellow mollusks and scavenges, as does its knobbed relative.

Powerful predators, whelks pursue clams, oysters and many other living shells. To open inflexible clam shells, a knobbed whelk grabs its prey with its foot and hammers the clam shell with the aperture of its own shell. The repeated blows chip away chunks of the clam shell and the whelk inserts the sharp edge of its shell into the damaged margin of the clam. A single large clam may be enough to keep a whelk going for a month. Meanwhile, the whelk may work on repairing its own shell, likely to be chinked in the dinner fight. Oysters are somewhat easier fare. The whelk simply waits until the bivalve is slightly open then inserts its aperture. Using its shell as a wedge, the whelk reaches in with its tubular proboscis, an extension of the head that ends with a mouth. Little wonder that oyster beds are often a good place to observe live gastropods on the prowl.

Excavating an indented trail may produce a lettered olive, South Carolina's state shell. The elongated, glossy shell with a pointed spire has elaborate reddish-brown, brown, grayish or nearly black hieroglyphics that are handsome if illegible. Olives rest just under the sand with siphons upward in the water. But low tide may leave an olive in exposed sand, where it continues its search for such favorites as coquinas and egg cockles. Olives like sand bars and often lurk, partially buried, along the ocean side of a bar.

Feeding at night, an olive grabs its prey, encircles it with the back of the foot then drags it under the sand for a leisurely dinner. Growing to nearly 3 inches, olives have been known to crawl onto fishermen's bait such as crabs for a snack. The mollusks have even been lured out of hiding by a fresh chicken neck. The light brown, mottled animal with eyes on its tentacles usually keeps its mantle and part of its foot over the shell, which is continually polished to a high sheen.

In 1984, South Carolina adopted the lettered olive, making the state the third in the nation to choose a state shell. (North Carolina has its scotch bonnet and Florida its horse conch.) The species was named by Charleston physician Dr. Edmund Ravenel, an acclaimed conchologist of the 19th century who was the first to discover or describe a number of shells to science.

From winter into spring, South Carolina beaches may bear the marks or trails of many other live mollusks including shark eyes, augers, wentletraps, giant Atlantic cockles, incongruous arks, surf clams and angel wings.

A common find on Lowcountry beaches, the shark eye is a rounded shell shaped much like a land snail. Tan to gray, the shell is sometimes

Bivalve (right) with hole drilled by Shark Eye (left).

delicately or boldly ringed with color; because the earliest whorls often are darker, the entire shell may resemble a bull's-eye. The mollusk makes a track broader than the shell, which can grow to 3 inches in the Carolinas. The chunky eyes force sand up as they move so produce a mounded trail. If the shore abruptly drops a bit in shallow water, check the cliff face for live shark eyes. The amazingly large tannish animal forms a jellylike mass around and over the shell but quickly retreats if touched or moved.

Foraging for clams and other bivales in the sand, a shark eye uses its strong foot to hold prey. Then the predator sets to work with its radula, a file-like ribbon of minute teeth arranged in rows. Eating up to three or four small clams a day, the shark eye also secretes a corrosive acid to assist the radula, which forms a round hole as it drills into the valve of prey. Once the valve is broken, the bivalve is helpless and the shark eye has an easy meal.

Murexes, oyster drills and other drill shells use a similar technique and also leave a round hole. Carolina beaches are littered with victims, ranging from shark eyes to glittery jingle shells to coquinas and assorted clams. Less than 2 inches long, Atlantic oyster drills are probably second only to man in the amount of oysters they eat, but the drill also drives its radula into the shells of other bivalves, gastropods and even crabs. Then it inserts its proboscis to feed.

A little auger may disclose its hiding place by leaving the pointed tip of its shell exposed during very low tides or in shallow water. Measuring 1¼ to 2½ inches long, common American or Atlantic augers are very narrow shells with about 14 whorls ending in a sharp point. Bluish-gray to yellowish-brown, the shells may have axial ribs, running up and down the newer, larger whorls.

Some augers have radular teeth and poison glands to help the mollusks deal with marine worm meals, but the American auger has neither. It relies only on a proboscis to engulf slow, worm-like prey. Although little is known about its hunting tactics, this auger is often seen near acorn worm burrows so probably dines on that species. Piles of stringlike mud castings often surround the openings of acorn worm burrows in sand or mud flats; trails of augers may appear nearby.

Along the low-tide line, a mound may announce the burrow of a giant Atlantic cockle. Occasionally the entire clam pops into view, but more often only a pair of siphon holes is visible. The siphons circulate water

Giant Atlantic Cockles show a variety of markings.

in and out of the clamlike animal as it lies on its side. With a strong, narrow foot, the animal can burrow quickly or travel across the ocean bottom in a jerky tumble. A favorite food of assorted whelks, which may chase cockles, the giant stretches its foot ahead of its shell, anchors the foot into the sand then heaves the heavy shell forward.

Measuring up to 5 inches or more, this largest cockle on the Atlantic coast has a broadly oval, ridged pair of shells most easily recognized by their size and their beautiful but unpredictable markings. The background is whitish-yellow with assorted stripes, small spots and large splotches of reddish-brown, black, yellowish and bluish. The smooth interior of the tough shells, which often reach the beach in perfect condition, is pale reddish or purplish-brown but white toward the front.

Incongruous arks may dig in just below the surface with cockles. Usually measuring about 1 inch wide, the little arks may reach 3 inches and are about as high as they are wide. Generally white and plain, the broadly oval shells are furrowed with fairly deep ridges; the bivalve usually is partially covered with a thin, light brown, almost fuzzy periostracum. (The related, thicker ponderous ark wears a black, very hairy periostracum over much of the shell.) The incongruous species gets its name from the fact the left valve is larger than the right and overlaps it slightly. Gulls are fond of the arks and leave many a nice, fresh specimen well cleaned and just waiting for a sheller. Or look for a mound of sand and a line streaking away from the mound, sign of a live ark below.

Rather than a mound, surf clams leave a depression in the sand. Several varieties may appear on Carolina beaches, including Atlantic, dwarf and fragile surf clams. The most common of these undramatic shells are ½ to 2 inches long, smooth, oval and brownish. Unlike most bivalves, the surf clam has quite durable hinges so the entire shell may arrive on the beach intact. More often seen in North than South Carolina, the Atlantic surf clam measuring 2 to 7 inches is yellowish-white to grayish and at least partially covered with a brownish periostracum. This thin, paper-like coating often is peeling off the shell, which is marked with growth lines.

Angel wings, delicate white shells shaped like wings, seldom reach the beach intact. But the mollusk may spend nearly its entire lifetime buried in mud or sand and protected from the rigors of waves and hard objects. Angel wings routinely bury 1 foot beneath the surface and sometimes 2 feet. A surprisingly long white foot moves the shell up and down its burrow. Often called an elephant nose, the tubular siphon that brings in food hints at the shell below. But pursuit is fruitless. Angel wings can rapidly outdig a human. In addition, a shovel or other implement is likely to shatter the shell and harm the animal rather than uproot it. The elongated wings, reaching 4 to 8 inches, are ribbed with lines of small, blunt spines that are quickly sanded away by waves.

Live wentletraps sometimes are captured in ponds as the tide recedes. The beautiful, glistening, little white shells are unmistakable: They have bladelike ribs running along whorls, the oldest whorl forming a sharp point atop the shell. The angulate wentletrap, similar to its relatives and particularly common along the Atlantic Coast, lives in sand or rubble beneath shallow water and often near anemones, a mainstay of the wentletrap's diet. These carnivores use pairs of filelike jaws to rip tissue from sea anemones, corals and other animals. Wentletraps secrete a substance that turns purple and may act as an anesthetic, perhaps making the fate of prey a trifle less painful.

While any beach will offer its best shelling in winter, some spots usually prove more rewarding than others. Among the best in South Carolina are Edisto Beach including Edisto Beach State Park, Folly Beach near Folly Beach County Park, Beachwalker Park on Kiawah Island, Breech Inlet between Sullivan's Island and Isle of Palms, Litchfield Beach, Huntington Beach State Park near Litchfield Beach and the south end of Pawley's Island. Shells and starfish are sometimes caught in the rocks at Myrtle Beach as tides fall. Cape Romain National Wildlife Refuge, Bull's and Capers islands and Raccoon Key are excellent shelling sites but accessible only by boat.

Screech Owl.

Owls—

While other birds are quietly quelled by winter, owls are in their vocal glory. From fall through spring, these nocturnal raptors are hooting and hooing, but winter inspires the peak of enthusiasm. Like songbirds in spring, owls in winter are courting and declaring their territory. Adding to the year-round population of barred, screech, great horned and barn owls are several varieties of winter visitors, swelling South Carolina owl numbers to their maximum.

Such owls as the short-eared, long-eared, snowy and saw-whet will spend the winter silently hunting then head north to nest. But permanent residents will have a long and vocal season, announcing territory as early as October and still teaching young about hunting well into summer. Each variety has its own distinct call, heard far more often than the cagey birds are seen. Females, slightly larger than males but almost identically colored, have somewhat higher voices so a listener can tell whether a duet is owl romance or the challenge of two rival males.

Little Southern screech owls, the most common variety in South Carolina, are at home even in subdivisions with a good cover of trees. Often allowing people to come quite near, the gray or rust-colored owls wail a wavering, tremulous, descending, plaintive and sad moan that sounds nothing like a scream. Like many owls, the screech also makes assorted other sounds, including purrs and trills.

Also common, particularly in swampy areas, the large Florida barred owl gives eight hoos then trails off with "aw," the Southern accent of the owl world. The call is usually very precise with a short pause between the fourth and fifth barking "hoos." But during the height of the courtship season, a pair of barred owls will put on a non-stop concert that defies description, a wondrous mixture of cackles, hoos, barks, laughs, aws, chortles, chuckles and other ecstatic glee. In winter some barred owls routinely begin calling in late afternoon and year-round may start hunting well before dark.

Preferring the wild pinelands but occasionally nesting near houses, the ferocious great horned owl gives three, five or six uninflected "hoos," the second and third being shortest, the last two strongest. Often hooting in the daylight, this largest American owl with horns or ears gives low, resonant, far-carrying calls that rise slighly at the end.

The barn owl not only is more difficult to find but harder to hear even near his nest. Often mute, the light-colored owl sometimes gives rapid grackle-like clicks, bill snappings, screams, hissings and grunts.

The short-eared owl, a fairly common winter resident from late October to late May in Eastern South Carolina, is normally quiet except on his nesting grounds, where he makes assorted hisses, squeals and barks. Long-eared owls, rare winter residents in most of South Carolina from late October to mid-March, court with various soft hoots, whistles, whines, shrieks and meows. Saw-whet owls, rare winter residents in most of the state from November to February, utter a series of whistles only in late winter and spring. A rare and irregular winter visitor in most of South Carolina, the snowy owl gives hoarse croaks and shrill whistles on his breeding grounds.

The barred owl, in contrast, is anything but silent. If he lives nearby, his calls become a regular part of the evening's events. He may even call and leave the woods at the same time each afternoon or evening, fly through a yard and land on a favorite tree perch. Not being shy, he lets people approach him and seems comfortable enough searching for prey near a house in the country.

If a barred owl has not established his territory nearby, search for him in a swamp or damp preserve such as Francis Beidler Forest near Harleyville or I'On Swamp in Francis Marion National Forest. Huntington Beach State Park near Litchfield Beach and Santee National

Wildlife Refuge near Santee are good sites to scout owls preferring drier habitat.

At 18 to 24 inches, the barred is brown, broadly barred with white or buff on his upper parts. Lower parts are white, buff or grayish-white barred and streaked with brown. Wearing a banded collar around his neck, the owl has unusual dark eyes and a surprisingly placid, gentle-looking face for an owl. Fond of river swamps, heavy woods, mixed forests and pinelands, the owl breeds and nests early as does the great horned.

The barred often lays eggs in early February in the Lowcountry and has newly-hatched young in mid-March in the Piedmont. The female,

Barred Owl.

perhaps with help from the male, spends about a month incubating her two or three pure white eggs. She typically chooses an unlined tree cavity or the hollow top of a tree stub. But she readily takes to the abandoned nest of a hawk or crow and on occasion will build her own platform or use an abandoned building. A couple often nests in the same area for years, 34 years in the case of one pair studied.

Little white fluffballs of young are brooded for 3 weeks but at 4 to 5 weeks may leave the nest for nearby branches. Fed and tended by both parents, young can fly at about 6 weeks. But fledglings often accompany their parents through the spring and summer. A parent may stash each youngster in a safe place, go hunting and return to present his catch. A lonely, hungry young owl coughs out a high-pitched, tremulous beg, more like the call of a screech owl than an adult barred. The fledgling barred owl wails repeatedly and often until dinner arrives.

Meals consist of rodents, insects, small birds, frogs, crayfish, squirrels, shrews and rabbits. Cotton rats seem to be a favorite and barred owls probably help farmers much more than they harm by taking poultry, a common accusation but a rare occurrence. Also on the diet are screech owls.

The screech owl primarily eats small rodents, but often dines on insects and sometimes small birds such as sparrows and warblers. At only 7 to 10 inches with a wingspread of 21 inches, the impressive hunter can capture prey his own weight. The screech shows little fear and will attack a human passing near the nest at night. During the day, screech owls hide behind their camouflage coloring and let people approach unmolested.

The mottled owls have very distinct ear tufts and yellow eyes but vary in hue. Red phase screech owls wear cinnamon feathers while gray phase have brown streaked and barred with black. Neither color predominates and siblings may be of both color phases.

The screech owl makes her nest in a natural tree cavity, the abandoned nest hole of assorted woodpeckers, birdhouses or even crevices in buildings. The female often returns to the same tree year after year and will settle near houses, in parks, in woods or in small groves. She usually lays four or five white eggs in early April in the rotted material, rubble or feathers already lining the cavity.

Incubation, from 21 to 30 days, is mostly, if not entirely, by the female. But the male brings his mate food at night and the couple often spends the day together in the nest cavity. Covered with thick, white down, nestlings are brooded by their mother for two weeks while their father delivers food to the rasping demands of young. At 10 days, chicks can feed themselves; they leave the nest at about 5 weeks.

More challenging to find, see or hear are great horned owls. The fierce raptors are fairly common in South Carolina but prefer woods, cypress swamps and open country far from man. The owl thrives from barrier islands such as Bull's Island to the mountains and occasionally nests in a suburban back yard if stands of large trees remain. The dark brown owls are finely mottled with white or yellowish tones above; underparts are white or buff barred with dark brown or black. Even more distinctive are the very long ear tufts or horns, the yellow eyes and a broad white collar, or throat, that sometimes may be hidden.

The fiesty bird is about 2 feet of sheer power, giving him the nick-

Great Horned Owl.

name flying tiger. An adult can kill no lesser raptors than bald eagles, peregrine falcons, barred and barn owls. The diet of the horned includes enormous numbers of rats and mice as well as cottontail rabbits, weasels, mink, woodchucks, opossums, porcupines, snakes, gophers, squirrels and sometimes turkeys or ducks. Armed with powerful talons, the owl determinedly pursues his meal by night and sometimes by day. Even the best, most odoriferous defense of a skunk fails to slow him. If prey is plentiful, several of the owls may gather and hunt together in a relatively small area.

If left undisturbed, these owls may roost in the same tree for a 25-year lifetime. But if the food supply dwindles, the voracious owl will move to a new area.

The female sometimes builds a rather rough nest of sticks or uses a tree cavity but more often takes over the deserted nest of a hawk or

Young Great Horned Owl.

crow. With sheer daring-do, a great horned owl will even move into the nest of a bald eagle or osprey, birds that reuse their huge nests year after year. Eagles typically are nesting before the owl lays her eggs in January, but a female eagle and a female owl have been seen incubating eggs on different parts of the same nest at the same time. Returning from wintering quarters much later, an osprey will forego nesting until an interloping owl and her fledglings leave.

Mates appear loyal to one another during the season, males flying to the nest at the same time late each afternoon. Before nesting, couples may roost in separate trees by day but call to one another when they waken for the night. Hoots grow increasingly excited as the owls flap nearer one another and finally meet.

When it comes to barn owl courting, the female takes the initiative, catching prey such as mice and presenting them to her chosen male.

The heart-shaped, brownish-white face looks something like the face of a monkey, but feathers rim the eyes and form a disk. The upper parts of the 14 to 20-inch owl are yellowish-buff mottled with gray and white. Undersurfaces are the same color or white spotted with black. In the dark of night, the silent owl appears almost white and ghost-like.

Being extremely nocturnal, the barn owl is seen by few people. And few hear his clicks, hisses, screams, grunts and bill snappings. Yet the owl lives in cities as well as the country, in belfries, deserted buildings and hollow trees.

Dining almost entirely on rodents but also taking a few shrews and insects, the barn owl often has been called the single most beneficial bird in the world. An experienced hunter with a 4-foot wingspread is said to outstrip the work of a dozen cats. Willing to fly considerable distance to find food, the owl even hunts in garbage dumps, overgrown cemetaries, large city lots, marshes and farms. One study of barn owls found it took parents more than 750 rodents (and one bird) to raise their family from egg laying to fledging. Other estimates range up to 1,000 field mice or voles.

By day the barn owl often roosts in the woods or in old buildings. The female lays her eggs on bare wood or stone in barns, attics, empty buildings, church steeples, silos, sides of wells, hollow trees, caves, duck blinds, nesting boxes, even construction sites and occasionally burrows. She normally produces five to seven white eggs, usually one every second day. When food is not plentiful, barn owls may lay fewer eggs or may not breed at all.

The male feeds his mate regularly as she incubates the eggs, the first of which may begin hatching in just three weeks but the full clutch not for a month or more. With some nestlings two weeks older than others, larger young may devour their siblings. Able to consume their own weight and more in food every night, the youngest may starve, unable to compete for food delivered by both parents. Barn owls can and often do raise two broods in a year, which could account for the seemingly unpredictable breeding and nesting season in South Carolina. Barn owl eggs have been found in the Lowcountry in early February, early April, mid-September and assorted times in between.

Unlike other owls, the nestlings wear short, white down for about 12 days then molt and grow longer, thicker, cream-colored down. Feathers sprout between 3 and 7 weeks. The young begin pumping their wings for exercise at about 6 weeks, fledge at 2 months and are independent in about 10 weeks.

The winter population of barn owls swells as migrants join year-round residents. Although common throughout much of the South, the barn owl recently has been disappearing in some of his former range and is listed as endangered in a growing number of Midwestern states.

All owls are well adapted to their night life although their eyesight is excellent by day as well. The iris opens up to see in virtual darkness or closes down in bright sun. The eyeballs do not move, but owls are able to rotate their heads about 270 degrees.

Eyesight aside, owls have such outstanding hearing that many could catch meals without the aid of sight. Studies show owls capture more prey in drought than in rainy weather because the scuffling of rodents is more evident in dry leaves. The large ear openings of some species nearly cover the side of the head. Because the ears are set far apart and usually at different heights, sound waves reach one ear slightly before the other and at a different intensity so the owl can judge direction. Most have a disk of curved feathers around their faces to funnel sound to their large eardrums. And owls can control these stiff feathers with facial muscles.

The flight feathers are equipped with teeth on the front side and soft edges at the back, damping sound so the raptor flies almost silently and sneaks up on alert prey. (Some owls in other parts of the country feed mostly by day and have stiffer feathers.) To catch prey, the owl uses four very sharp talons; a tendon keeps them embedded in prey as long as the owl's legs are bent. The raptors carry most food in their beaks but large catches in their talons.

Owls swallow small prey whole although parents have to shred food for young. Enzymes go to work on the often furry meal and the owl uses virtually everything but bones, fur, teeth, nails or feathers and mandibles. About eight hours after eating, the owl has formed a pellet of bones wrapped in fur or feathers. Within a few hours, the owl regurgitates the pellet at the base of the roosting spot or within the nest; barn owl nestlings and eggs frequently rest on a soft base of owl castings. These pellets are a favorite of biologists because a perfect skeleton is preserved inside.

In days gone by, man almost routinely shot any owls he could spot, at least in part on the mistaken assumption that owls kill poultry or other domestic animals. Yet these well-camouflaged birds have endured. Protected by law now, owls sometimes fall victim to barbed wire fences or passing cars. If in the open and visible by day, the nocturnal raptors are harassed or attacked by virtually every other species of bird, from hawks to songbirds to ducks.

Raccoon family at mouth of den.

Raccoons—

Adorable, curious and undoubtedly intelligent, raccoons have a way of winning most people over. Dextrous enough to pick up a small coin and twist a lid from a jar, the bandit-faced mammals look well-groomed and even appear to wash their food before dining. If permitted, a raccoon will watch television for hours and will change channels if a program proves boring. At least some 'coons have a decided taste in music, too. One raccoon showed up at a house each time a certain classical piece was played then returned to the woods when it ended.

Yet this cute, cuddly-looking animal is indeed a thief of the worst sort. He will ravage garbage cans and spread debris around a yard, munch out every night at a bird feeder or dog dish, invade the garden just hours before the corn is ready to pick and retaliate if his food supplier grows stingy. Raccoons are quite capable of unlatching doors or turning knobs, walking into a house and opening refrigerators if expected food fails to appear one night. In the natural world, raccoons have gained a bad reputation for taking sea turtle eggs and thus diminishing already threatened and endangered species.

All in all, raccoons are much like other wildlife and human beings. Almost everyone has at least a few admirable traits and a few that seem less than appealing. Unlike many wild mammals, however, raccoons are relatively obvious and easily observed in subdivisions and in the country. If a neighborhood offers a bit of food and water, large hardwood trees, cavities or even sewers for den sites, then raccoons are likely to settle in. They are bound to be found on coastal islands, in swamps, along streams or in moist mountain areas.

The masked marvels are active year-round in the Carolinas but may be particularly visible in winter. Cold weather may bring hungry raccoons to yards in search of bird food, nuts, berries or table scraps. And in winter romance runs high.

In January, if not December, a male leaves his territory to search for a mate. Raccoons defend their overlapping territories in a somewhat passive way. When two adults cross paths, they usually lower their heads, growl, bare their teeth, flatten their ears and raise the fur on the back of their necks and shoulders. After the display, both are likely to back off and lumber away. During the mating season, however, males may stage ferocious battles. The fight may be to no avail. The female raccoon is very choosy and may not select the winner or the loser. Once she accepts a mate, she invites him to share her den for a honeymoon lasting a week or more. Then she suggests he leave. He goes searching for another mate, but she will not be receptive to other suitors.

Males are still looking for invitations in March, but by then some females are giving birth. During the two months' gestation, the mother-to-be spends considerable time in her den, often a leaf-lined tree cavity. That den becomes the nursery for an average of four or five cubs, born a mere 4 inches long and 2 to 3 ounces. Living two to six years in the wild but up to 17 in captivity, adults in the Carolinas usually measure 28 to 33 inches including 7 to 16 inches of striped tail. Weighing 8 to 20 pounds, males are generally heavier than females but smaller than Northern raccoons. A world record animal weighed in at 62 pounds and 55 inches.

The female thoroughly licks each newborn, opening air passages, encouraging him to breathe and cleaning his soft fur. The ears and eyes of young are sealed, eyes not opening until 3 weeks old. Left alone for long periods, the litter mates become good companions while their mother spends nights scouring the area for food. If she is late returning, young may complain with a whimpering entirely distinct from such adult sounds as contented purrs, less blissful whines, squeals, screams, snarls, growls, hisses and churrs. Young also may scream if scared or peeved and will chirp to beg for food.

If she senses danger, the female will choose a new den. She carries each youngster, one at a time, by the scruff of the neck. At 1 month, young weigh about 2 pounds and rely on their mother to move them.

At 7 weeks, cubs are usually hanging out at the mouth of the den; they can run and climb and may even frighten themselves by clambering high up in the den tree. About three weeks later, by June in South Carolina, they emerge to follow their mother on nightly food hunts although youngsters are not weaned until about 16 weeks old. Fiercely protective of her young, she will hoist them up a nearby tree for safety and will attack any source of threat. In addition to man and dogs, a raccoon's chief predators are large mammals such as bobcats, mountain lions and coyotes. A great horned owl may try to flap off with a youngster.

The family at first spends days in the den but later wanders more widely. Mother and young may sleep in any convenient tree or other crevice on the home range, an area from 12 acres to two miles wide. In the heat of summer, 'coons may sprawl over a limb with all four feet dangling.

In the South, young weighing as much as 10 pounds usually disperse in fall to find their own dens. But where snow covers the ground and 'coons den up for the winter, young may not leave their mother until a gentleman caller arrives to court. Winter den sites range from cavities in trees to groundhog burrows, culverts, caves and overturned trees. Climbing well, raccoons may choose a spot 30 to 40 feet up a tree trunk, which they descend either head or tail first.

Being water oriented, raccoons are fond of crayfish, frogs, salamanders, fish, worms, snails, dragonfly larvae, oysters, clams, crabs, turtles and minnows. But the nocturnal nibblers also feast on eggs, young birds, grasshoppers and crickets, voles, squirrels and other small mammals, assorted fruit, tender shoots, acorns and other seeds, corn, melons, tomatoes and (near civilization) refuse from garbage cans or dumpsters. Young watch their mother's foraging and learn what foods are most tasty and where to find or catch delicacies. Excellent swimmers that can fight off and even drown a hunting dog, raccoons readily explore water and mud for meals.

Formally known as *Procyon lotor*, the raccoon has a species name meaning "washer." But a 'coon does not wash his food so much as he examines it and his very dextrous paws are all the more sensitive when wet. He thoroughly handles and tears at his food then discards inedibles. His more appropriate common name, in fact, is an Algonquin Indian word meaning "he scratches with his hands."

Beyond the ringed tail, 'coons are covered in a coat of grizzled gray to brownish fur, so long and thick that the animals appear pudgy even when lean. From the masked face, eyes glow bright yellow in a flashlight or headlight. Living in almost every state and throughout the Carolinas, raccoons are far more plentiful in the coastal plain, where their fur may be brownish, than in the mountains and Piedmont, where fur is usually gray.

Because raccoons can carry rabies, their appearance near homes sometimes causes alarm. Any 'coon showing signs of sickness, weakness, stumbling or aggression should be avoided. Although raccoons are cute and clever, they should not be adopted as pets. Not only is there danger of rabies, but 'coons as well as other critters are happiest and usually healthiest when left to follow their natural inclinations in the wild.

Foxes—

Winter nights are the time for foxy carryings-on. Both red and gray foxes begin courting early in the season and remain romantic well into March. The sly, intelligent mammals seek dens where females will give birth to four or five pups. The red fox heads for her maternity den soon after mating but otherwise shuns protection. Even in colder climates in this country and Canada, *Vulpes vulpes* will sleep in the open, sometimes buried in snow, with his bushy tail tucked around his nose and foot pads. Gray foxes tend to den up in the winter, for shelter and safety. But both species remain active, hunting and wooing all winter.

Other than color, the two dog-like animals look quite similar. Yet their habits and dens differ just as their talents do. The red is the wilier and faster of the two, good at backtracking and confusing pursuers. The gray, more common throughout South Carolina, climbs expertly, making him the only good climber among the *Canidae* family of wolves, foxes, coyotes and dogs.

Soon after mating in January or February, reds establish their dens in open fields, ditch banks or piles of spoil. These foxes are content in a variety of habitats but particularly like cultivated areas, brushlands and mixed areas. Edges between woods and crops or trees and old fields offer a variety of cover and prey. For the maternity den, a red frequently chooses an open field or other site with sparse ground cover;

Charleston Museum specimen.

Gray Fox

she often takes over the den another mammal has made on a slight rise, which gives a view on all sides. On occasion, a female will even use a hollow tree or log. A good digger, she will excavate new tunnels or remodel old ones. The burrow may be 8 to 10 inches wide but as long as 75 feet. She may build as many as eight entrances, two or three for each of several chambers, just to guarantee escape and confuse predators. Since the red reuses and extends her tunnel system each year, an older red may have a den covering 20 to 30 square yards. The main entrance, up to 1 foot wide and slightly higher, is marked by an earthen mound with a fan or mound of packed earth. Cache mounds where food is buried, holes where food has been unearthed, bones and feathers all decorate the entry area.

The red's maternity den will remain busy until late August, when families disperse. The female carries her young for about 52 days and gives birth to an average of four to eight kits from March to May. Pups are ready to leave the den at about 1 month but nurse for eight to 10 weeks. Reds mate for life and the father devotedly brings prey to his mate during her confinement. And he supplies most of the food for the young until they are old enough to be left alone during hunting forays. At first the mother predigests food for her kits and regurgitates their meals. But before long, parents are bringing live prey so youngsters can practice killing as well as devouring fresh food. By 3 months of age, young are exploring around the den.

Communicating with assorted barks, growls and yaps, foxes remain very social families from spring into fall. Playful youngsters romp around the den and parents sometimes join in the apparent games. Fox families have been seen running along the trail of a rabbit and barking almost like dogs. At about 4 months, between late summer and early fall, the kits are independent, able to hunt on their own and ready to seek out their own homes. Males may travel 150 miles or more from their birthplace, but females usually settle closer by. About the same time, adults also part company until winter reunites the pair.

The gray fox, *Urocyon cinereoargenteus*, follows a similar outline in raising young, but grays do not appear to mate for life. Preferring wooded and brushy areas more than reds do, the gray fox also likes boulders and ridges. Grays dig only if they have to and may enlarge a woodchuck burrow to suit them. But they much prefer a ready-made den for the winter and the kits. Slash piles, hollow logs, hollow trees, sawdust piles, old buildings, rock piles and such suit grays well. They sometimes den in hollow limbs or tree cavities as high as 25 feet above the ground. Oak trees seem to be a special favorite. The den sites are not conspicuously marked, but snagged hair or bone scraps may be obvious. Only on occasion is there a mound of dirt at the main entrance, several escape dens usually are nearby.

A gray fox father helps raise his young but does not share the den with them. The mating season runs from December into March with an average of three to four kits being born from March to May. Weaned at 3 months, they are hunting for themselves at 4 months, when they weigh about 7 pounds.

Quite comfortable up a tree, the gray fox sometimes forages aloft and eats more plant food than does the red. Wild berries, grass, apples, persimmons, cherries, grapes, pokeweed fruit, corn and nuts flush out a meat diet. Rabbits and mice head a menu that also includes other small mammals, birds and insects. Although primarily nocturnal, a gray sometimes will feed during the day in brush, thick foliage or timber.

The red takes almost anything that presents itself including rabbits, mice, squirrels, birds, woodchucks, crayfish and insects ranging from

Red Fox at Charles Towne Landing.

crickets to caterpillars. The diet is rounded out with assorted berries, apples, grapes, acorns, peanuts, grasses, rushes and corn. A mouser whose talents any cat could admire, a red fox dines heavily on mice in winter, when insects and fruit are less available. Where man has recently developed an area, foxes are even lured into yards by nightly food offerings and will appear singly or in pairs at precisely the same time for snacks. What the fox does not eat immediately he hides or caches under leaves or dirt.

Like the gray, the red usually begins searching for food about two hours before dark. The mammals characteristically head for a likely spot from downwind then sniff the air. Equipped with excellent sight and hearing, foxes depend on their very fine sense of smell to find prey and also to identify the messages left behind on scent posts that various species use. Foxes rely on stalking and pouncing as well as chasing prey. A fox may tirelessly sit and listen until he figures out the precise location of a future meal. Then the predator pounces, stiff-legged, and pins the prey under his front paws.

While very nocturnal, a red may begin hunting toward dusk and continue into dawn. On dark days, he may be searching for food at almost any hour. Typically, he takes a respite away from his den during the middle of the night then resumes hunting. If he has a den, he returns to it several hours after dawn. Reds sometimes are seen prowling along old roadways, railroad beds, pastures, croplands and field edges particularly in mixed or cultivated woods or brushlands.

Gray foxes live throughout the Carolinas including many coastal islands but are less common in high mountains and right along the shore. These natives will stay surprisingly near man and may be seen in suburbs not far from cities. Measuring 33 to 40 inches long, they weigh 7 to 10 pounds. Primarily gray, the fox has a white throat and underparts but a black tail tip and stripe along the top of the tail. The animal often has reddish patches of fur on his legs, flanks, neck and underside of tail.

The red fox, however, is more uniformly rich reddish-yellow with white underparts, chin and throat. At 39 to 41 inches including up to 17 inches of tail, the red weighs 9 to 12 pounds, males being slightly larger than females. The very bushy, white-tipped tail may seem as large as the slender body. There are also black and silver phases of the red and a cross phase is reddish-brown with a dark cross across his shoulders. Reds are common in the mountains and the Piedmont but rare in the coastal plain.

Reds fit the typical cunning fox image better than grays do. Yet many observers think the animals are less cunning than shy, cautious and smart enough to learn from experience. When chased, a gray will run up a tree or otherwise hide as quickly as possible. But a red will lead pursuers on a long, fast and (for hunters and hounds) merry chase full of double tracks and back tracks.

Hunters in Colonial America remembered the gambits of English red foxes and found the slower, furtive gray fox rather boring in comparison. So in the mid-Eighteenth century, landowners from New York to Virginia were importing reds and releasing them as future targets. Hunters also introduced reds into several South Carolina counties including Aiken, Edgefield, Fairfield and Saluda. Despite hunting, reds took hold.

Meanwhile, American red foxes began spreading south from Canada as forests were felled and land opened. Today's reds probably bear the genes of both foxes. Now numbering between 3 and 4 million nationally, reds live in much of this country except the West and seem to be adapting fairly well to man's encroachment. Native grays thrive throughout the South, East, Midwest and along the West Coast, but they are absent in a large chunk of the mid section of the country and the North.

In part because they will grab chickens, reds once suffered from poisoning, bounties and unregulated trapping. Regulations have now reduced hunting and trapping of both fox species. About 2,000 grays and 1,500 reds are taken in South Carolina each year.

Reds now may be expanding their range but seem to be facing competition from coyotes, which are spreading to the south and east. Coyotes have been introduced into Aiken County, released on Edisto Island about 1924 and brought into Georgia in the 1950s. Coyotes are increasingly seen in South Carolina, particularly in the Piedmont, Abbeville and Union counties. The animals kill and feed on foxes as well as rabbits, mice and other prey that foxes take. Also breeding in winter, coyotes like essentially the same habitat as reds. When coyotes increase in an area, the fox population usually decreases. Since foxes need diverse habitat with plenty of open land for rodents and fruiting plants, the animals could lose ground as farmers convert small fields and fencerows into large fields groomed with clean farming techniques.

In addition, bobcats occasionally seize young foxes while dogs and man take adults. Automobiles and farm equipment kill many foxes and illnesses, such as mange, claim others. The very diseases that kill dogs — distemper, parvovirus and rabies — can destroy large numbers of foxes quickly. Grays have been more widely blamed than reds in the spread of rabies. A rabid fox may appear sick and weak or may act aggressive and try to bite. A healthy fox usually will flee man or be cagey enough to avoid being seen.

Beavers—

Nature's master carpenters and builders seem to enjoy the chill of winter. Protected by heavy coats and thick layers of fat, beavers are busy marking their home range, swimming the invigorating water and getting romantic with life-long mates.

Year-round, the largest native rodents in North America continually build lodges, repair dams and cut such favorite trees as ash and sweetgum. The beaver's constantly growing teeth have been known to fell trees 110 feet tall and more than 5 feet thick. A 5-inch-diameter willow goes down in 3 minutes' chewing.

The dam is usually made of such beaver delicacies as willow, preferably small trees 2 to 6 inches in diameter. The beaver first gnaws around his chosen building material then bites out chips in a deep grove. Once the tree is down, the beaver begins removing branches and chomping them into manageable lengths, usually about 6 feet long and 1 to 2 inches thick. An adult beaver, weighing from 35 to 60 pounds and 35 to 49 inches long, uses his mouth to haul wood back to the dam. If hungry, he may grasp a branch in his front feet and turn it around and around as he munches, much as a person eats an ear of corn. If not, he will add the branch to the dam or residence by wedging the tip in the bottom of the pond.

Sticks, branches, saplings and reeds serve as home and larder for beavers. During warmer months, the tough diet is supplemented with tender green plants. The clean, neat critters are willing to travel considerable distance for a nice ash, alder or privet. Lake Murray beavers routinely swim a mile each night.

A beaver can use his flexible, five-toed front paws to hold branches directly against his chest or to push debris aside. Webbed hind feet and the scaly, black, rudderlike tail enable the beaver to cruise at up to 6 miles per hour. Adapted for underwater construction work, the gentle creature has valves to close off nose and ears, clear membranes to slide over eyes and skin flaps to seal his mouth. Only the front incisors remain exposed to carry branches. The animal's large liver and lungs allow him to stay under for 15 minutes. The very dense, soft underfur, covered by coarse guard hairs, keeps his body dry.

The architects come up with a variety of dam designs to control water flow. In fast-moving streams, for instance, beavers may bow their dam upriver to reduce water pressure. Each day a cohort or group of resident beavers repairs their dam and calks it with mud. Should a flood strike, the flat-tailed mammals may quickly add spillways to protect their home. Dams may be small or impressive. One industrious cohort built a dam three-fourths of a mile long.

If living along a river, however, beavers forego their dam work and instead excavate burrows in the bank. Using underwater entrances, the animals often come and go unnoticed as they gradually undermine a riverbank. When an unsuspecting farmer arrives to do his spring plowing, the tractor may drop into a collapsing beaver den.

Standing as high as 6 feet, the domelike lodge is built of the same materials as the dam. One or more underwater entrances lead to the lodge or hut, where the beavers live in an upper hollow area. The floor is covered with wood chips, which absorb moisture, and a vent above lets in fresh air. The lodge is home to a male, a female and their offspring, a cohort of four to 10 beavers.

Family members communicate in a variety of ways, the most famous being a loud, carrying slap of the tail on the water, which sends beavers diving for safety. More than one family may share a pond, but each will have its own lodge.

The lodge, or den, also serves as nursery. In spring, the female lines a cavity with fresh greenery including moss and grass. In the cavity, sometimes visible from the top of the lodge, she will give birth to three or four fully furred kits in late May or June. Weighing about 1 pound, young are born with eyes open, teeth cut and a good coat of fur.

The devoted mother seems to dote on her young, which remain in the cavity for three or four weeks and are weaned at 6 to 8 weeks. Kits may go swimming inside the lodge just half an hour after birth and are excellent paddlers in a week. Nonetheless, the kits often ride their mother's back as she swims. She will carry them across dry land on her broad tail or even walk upright with her young in her forepaws.

For two years, youngsters remain with their parents. As nesting time arrives and young females mature, however, push literally comes to shove. Parents often run off the 2-year-olds while the immature yearlings stay peacefully at home. In the wild, adults seldom live beyond about 5 years. In time, mother and father will confront a strong son or daughter and be forced to abandon dam and lodge to the children. Fights may leave the parent so badly hurt that he dies from wounds and infection. If the parents win, however, the young move, usually along a water route. The 2-year-old may travel quite a distance or may build a new dam just down the river, outside the parents' home range.

Beavers mark their home range, usually a couple of hundred acres, with a strong scent from castor glands. Particularly during the breeding season, which lasts from January into March, the beaver squirts this oil on leaves he scratches into tufts shaped like softballs. The territory of an entire family is marked by larger scent mounds, heaps of mud, sticks, grasses and sedges often 1 foot high and 3 feet wide.

The oily secretion also helps waterproof the beaver's dark brown fur, which he conditions by combing with the split nails on his hind feet. This castoreum takes its name from both the genus and the family of *Castor canadensis*. The beaver is the sole species of the family, which lives only in North America.

The strong scent is easily detected in swamps during late winter and is tracked by man and predators such as otters, red foxes and bobcats. Trappers use the oil to attract beavers and also sell it to perfume companies. Fur commanded a higher price than oil, however. Beaver pelts built many a fortune and inspired the exploration of this country's wilderness. Between 1860 and 1870, two fur companies alone took 150,000 beaver a year. An estimated 60 million were thriving in this country before Europeans arrived, but the drive for fur nearly exterminated the animals by 1890.

Beavers have been reintroduced in northeastern South Carolina and in the 1940s, the Carolina Sandhill Wildlife Refuge at McBee stocked the animals. The furry relatives of porcupines and rats now thrive in 38 of the state's 46 counties, are doing well along the coast and are missing primarily in the center of the state.

Difficult to census, beavers are thought to number 6 to 12 million nationally, several thousand in South Carolina. With the exception of Florida, Nevada and Southern California, beavers are now in residence throughout this country and most of Canada. A few hundred beavers are taken in South Carolina each year although their fur no longer brings a high price. Because beaver construction winds up flooding woodlots, farm fields, roads or sometimes houses, the state grants some nuisance permits each year and unwanted beavers are dispatched.

On the other hand, the beaver is a water conservationist. His dams slow erosion, retain water in ponds and provide new homes for other wild creatures. Over the years, a beaver dam completely transforms a stream into a series of ponds. As water stops moving, the ponds silt in. Trees die if flooded or girdled by hungry beavers and varieties such as willows spring up. The changing habitat draws raccoons, muskrats, minks, otters, water snakes, ducks, wading birds and even cavity-nesters such as wood ducks and woodpeckers, which drill for dinner in the dead or dying trees. Beaver ponds even hold water during rainy periods so may help control flooding.

As these architects munch on branches forming the dam or lodge, shards fall to the bottom and decompose. Slowly but surely the floor of the pond rises until, in time, a meadow stands where a waterway once flowed.

Slimy Salamander.

Salamanders —

Most amphibians and reptiles spend the winter in quiet hiding. An alligator, snake or anole will come out to sun on a warm winter day, but reptiles generally hide in a protected spot until spring arrives. Amphibians, such as frogs and salamanders, also are careful of the cold. Unlike birds and mammals, amphibians and reptiles cannot regulate their body temperatures. So amphibians must hide where the frost will not intrude. If the animal misjudges the frost line, he may pay with his life. As weather grows cooler and drier in the fall, amphibians burrow in leaf litter, under bark, into the soil or deep in the grass.

Some amphibians, however, are more active in winter than at any other time of the year. A handful of frogs and most Carolina salamanders emerge only in the rainy, cold darkness. What seems like the most inauspicious of times stirs these animals to breed and provides the only chance to catch a glimpse of salamanders.

More difficult to spot than a shy frog hiding in a clump of cattails, salamanders are lizard-like animals with moist, rather than dry, skin. Like frogs and other amphibians, salamanders easily become dehydrated and may die of desiccation. Most of North America's 80-plus species of salamanders live in the Eastern mountains, a few in the Lowcountry of South Carolina.

Salamanders have moist skins and a few secrete a slimy mucus when disturbed. The mucus of the slimy salamander species, a shiny black animal spotted with white or gray or yellow, is so persistent that it slowly has to wear off human skin. Poison glands, which release alkaloids, also dot the skin and are particularly numerous in the tail. If a predator grabs the salamander, he can shed his tail and flee to safety.

The enemy is left with a thrashing, foul-tasting meal that will make him shun salamanders the rest of his life.

Salamanders feed on a variety of food, but earthworms are their filet mignon. Entirely carniverous as larvae and adults, salamanders take grubs and almost any other animal food of the right size. When the winter breeding season arrives, appetites seem to decrease.

Usually hidden away in a burrow of leaf litter, a salamander returns to the same pond each year to breed. Even if moved to a new spot, a salamander will find his way to the pond, perhaps with guidance from landmarks or a keen sense of smell. Vision and hearing are not particularly important to silent salamanders, at least not on nuptial nights. Females look almost identical to males and both sexes rely on scent to find each other.

After courting, a ritual that varies from one species to another, the male deposits sperm sacs. The female, following behind, picks up the sacs from the water and lays from 50 to 200 eggs in a mass. Males are thought capable of breeding more than once in a season although a single mating probably fertilizes all of a female's eggs. Most species choose a shallow pond or ditch in which to lay several different egg masses, each in an envelope of jelly.

Aquatic salamander eggs have a symbiotic or mutually beneficial relationship with a single-celled green algae known to live only in salamander egg masses. When in full bloom, the algae turn the egg mass as brilliant as lime gelatin. Algae produce protein from the ammonia which salamander embryos expel as waste. The algae in turn appear to stimulate embryo growth and may increase hatching rate. Eggs normally hatch in a few weeks, more quickly if the weather is warm. Larvae remain in the water to feed and grow. But by late spring and early summer, ponds begin to dry up and larvae emerge as small copies of their parents. Although a severe drought may prove fatal, larvae appear able to speed up the metamorphosis and move to land more quickly if their pond is evaporating earlier than normal. Youngsters do not mature until they are about 2 or 3 years old.

Salamander species follow a precise order each winter. The marbled salamander starts the season late in the fall and eggs usually have hatched into tadpole-like larvae by February. The flatwoods is next to court and lay eggs then the spotted, mole, tiger and finally Mabee's salamanders. The amphibians usually remain active into early March while eggs and larvae are visible long after.

In fall marbled salamanders, with light markings or crossbands on a dark background, court and mate in ponds. The marbled is a terrestrial, burrowing species and the female lays her eggs near a pond in a moist depression under leaves or other protection. Measuring up to 5 inches, she usually curls around her eggs until they hatch. The aquatic larvae emerge just after winter rains fill the pond. Should the rains come late, the development of the eggs slows to wait for a full pond.

The eggs of the tiny dwarf salamander also hatch after a rain, but the female abandons the eggs she lays in late fall under a log or in a clutch of rootlets.

Listed as a species of special concern in South Carolina, the flatwoods salamander breeds in November and abandons her eggs on a pond bank, the edge of a pitcher plant bog or savannah. The mysterious dark bluish-gray salamander with silvery flockings on his back and sides reaches up to 5 inches. Triggered by rain to migrate to dry pond basins and roadside ditches, the female lays her eggs under debris or on bare soil that will later flood. Drainage and development have destroyed much of the habitat of the flatwoods, known to live no farther north than Charleston County.

Spending most of his life underground, the stout spotted salamander may grow to 8 inches and 20 years. The only salamander with two rows of large, round, yellowish spots on a bluish-black back, the spotted lives

Spotted Salamander.

in woodlands and migrates to nearby breeding ponds after heavy rains. The female lays one or more clear or milky egg masses of about 100 eggs. They cling to submerged branches and hatch in one or two months. Spotted larvae emerge from the water in two to four months as 2½-inch-long replicas of their parents.

Mole salamanders live up to their name by burrowing and seldom showing their noses above ground. They also lend their name to the family of salamanders which includes the flatwoods, Mabee's, spotted, marbled and tiger. The larvae of all the family members have obvious tail fins and long, plumelike gills. The mole species dwells primarily in pine flatwoods and only reaches into Southeastern South Carolina. The 4-inch-long, grayish-brown spotted moles head to shallow ponds after a heavy rain and drop in temperature. Small egg masses are transformed in late spring or early summer in the same depressions that may hold marbled, spotted and tiger relatives.

Tiger salamanders, which can survive for 25 years, may grow to 11 inches. Resembling the spotted, the tiger has larger yellow to yellowish-brown spots on a dark background. The rare salamander, which breeds in January and February, is known from only 15 spots in South Carolina and is listed as a species of special concern in the state. Hiding under debris near water or in crayfish or mammal burrows, some tigers feed on mice and amphibians as well as insects.

Although not rare, Mabee's salamanders are difficult to spot. Slender with a rich brown body, the Mabee's is marked with small groups of grayish-yellow flecks on his back and sides. Living only in the pine flatwoods and savannahs of the Carolina coastal plain, this salamander lays loose chains of two to six eggs. Larvae of this 3 to 4-inch salamander may fall prey to tiger salamander larvae.

Eel-like salamanders, members of the amphiuma family have four tiny, useless limbs. The two-toed species may live 27 years and reach 46 inches, making him the longest salamander in the world. Almost entirely aquatic, the animal may venture out of streams, ditches, swamps and shallow ponds to cross the land but only on rainy nights. Nicknamed the Congo or ditch eel, the nocturnal amphiuma can bite viciously with short, very sharp teeth. Hiding in fallen leaves with only his eyes peeking out, the speedy amphiuma waits to nab passing fish or may take the bait on a fisherman's hook. Amphiumas also prowl the shallow water for frogs, small snakes and crayfish. In summer the female lays her 200 eggs in a damp cavity under debris then coils around them until they hatch five months later.

A search for salamanders in the winter may also turn up frogs. But as in spring and summer, courting croakers are heard more than seen. Spring peepers, leopard frogs and four varieties of chorus frogs are the only winter breeders, inspired by wet weather and more noisy on warmer than cold nights. Winter frogs lay their eggs in temporary pools, where there are no predators such as fish to threaten eggs or tadpoles. The evaporating water permits only a short tadpole stage and provides only algae as food.

The same species that announces spring in the North, peepers give their high piping whistles or peeps from late fall through winter in the Carolinas. A single peeper whistles his clear note at one-second intervals, but choral assemblies ring as jingle bells in swamps, roadside streamlets, damp forests and woodlands. The wetter the night, the more intense the peeping by males, whose nuptial embraces may last as long as 34 hours.

A frog sounds out as air passes from lungs across vocal cords. The sound rises from a resonating vocal pouch so the frog sings with his mouth closed. The pouch usually is in gathers of loose skin at the throat of the frog although some varieties such as the leopard frog have two vocal pouches, one on each side of the head running forward from the edge of the jaw. The aptly spotted leopard groans in freshwater marshes and ponds from December through February or early spring. In choruses or singly, males give a long, low, gutteral moaning, chuckling or rattling and a grunt that sounds like a deep, musical "ker-r-r-r-ock."

Appearing about the same time as peepers, ornate chorus frogs give shrill, birdlike peeps. Southern and Northern chorus frogs emerge next, the Southern in pine woods nearer the coast and the Northern in hardwoods and disturbed habitat in the Piedmont. Southern males orchestrate a musical or rasping trill from roadside ditches, ponds or floating vegetation. Both the Southern and the Northern climb poorly so instead burrow into banks of ponds and ditches. The Brimley's chorus frog repeats his short, rasping trill very often in marshes, swamps and ditches, particularly in late winter and early spring. Found in the Eastern half of the Carolinas, the nocturnal frog changes color rapidly in response to temperature and activity.

Not coldblooded, frogs have a body temperature near that of the environment. Enzymes are thought to affect the frog's tolerance to cold or heat and frogs apparently produce a different variety of the same enzyme when temperatures plummet. If a leopard frog were tossed into a bucket of ice water in summer, for instance, he would die. But the same frog given the frosty ice water in winter will have a thoroughly delightful swim.

Red-Tailed Hawk.

Hawks—

Birding has particular joys in winter. The drop in temperature, humidity, mosquitoes and chiggers makes outings more comfortable and several groups of birds are far more abundant in winter than at other times of the year. Hawks, woodpeckers, sparrows and waterfowl, such as ducks and geese, all increase dramatically as wintering species arrive and visitors flush out populations of year-round birds. Also look for new wren species, kinglets, finches, juncos and blackbirds when the weather turns cold. Of all the groups, hawks become especially obvious and showy during winter as they soar overhead or perch in conspicuous places.

Increasing in number are the more common, year-round varieties of South Carolina hawks — red-tailed, Florida red-shouldered, sharp-shinned, Cooper's and marsh hawks. Bare trees and hungry hunting forays also make the raptors more obvious. Falcons, known as Eastern pigeon hawks or merlins and American kestrels or sparrow hawks, become common only in winter. And the endangered peregrine falcon or duck hawk, recently reintroduced as a summer resident, is almost never seen except during the winter. The falcons may be joined by rough-legged and Northern red-shouldered hawks and by such accidental winter visitors as the Florida red-tailed. Only the broad-winged hawk, an uncommon permanent resident, decreases in winter.

True hawks are divided into two groups, each with its own lifestyle and hunting technique. Accipiters, namely sharp-shinned and Cooper's hawks, dart for their prey and often hunt in heavy growth and along edges. These scrappy raptors are less commonly seen than their relatives the buteos. Magnificent soaring birds, the buteos often spot their prey while far above or brazely sit in plain sight on bare branches. Red tails, red shoulders, broad wings and the assorted rare or accidental winter visitors are buteos. These more obvious birds rarely if ever take poultry yet routinely are blamed when a less evident hawk kills a chicken. Marsh hawks, belonging to the group known as harriers, have their own hunting method; they fly close to the ground and surprise small animals. Falcons use a variety of techniques.

The red-tailed hawk is often referred to as the hen-hawk. But when the stomach contents of 754 of these birds were analyzed, all but 100 of the birds had eaten rats, mice and rabbits. Measuring 19 to 25 inches long, the dark brown hawk with streaked white breast and bright rufous tail hunts over meadows, fields, marshes and other open areas. Making large circles, he soars on unmoving wings and may scream a shrill "kreeeee" note. Like other hawks, red tails can pick out a mouse half a mile away with eyesight eight times better than man's. At other times, the bird may perch on top of a dead tree or telephone poll and scan the countryside in every direction. Particularly when hungry in winter, red tails may zip down to devour road kills and in the process be struck by a car themselves.

From his high perch, the red tail often drops forward and glides directly toward a passing mouse or rat. As he nears his meal, the hawk draws in his wings and speeds up without flapping and perhaps even without alerting the victim. Just before contact, the bird spreads his wings and tail, slows down and extends his talons to make the kill.

Rabbits demand different tactics. The red tail zips slightly above or even past a speeding rabbit. When the hawk senses everything is right, he may do a speedy wingover and come crashing down on top of the rabbit. But sometimes the intended dinner is more experienced than the diner. Worldly bunnies have been known to outfox hawks by running tight circles around a bush. The hawk tries to follow and, as the circle shrinks and flight slows, the bird may stall and fall to the ground. The rabbit, of course, scampers away to safety. Pursued by a hawk, a rabbit also may run along a barbed-wire fence. When the bird prepares to strike, the rodent darts under the fence and the predator dives right into the teeth of barbed wire.

Red-shouldered hawks use the same hunting techniques as red tails. The Northern subspecies is an uncommon winter resident along the fall line and above, but the Florida subspecies, having the same habits and appearance, covers the entire state year-round. Dark brown marked with white or buff above, dull white barred with light rufous below, the lighter-headed bird is most easily identified by the bright rusty shade of his shoulders and the black tail barred with white. At 17 to 19 inches, the red shoulder is smaller than the red tail yet may do an even better job of killing pesky rodents. In short, these two buteos help farmers, who instead sometimes accuse the raptors of stealing chickens. Very rarely taking poultry or wild birds, red shoulders do dine on mammals and occasionally snakes, frogs and insects.

In February, red shoulders begin courting in the air, calling "kee-yer" and making dives from great heights. That same month the pair may begin building or repairing a bulky nest of sticks and twigs lined with inner bark, dry leaves, evergreen sprigs and feathers. The pair usually returns to the same territory or nesting site each year and year-round residents usually repair and reuse their former nest. Young become active just a day after hatching, much more quickly than young red tails. Red shoulders are flying in six or seven weeks, learning to hunt about three weeks later.

Sharp-shinned and Cooper's hawks, as well as fellow accipiters, make short hunting flights but turn on bursts of power. These aggressive birds often hide from sight and hunt in the woods. The Cooper's silently lurks near a tree trunk or other camouflage then launches a sneak attack on prey such as birds, mammals, reptiles, insects and even small fish. Small hawks with short wings, accipiters often follow birds on the wing, drop below and attack from beneath. When the victim instinctively flies up, the hawk may roll backwards, extend his claws forward and snatch the bird by the chest.

An explosion of top speed may carry the Cooper's hawk 100 yards out of hiding and into prey. The Cooper's, which can easily streak through even thick cover, often performs tail chasing, flying atop the tail of such victims as green herons, ring-necked ducks, clapper rails or songbirds. The hawk is equally adept at grabbing a bird from the air or from a limb. Unlike most other hawks, the Cooper's runs well and will even pursue such prey as quails into brush. Although a female Cooper's weighs only a pound and her mate slightly less, the birds seem fearless. If his preferred food is hard to find, a Cooper's will take a half-grown hen.

The smaller sharp shin would prove awesome if he were larger than his 10 to 14 inches. The fiesty bird takes prey his own size and hunts in barnyards and city gardens alike. Occasionally taking insects or small mammals, sharp shins dine primarily on birds, ranging from sparrows, warblers and thrushes to poultry. To the despair of some bird enthusiasts, a sharp shin will adopt a bird feeder as hunting territory and grab birds that stop by for a meal of seed. He usually hangs out in the edges of clearings and woodlands and attacks with lightning speed, before a cardinal knows what struck. He can swiftly maneuver through thick trees and branches as well as any wood duck can.

Rare in summer in South Carolina, sharp shins begin arriving in early October and stay until late April, precisely the season people most often put food out for songbirds. Bluish-gray above and nicknamed the little blue darter, the sharp shin is white below barred with rufous. His long tail is square at the end while the tail of the Cooper's is rounded. The two otherwise look very similar except the Cooper's measures 14 to 20 inches, giving him the nickname the big blue darter.

Until 1985, the Cooper's was listed as a threatened species in South Carolina, where relatively little was known about the hawk and few were seen except during the winter. Farther north, where the birds nest and have been studied in more detail, the Cooper's has been increasing in recent years. The effects of DDT have worn off, breeding apparently has increased and illegal shooting of the raptors has declined. The Cooper's is now more abundant in South Carolina as well; some of the hawks nest and far more arrive to spend the winter.

Marsh hawks or harriers, more rare in summer but common in winter, are easily identified by the white patch on the base of the tail. The white shows as the hawk flies, his wings forming a shallow "V." Measuring 16 inches to 2 feet, males are primarily bluish-gray while females and young, which seem much more abundant than males in winter, are brown above and streaked below. These harriers fly back and forth over fields and marshes, barely above the top of the grass.

Marsh Hawk.

The marsh hawk is thought to have keener hearing than other hawks do and his disk-shaped face may amplify sound much as an owl's does. When he hears a likely sound, the marsh hawk drops or pounces onto such prey as rats, mice and rabbits. Less often the marsh hawk takes wounded ducks, clapper rails and bobwhites. Almost silent in winter, the marsh hawk typically roosts on the ground and often returns night after night to the same favored spot in a field or marsh.

The peregrine falcon remains an endangered species on the federal and the South Carolina state lists. Although peregrines winter throughout the state, they had not nested in the South Carolina mountains for half a century. In 1985, the state released five hatchlings, marking the first time South Carolina had ever introduced birds of prey into the state. The project was expected to continue with new birds arriving each summer for about five years. After maturing at age 2, these peregrines could begin breeding in the mountains.

Peregrines have suffered from shooting and from contamination of prey. Extremely sensitive to pesticides, the Eastern subspecies of peregrines was entirely wiped out by DDT and other chemicals. A very similar subspecies, the tundra peregrine falcon, clung to life in Alaska.

Eggs from tundra peregrines have been raised in captivity by Cornell University's Peregrine Fund, which has supplied young to re-establish populations in several states. Birds stocked into the Appalachian Mountains were adapting well in the mid-1980s.

At their glorious best when hunting, peregrines like to soar over lakes and open fields. Climbing high into the air, the falcon makes spectacular dives at speeds said to reach 200 miles per hour. A pilot travelling 175 miles per hour once reported a peregrine flashed past as if the plane were standing still. Sheer impact may kill a duck, shorebird, gull, dove or pigeon outright in mid-air or may simply stun the prey and knock it to the ground. (The fearless raptors also have been known to steal a dead duck right out of a hunter's hand.) The falcon's slender, pointed wings are made for speed. And he is so fond of speeding that in play he will even fold his wings and plummet down. Close relatives, European peregrine falcons were the birds most often used in falconry because of their extraordinary speed.

Before numbers fell so low, North American peregrines used to nest on ledges of skyscrapers in large cities. Resident pigeons made up the bulk of the streamlined bird's diet. The buildings with their sheer drops resemble the mountain ledges peregrines normally choose, assuring their eggs and young are safe from predators.

Adult peregrines, 15 to 21 inches long, are slate colored above with black barring on their backs. Undersurfaces are white or pale buffy with heavy blackish-brown spotting or barring. Immature birds are darker below and browner. Much like a football player, the raptor has a black mark under each eye to reduce glare. In winter along the coast, peregrines are seen along barrier islands, salt marshes and high bridges, where the birds may perch and look for flying prey.

The smallest and most colorful member of the falcon family, kestrels also are adaptable birds. In cities, they primarily catch house sparrows. But the raptors also live in towns, parks, farmland and open country. There the kestrel preys on insects, spiders, small birds, rodents and sometimes reptiles. Grasshoppers are a special favorite as the bird hunts the open fields and meadows he prefers.

American Kestrel or Sparrow Hawk.

Kestrels perch conspicuously at the top of trees, on exposed branches, on wires or poles. The bird dives for prey on the ground and often returns to his perch to watch for the next meal to come along. The kestrel also hovers in the air with body almost motionless, almost like a kingfisher. Apparently not bothered by smoke, kestrels sometimes gather near brush fires to capture insects and other animals fleeing the fire.

Because kestrels have declined in number, South Carolina state biologists have begun putting up nesting boxes, resembling large bluebird boxes. Although kestrels ignored the boxes at first, the birds later moved in and raised young. Normally using abandoned woodpecker holes in trees, the birds nest during April and May in South Carolina. But kestrels become far more abundant in fall and winter as individuals from northeastern states arrive to spend the cold season.

Calling a shrill "killy-killy-killy," the jay-sized birds have a rusty tail, back and crown. The wings of the female also are rusty but pale bluish-gray in the male. The kestrel wears a black stripe under each eye, similar to a peregrine.

Also common only in winter, the merlin visits South Carolina from September into May. Most often wintering near the coast, the falcon is also seen during migration along the larger rivers and marshes that attract water birds. At 10 to 14 inches in length, the merlin is not much larger than a robin. Males are recognized by their bluish-gray, pointed wings and long, striped tail; slightly larger females are brownish above and streaked below.

Living in open country such as fields, beaches and marshes, the merlin may sit almost endlessly on a high branch, much as a kestrel would. The merlin alternately flaps and sails but can reach speeds almost as impressive as those of the peregrine. A daring, aggressive bird, the merlin readily takes birds larger than himself, such as pigeons, ducks or shorebirds and even seizes mammals. Smaller birds, such as warblers, sparrows and vireos, more often fall prey to the merlin. In the cold months, the falcon stays busy not only hunting a wealth of wintering ducks but also harassing the many larger hawks that spend the winter.

Groundhog or Woodchuck.

Groundhogs—

Seldom does a species of wildlife have a day all its own, a day the nation's attention focuses on its slightest move. But on Feb. 2, eyes all turn to the groundhog. Be it the famous Punxsatawney Phil or a cousin burrowed into a meadow by a house, the groundhog, or woodchuck, is said to predict how much longer winter will endure.

However, the grizzled brown rodent with the bushy tail and short, powerful legs has no more meteorological ability than any other animal. Europeans believed badgers or bears could forecast the weather on Candlemas Day, Feb. 2, and adapted the tradition to groundhogs in this country. But there may be a bit of truth to Groundhog Day. Unlike other animals that hibernate, groundhogs are early to waken. In the Carolinas and throughout the southern portion of their range, the marmots emerge from their burrows in early February and may appear on their big day.

Marmota monax lives from Canada as far south as upper South Carolina. A groundhog skull has been found in the Lowcountry and on occasion a live groundhog has been seen in coastal South Carolina. But these are thought to be escapes rather than wild residents, which like the mountains of Western South Carolina. In North Carolina, the animals live from the western mountains to the central Piedmont and the northeastern tier of the coastal plain. After a short winter's sleep, the groundhog seems totally disinterested in his shadow. Males, averaging 2 feet or more, even shun food although their weight may have plummeted by a third to a half since fall. Late winter is courting time and a newly wakened male quickly sets out to find other groundhog dens in the area.

Pausing at the entrance to a burrow, the master digger sniffs. If he detects another male or a pair, he discreetly disappears. But if he senses an available female, he creeps into her burrow with tail wagging like a hesitant but affectionate puppy. The female probably will chase him out of her lair at least once and maybe repeatedly. But groundhogs are persistence personified. Eventually he gains a mate and a new home. During courtship and early in the female's pregnancy, he will stay with her, the only time groundhogs live in pairs. As the female's time draws near, she firmly insists her boarder depart. He usually takes up his search for a receptive female, but he probably will be rebuffed time and again by groundhogs already in the family way.

The fastidious female turns her attention to her homey burrow, up to 5 feet deep and 30 feet long. An amazingly fast digger, the woodchuck can toss soil a yard with her front paws. Deeper into the hole, she digs with her front legs and pushes dirt out with her back legs. Periodically, she shoves the growing pile out the entrance, which forms the large mound characteristic of woodchuck holes. The animal's constantly growing white incisors can gnaw through obstacles such as roots and a groundhog can heave a rock more than her own weight out of the tunnel.

Able to excavate an entire burrow in a day, the groundhog digs in several feet, angles up then continues along a straight path, assuring the burrow will not flood. One side tunnel leads to a small pit, used only for excrement and sealed off when full. A second tunnel ends at the nest, the site used for raising young, sleeping or hibernating. (A female opossum, raccoon, skunk or fox often takes over a deserted groundhog den and enlarges it for her own nursery.) The mother-to-be removes old nesting material and brings in new dried grasses or weeds before her young arrive.

From three to six 1-ounce, 4-inch-long kits are born blind, naked and helpless to a mother measuring from 16 to 32 inches and weighing 5 to 10 pounds. On their mother's rich milk, the young double their weight within a week and grow a sparse coat of hair. At 4 weeks and 8 inches, the furry kits open their eyes and start crawling. In another two weeks, the 8-ounce youngsters begin leaving the den with their ever watchful mother. Weaning themselves, they munch on their mother's favorite foods such as clover, grasses, herbs, alfalfa, plantain, dandelions, fruits and such garden goodies as corn, lettuce, beans and peas.

The upper and lower incisors are continually worn and sharpened against one another as the groundhog gnaws. Chucks do not work on wood. Their name comes from the Cree Indian word "wuchak," used to identify several different animals, and not from any ability with wood.

Woodchucks give a high-pitched whistle, their most common call, at any sign of danger. Young quickly dodge into the burrow when their mother whistles, but adults also heed the warning. When angry, groundhogs chatter or grind their teeth, making a rapid clicking. The sun-loving animals also can make an assortment of growls, snarles, hisses, chirps and squeals.

Excellent swimmers and climbers, woodchucks learn about safety at an early age. Less than speedy, the mammals probably cannot top about 9 miles per hour so resort to scampering up a tree if danger looms. Safety lies in staying near an entrance to the burrow. Woodchucks build as many as five small side entrances, usually concealed and lacking the mound of earth at the main entrance. If a predator, such as a fox, dog or human appears, the woodchuck may vanish down the main burrow entrance but quietly pop up for a second look from a less noticeable exit. Although armed with well-developed sight, hearing and smell, a woodchuck still finds his burrow his best defense.

Because groundhogs do not wander far from their burrows, the mammals tend to den in the middle of a nice buffet such as a meadow, pasture, abandoned field or even a back yard near a source of food. Most active in early morning and late afternoon, a woodchuck is often seen sitting on his haunches surveying his home range, an area shared by other woodchucks. An adult does defend his territory, the area around his burrow, and uses scent as well as whistling to notify intruders they should leave.

Young gradually depart from their mother's den and begin dispersing at about 2 months. At first youngsters move into a temporary burrow their mother has previously dug. She visits each offspring daily and whistles them into their dens if she senses a threat. In time, each moves out and establishes his own territory. Able to breed at 2 years, the animal may take over an empty burrow or excavate a new one. Youngsters are well established in their own homes by fall, and adults are gobbling almost every piece of greenery in sight, as much as a third of their weight in a single day. By the time they hibernate, groundhogs may weigh 12 to 14 pounds and literally drag the ground.

Up to two weeks before going underground for the winter, groundhogs stop eating and snooze lazily in the sun. Probably in November — the dates are not well known in South Carolina — the groundhog curls up on a mat of grasses in a winter burrow dug for just that purpose. Body temperature falls from nearly 97 degrees to less than 40, breathing decreases from 2,100 breaths per hour to as few as 10, heartbeats from more than 100 per minute to four or five. Warmed by the extra fat put on during fall feeding, groundhogs are thought to waken briefly on occasion and to take several deep breaths. In late winter, the groundhog's body begins to warm up gradually. Heart, lungs and brain come to life first, hindquarters last.

While farmers and gardeners may complain about groundhogs' appetites, the rodents fertilize the soil with their wastes, loosen and aerate soil with their digging and dredge up new topsoil from underground. In New York state alone, groundhogs are said to turn over 1.6 million tons of soil each year.

Living about four or five years in the wild, a groundhog may perish at the hands of man, in the form of hunters, automobile drivers and aggravated farmers or gardeners who feel a resident woodchuck is getting a free lunch. Such large predators as dogs and red foxes also take adults and birds of prey may take young. Yet the animals have survived and prospered at a time many other wildlife species have declined. The mammals may have been scarce when settlers first started to clear land, but the fields and meadows man produced were just what groundhogs needed. The animals have even taken to burrowing under old buildings, along the edges of roads and by rights of way. Woodchucks are doing so well that they have even extended their range in recent years and could become more common in the Carolinas.

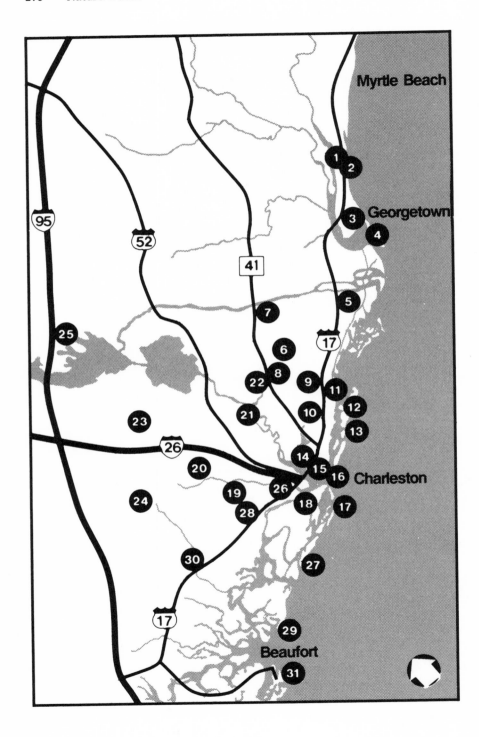

Appendix 1 —

The South Carolina Lowcountry offers numerous opportunities for watching nature. A number of the more important sites, arranged by area, are listed below. However, there are many others, and visitors are advised to inquire at local tourist centers for the latest information.

1. **BROOKGREEN GARDENS**: On Highway 17 north of Litchfield Beach. Admission charged. Wildlife Park featuring animals in natural settings including a deer savannah, fox and raccoon glade, alligator swamp, otter pond; large aviary with ducks, herons, ibises and egrets; nature trail connecting animal habitats; daily natural history films and guided tours of the Wildlife Park; former ricefield area with walking dike through habitat for birds, alligators and other animals; formal garden featuring sculpture, frequented by songbirds.

2. **HUNTINGTON BEACH STATE PARK**: Off Highway 17 just north of Litchfield Beach. Boardwalk and nature trails; lagoon, saltmarsh and beach areas; excellent birding on dike between brackish marsh and freshwater diked area; waterfowl in fall and winter, the quietest seasons at the park; birding along the beach and dunes at the north end of the park; more than 255 species listed on a checklist available at the park office; camping and picnic areas.

3. **BELLEFIELD NATURE CENTER**: Just east of Highway 17, 1½ miles north of Georgetown. Center operated by Belle W. Baruch Foundation offering aquariums, terrariums, saltwater touch tank and other exhibits of live coastal wildlife. Staff-guided tours, programs and field studies within the 17,500-acre wildlife refuge by advance reservation only; contact Bellefield Nature Center, P.O. Box 1413, Georgetown, S.C. 29442.

4. **TOM YAWKEY WILDLIFE CENTER**: On Cat, South and North islands; transportation from the mainland by state-owned ferry. Half-day field trips of this South Carolina Wildlife and Marine Resources Heritage Preserve by advance reservation only; send choice of dates and preference for morning or afternoon tour well in advance to: Tom Yawkey Wildlife Center, Route 2, Box 181, Georgetown, S.C. 29440. Marsh, diked waterways, ocean beach, pineland and maritime forest, forest openings; dedicated to the management of waterfowl, wild turkey and deer habitat and to nongame wildlife research; wide diversity of wildlife including alligators and fox squirrels; birds ranging from osprey to herons, songbirds and vast numbers of ducks in fall and winter.

5. **SANTEE COASTAL RESERVE**: Off Highway 17 just south of the Santee Rivers; signs show the way to this South Carolina Wildlife and Marine Resources Department preserve. Brackish delta, freshwater wetland and uplands; boardwalk into cypress-tupelo swamp; nature trails, canoe trail and bike-hike trail; good birding for ducks and other water birds; shorebirds along 11 miles of beach; habitat for snakes, raccoons and deer. Washo Reserve section excellent for wading birds, nesting ospreys in spring and summer, nesting eagles in winter, alligators and other freshwater wildlife.

6. **FRANCIS MARION NATIONAL FOREST**: Extensive hiking, canoe and nature trails with various wildlife, plants and habitats; nesting habitat for endangered species including red-cockaded woodpeckers and swallow-tailed kites. Maps available from the Wambaw District office, P.O. Box 106, McClellanville, S.C. 29458 or the Witherbee District office, Route 3, Box 630, Moncks Corner, S.C. 29461.

7. **GUILLARD LAKE SCENIC AREA**: Take Highway 17 north from Charleston, turn left on Highway 45 then right on U.S. Forest Service Road Number 150. Hiking trail along the Santee River; birding good for upland species; primitive camping and picnic area.

8. **SWAMP FOX TRAIL**: From Highway 17, take Highway 41 to Huger then Highway 402 to the campground at Santee Experiment Station. Trail through second growth forest, about 30 miles to Buck Hall Landing but easily walked in shorter sections; wildflowers including orchids especially in spring; camping and picnic area near Huger. Part of Francis Marion National Forest; maps available from the U.S. Forest Service or Francis Marion offices.

9. **BUCK HALL LANDING**: On Highway 17, 20 miles north of Mount Pleasant. Boat ramp access to Cape Romain National Wildlife Refuge; picnic and primitive camping areas.

10. **I'ON SWAMP**: Off Highway 17, take U.S. Forest Service Road Number 228 (I'On Swamp Road) left, about 15 miles north of Mount Pleasant. Many small logging roads for good birding; warblers in spring, excellent for upland birds including the endangered red-cockaded woodpecker; owls on fall and winter nights; orchids and other wildflowers in sping and fall; part of Francis Marion National Forest; maps available from U.S. Forest Service.

11. **MOORE'S LANDING**: Highway 17 off Seewee Road, about 10 miles north of Mount Pleasant; follow signs to Cape Romain National Wildlife Refuge. Long dock extending across mudflats; good for shorebirds, wading birds, gulls and terns especially at low tide to half tide; refuge property around the landing good for upland birds and migrating warblers.

12. **BULL'S ISLAND**: Boat trips depart from Moore's Landing to the island; there is a fee for transportation. Untouched barrier island with

hiking trails, beach, excellent shelling and birding; good for wildlife observation and photography; excellent for freshwater birds particularly waders, waterfowl and rails; good for resident and migrant land birds; birding best in fall, winter and spring; shelling best in winter; picnic area.

13. **CAPER'S ISLAND**: Barrier island between Dewees and Bull's Island, accessible only by private boat; dock available. About five miles of hiking trails through 2,000 acres of oak and magnolia forests, saltmarshes, brackish marshes, freshwater ponds and creeks; wildlife including deer, raccoons, alligators, feral hogs, loggerhead sea turtle nesting; good for birding, especially for shorebirds and wading birds in 100-acre diked, flooded area; nesting osprey; shelling best on the north end; beach a favorite of photographers; most pleasant in cooler weather when insects are less troublesome. Free camping year-round in designated areas along beaches, by permit only, call or write the South Carolina Wildlife and Marine Resources Department, P.O. Box 12559, Charleston, S.C. 29412.

14. **PALMETTO ISLANDS COUNTY PARK**: Highway 17, Mount Pleasant. Admission charged. Self-guided and unmarked nature trails, boardwalk, observation tower; docks, canoeing, picnic area; one of the largest palmetto groves in the Southeast; saltmarsh, ponds, creeks, wildflower meadows and woodlands; Nature Island offering short and long trails with markers identifying plants; good for bird and wildlife observation including nesting osprey in spring and summer.

15. **PITT STREET BRIDGE**: At the end of Pitt Street in Mount Pleasant. Causeway extending several hundred yards across marsh and mud flats to abandoned bridge. Excellent for shorebirds including gulls, terns, waders, sandpipers, plovers and ducks; best at half tide, especially in fall and winter.

16. **FORT MOULTRIE**: At the south end of Sullivan's Island. Beach and groins behind the fort good for small shorebirds, especially in fall and winter, as well as saltwater ducks.

17. **FOLLY BEACH COUNTY PARK**: On Folly Beach at the end of Folly Road. Parking fee. Barrier island beachfront site excellent for observation of pelicans and shorebirds; excellent for migration in spring and fall; beach plants, shelling and beach creatures.

18. **JAMES ISLAND COUNTY PARK**: Off Riverland Drive on James Island. Admission. Nature trails through former plantation site; marsh, live oak forests, lowland ponds; birds ranging from hawks to kingfishers; deer and other wildlife in residence.

19. **DRAYTON HALL**: Highway 61, Charleston. Admission charged. Botanical trails; walking guide listing botanical species available at gate; low fern areas, ditches, dikes through marshes, high ground beech

forest, dry wooded areas, garden near 1738 Georgian Palladian villa; birds and diverse wildlife along botanical paths.

19. **MAGNOLIA PLANTATION AND GARDENS**: Highway 61, Charleston. Admission charged. Nature trails, bird observation tower on Ashley River, dike into river and nature trail through wetlands excellent for birding; waterfowl in fall and winter, migrants in spring, wading birds year-round; formal and informal gardens blooming year-round but peaking in spring.

19. **MIDDLETON PLACE**: Highway 61, Charleston. Admission charged. Formal and informal gardens peaking in spring; informal nature trails, paths offering diverse birding in habitat ranging from riverfront to woods; birding best during fall and spring migrations; observation blinds in woods and by ponds available with advance reservation; guided nature walks and canoe trips available with advance reservation.

20. **OLD DORCHESTER STATE PARK**: 300 State Park Road, off Dorchester Road, Summerville. Nature trails, picnic area and historic site of former fort.

21. **CYPRESS GARDENS**: Off Highway 52 north of Goose Creek. Admission charged; operated by the City of Charleston Department of Parks. Trails through cypress swamp, cultivated gardens and nature preserve; blackwater swamp, woodlands and riverfront; birdlife ranging from wading birds to hawks to land birds; diverse wildlife and wildflowers; self-guided walking tour with pamphlet available at gate.

22. **BLUFF PLANTATION WILDLIFE SANCTUARY**: Off Highway 52 near Moncks Corner, off road to Cypress Gardens. Some 2,000 acres of virtually every type of Lowcountry habitat from woods to marsh; pitcher plant bog, seepage bog area, remnants of inland ricefields; about 10 miles of nature trails; serves as sanctuary where rare plants have been introduced; red-cockaded woodpecker colony; more than 200 bird species in residence; extensive field guide and bird check list available; advance reservations required for guided tours or self-guided visits; call Bluff Plantation in Moncks Corner.

23. **FRANCIS BEIDLER FOREST IN FOUR HOLES SWAMP**: Harleyville; take Interstate 26 north, exit left on Highway 27 and follow the signs to this National Audubon Society sanctuary. Admission charged. Interpretive nature center with 1.5-mile self-guided boardwalk through virgin cypress-tupelo swamp; excellent birding especially in spring and during nesting season; wildflowers in swamp and on upland habitat nearby; giant bald cypress trees and cypress knees in blackwater sloughs; varied wildlife ranging from alligators, snakes and turtles to deer, raccoons and bobcats to warblers, herons and owls.

24. **GIVHANS FERRY STATE PARK**: Highway 61 in Ridgeville. Nature trails; dramatic limestone bluffs dropping steeply to Edisto

River; threatened and rare plants in the limestone area; camping and picnic areas.

25. **SANTEE NATIONAL WILDLIFE REFUGE**: Just south of Santee off Highway 15 in Summerton, on the shores of Lake Marion. Wildlife observation tower and nature trail paralleling waterfowl habitat; fields planted to grain to attract waterfowl; dramatic numbers of ducks and Canada geese in fall and winter with geese peaking in January; good birding any time of year for birds ranging from shorebirds to warblers to raptors.

26. **CHARLES TOWNE LANDING**: 1500 Old Town Rd., Charleston. Admission charged. State park and wildlife sanctuary featuring an Animal Forest with such wildlife as pumas, black bears, wolves, alligators, otters and bobcats in natural settings; aviary and snake house; wild ponds and lagoons with resident turtles and alligators; marsh with wading birds; cultivated gardens; picnic area.

27. **BEACHWALKER PARK**: On Kiawah Island. Parking fee. Operated by Charleston County Park and Recreation Commission. Beach good for observing plants and birds such as shorebirds, ibises and herons; shells and sand dollars in season.

28. **TEA FARM COUNTY PARK**: Highway 17, three miles south of Rantowles Creek Bridge. Open only by reservation for nature tours; for reservations contact the Charleston County Park and Recreation Commission in Charleston. Former plantation site and tea farm with ricefields, dikes dividing freshwater ponds from tidal marsh, swamps with cypress trees, young and mature hardwood forests; virtually untouched in recent years but well crossed by paths; numerous birds including songbirds, ducks, herons, ibises and turkeys; alligators, snakes, deer and raccoons.

29. **EDISTO BEACH STATE PARK**: Highway 174, Edisto Island. Parking fee in summer. Excellent shelling and good fossil hunting, particularly in winter; good birding especially north of the campground and picnic area; nature and hiking trails.

30. **EDISTO NATURE TRAIL**: Highway 17 in Jacksonboro. Half-mile and one-mile self-guided nature trails owned by Westvaco; forest, field, swamp and former ricefield habitat; former railroad tram and former phosphate plant; forest of mature pine, hardwood and cypress with trees identified; diverse plants and wildflowers; birds and other wildlife with markers identifying den trees; swamps crossed by bridges.

31. **HUNTING ISLAND STATE PARK**: Off Highway 21 in Frogmore, 14 miles south of Beaufort. Nature trails and boardwalk; good birding; lighthouse for observation; highlands with palmettos, pines and live oaks; marsh and beach with shelling.

Eastern Cougar, one of many endangered creatures.

Appendix 2 –

The United States Fish and Wildlife Service and the South Carolina Wildlife and Marine Resources Department each has designated a number of land and sea creatures as endangered or threatened species. Endangered species are varieties whose number has fallen so low that there is fear of total extinction or of extirpation from a critical part of the animal's range. A threatened species is considered likely to become endangered. Federal and state laws make it illegal to harass, kill, possess or sell an endangered or threatened animal or any of its parts. Any project that receives government funding must not cause further reduction in numbers and special steps must be taken to protect the species and its habitats.

BIRDS

American peregrine falcon
Falco peregrinus anatum
Endangered, federal and state.

Arctic peregrine falcon
Falco peregrinus tundrius
Endangered, federal and state.

Bachman's warbler
Verminora bachmanii
Endangered, federal and state.

Bewick's wren
Thryomanes bewickii
Threatened, state.

Eastern brown pelican
Pelecanus occidentalis
Threatened, state.

Eskimo curlew
Numenius borealis
Endangered, federal and state.

Golden eagle
Aquila chrysaetos
Endangered, state.

Ipswich sparrow
Passerculus sandwichensis princeps
Endangered, state.

Ivory-billed woodpecker
Campephilus principalis
Endangered, federal and state.

Kirtland's warbler
Dendroica kirtlandii
Endangered, federal and state.

Least tern
Sterna antillarum
Threatened, state.

Piping plover
Charadrius melodus
Endangered, federal.

Red-cockaded woodpecker
Picoides borealis
Endangered, federal and state.

Southern bald eagle
Haliaeetus leucocephalus
Endangered, federal and state.

Swallow-tailed kite
Elanoides forficatus
Endangered, state.

Wilson's plover
Charadrius wilsonia
Threatened, state.

Wood stork
Mycteria americana
Endangered, federal and state.

MAMMALS

Eastern cougar
Felis concolor cougar
Endangered, federal and state.

Florida manatee
Trichechus manatus
Endangered, federal and state.

Indiana bat
Myotis sodalis
Endangered, federal and state.

Atlantic right whale
Eubalaena glacialis
Endangered, federal and state.

Blue whale
Balaenoptera musculus
Endangered, federal and state.

Bowhead whale
Balaena mysticetus
Endangered, federal and state.

Finback whale
Balaenoptera physalus
Endangered, federal and state.

Humpback whale
Megatera novaeangliae
Endangered, federal and state.

Sei whale
Balaenoptera borealis
Endangered, federal and state.

Sperm whale
Physeter catodon
Endangered, federal and state.

REPTILES

American alligator
Alligator mississippiensis
Threatened along the coast but endangered inland, federal;
threatened by similarity of appearance, state.

Coal skink
Eumeces anthracinus
Threatened, state.

Eastern indigo snake
Drymarchon corias couperi
Threatened, federal; endangered, state.

Gopher tortoise
Gopherus polyphemus
Endangered, state.

Green sea turtle
Chelonia mydas
Endangered, federal; threatened, state.

Hawksbill turtle
Eretmochelys imbricata
Endangered, federal and state.

Kemp's ridley turtle
  Lepidochelys kempii
  Endangered, federal and state.

Leatherback turtle
  Dermochelys coriacea
  Endangered, federal and state.

Loggerhead turtle
  Caretta caretta
  Threatened, federal and state.

AMPHIBIANS

Pine barrens tree frog
  Hyla andersoni
  Threatened, state.

Webster's salamander
  Plethodon websteri
  Endangered, state.

FISH

Carolina darter
  Etheostoma collis collis
  Threatened, state.

Sandhills chub
  Semotilus lumbee
  Threatened, state.

Shortnose sturgeon
  Acipenser brevirostrum
  Endangered, federal and state.

MOLLUSKS

Atlantic pigtoe mussel.
  Fusconaia masoni
  Endangered, state.

Brother spike mussel
  Elliptio fraterna
  Endangered, state.

PLANTS

Numerous South Carolina plants are proposed or are candidates for federal listing as endangered or threatened species; all are considered species of national concern, in limited number throughout their entire range. Others have been unofficially listed as plants of regional or statewide concern. As of 1986, the federal government had listed six plants as endangered or threatened species. Federally-funded projects are not permitted to impact these species and by law must make special provisions for their protection. Although species of regional and statewide concern are not protected by law, the South Carolina Heritage Trust Program attempts to purchase and protect sites where species of regional and national concern are growing.

Bunched arrowhead
   Sagittaria fasciculata
   Endangered, federal.

Canby's cowbane
   Oxypolis canbyi
   Endangered, federal.

Florida gooseberry
   Ribes echinellum
   Threatened, federal.

Persistent trillium
   Trillium persistens
   Endangered, federal.

Small whorled pogonia
   Isotria medeoloides
   Endangered, federal.

Southern spicebush
   Lindera melissaefolium
   Endangered, federal.

Bibliography —

GENERAL REFERENCES

Abbott, R. Tucker, *Kingdom of the Seashell.* Bonanza Books, New York. 1982.

Audubon, John James, and Bachman, John, *The Viviparous Quadrupeds of North America.* 3 volumes. Victor Audubon, New York. 1846, 1851 and 1854.

The Birds Around Us, Alice E. Mace, editor. Ortho Books, San Francisco, Calif. 1986.

Brown, Joseph E., *The Return of the Brown Pelican.* Louisiana State University Press, Baton Rouge, La. 1983.

Burton, Robert, *Bird Behavior.* Alfred A. Knopf, New York. 1985.

Chamberlain, E. Burnham, *Frogs and Toads of South Carolina,* Charleston Museum Leaflet No. 12. Charleston Museum, Charleston, S.C. 1939.

Dennis, John V., *Beyond the Bird Feeder.* Alfred A. Knopf, New York. 1981.

Durrell, Gerald, *A Practical Guide for the Amateur Naturalist.* Alfred A. Knopf, New York. 1983.

Gaddy, L.L., and Morse, J.C., *Common Spiders of South Carolina,* South Carolina Agricultural Experiment Station Technical Bulletin 1094. Clemson University Agricultural Experiment Station, Clemson, S.C. 1985.

Golley, Frank B., *South Carolina Mammals.* Charleston Museum, Charleston, S.C. 1966.

Graham, Frank and Ada, *Alligators.* Delacorte Press, New York. 1979.

Harrison, Kit and George, *America's Favorite Backyard Wildlife.* Simon and Schuster, New York. 1985.

Martof, Bernard S.; Palmer, William M.; Bailey, Joseph R., and Harrison, Julian R., *Amphibians and Reptiles of the Carolinas and Virginia.* University of North Carolina Press, Chapel Hill, N.C. 1980.

Pautz, Phyllis, *How to Decorate With Natural Materials.* Doubleday and Co., Garden City, N.J. 1973.

Reiger, George, *Wanderer on my Native Shore: A Personal Guide & Tribute to the Ecology of the Atlantic Coast.* Simon and Schuster, New York. 1983.

Rhyne, Nancy, *Carolina Seashells*. Fast & McMillan Publishers, Charlotte, N.C. 1982.

Seton, Ernest Thompson, *Life-Histories of Northern Animals*. 2 vols. Charles Scribner's Sons, New York. 1909.

Simonds, Calvin, *Private Lives of Garden Birds*. Rodale Press, Emmaus, Pa. 1984.

Sprunt, Alexander Jr., and Chamberlain, E. Burnham, *South Carolina Bird Life*. University of South Carolina Press, Columbia, S.C. 1970.

Squires, Mabel, *The Art of Drying Plants and Flowers*. Bonanza Books, New York. 1958.

Stokes, Donald W., *A Guide to Observing Insect Lives*. Little, Brown and Company, Boston, Mass. 1983.

Walker, Lewis Wayne, *The Book of Owls*. Alfred A. Knopf, New York. 1974.

Webster, William David; Parnell, James F., and Biggs, Walter C. Jr., *Mammals of the Carolinas, Virginia and Maryland*. University of North Carolina Press, Chapel Hill, N.C. 1985.

Westland, Pamela, and Critchley, Paula, *The Art of Dried and Pressed Flowers*. Crown Publishers, New York. 1974.

Westland, Pamela, *Decorating With Wild Flowers*. Rodale Press, Emmaus, Pa. 1976.

Wilkinson, Philip M., *Nesting Ecology of the American Alligator in Coastal South Carolina*. South Carolina Wildlife and Marine Resources Department, Columbia, S.C. 1984.

The Wonder of Birds, Robert M. Poole, editor. National Geographic Society, Washington, D.C. 1983.

FIELD GUIDES

Abbott, R. Tucker, *A Guide to Field Identification: Seashells of North America*. Golden Press, New York. 1968.

Amos, William H. and Stephen H., *Audubon Society Nature Guide to the Atlantic and Gulf Coasts*. Alfred A. Knopf, New York. 1985.

Audubon Society Master Guide to Birding. John Farrand Jr., editor. 3 volumes. Alfred A. Knopf, New York. 1984.

Behler, John L., and King, F. Wayne, *Audubon Society Field Guide to North American Reptiles and Amphibians*. Alfred A. Knopf, New York. 1979.

Bull, John, and Farrand, John Jr., *Audubon Society Field Guide to North American Birds: Eastern Region*. Alfred A. Knopf, New York. 1977.

Collins, Henry Hill Jr., *Complete Field Guide to American Wildlife*. Harper and Row, New York. 1959.

Conant, Roger, *Peterson Field Guide to Reptiles and Amphibians of Eastern and Central North America.* Houghton Mifflin Co., Boston, Mass. 1975.

Gosner, Kenneth L., *Peterson Field Guide to the Atlantic Seashore.* Houghton Mifflin Co., Boston, Mass. 1978.

Guide to Shells, Harold S. Feinberg, editor. Simon and Schuster, New York. 1979.

Harrison, Colin, *Field Guide to the Nests, Eggs and Nestlings of North American Birds.* William Collins Sons & Co. Ltd., New York. 1978.

Harrison, Hal H., *Peterson Field Guide to Birds' Nests: In the United States East of the Mississippi River.* Houghton Mifflin Co., Boston, Mass. 1975.

Little, Elbert L., *Audubon Society Field Guide to North American Trees: Eastern Region.* Alfred A. Knopf, New York. 1980.

Meinkoth, Norman A., *Audubon Society Field Guide to North American Seashore Creatures.* Alfred A. Knopf, New York. 1981.

Milne, Lorus and Margery, *Audubon Society Field Guide to North American Insects and Spiders.* Alfred A. Knopf, New York. 1980.

Niering, William A., and Olmstead, Nancy C., *Audubon Society Field Guide to North American Wildflowers: Eastern Region.* Alfred A. Knopf, New York. 1979.

Nonis, U., *Mushrooms & Toadstools: A Color Field Guide.* Hippocrene Books, New York. 1982.

Peterson, Roger Tory, and McKenny, Margaret, *Peterson Field Guide to Wildflowers.* Houghton Mifflin Co., Boston, Mass. 1968.

Petrides, George A., *Peterson Field Guide to Trees and Shrubs.* Houghton Mifflin Co., Boston, Mass. 1972.

Porcher, Richard D., *Field Guide to the Bluff Plantation.* Kathleen O'Brien Foundation, New Orleans, La. 1985.

Pyle, Robert Michael, *Audubon Society Field Guide to North American Butterflies.* Alfred A. Knopf, New York. 1981.

Rehder, Harald A., *Audubon Society Field Guide to North American Seashells.* Alfred A. Knopf, New York. 1981.

Whitaker, John O. Jr., *Audubon Society Field Guide to North American Mammals.* Alfred A. Knopf, New York. 1980.

Index —